Pacific Northwestern Spiritual Poetry

Pacific Northwestern Spiritual Poetry

Edited by

Charles Potts

with an introduction, "A Reason to Read"

Tsunami Inc.
Walla Walla, Washington

Library of Congress Catalog Card Number: 98-90363

Charles Potts, editor

Pacific Northwestern Spiritual Poetry

Cover painting by Robert McNealy

from the "Attempting to See the Flood" series, a wall of water, ice and debris 50 m high traveling 100 km an hour

ISBN 0-9644440-4-5

Printed in the United States of America

First Edition

2 3 4 5 6 7 8 9 10

Dedication

At every step of the way in my literary career, if that is what it has been, I've been helped. In Mackay by Larry Kent, Lin Hintze, Terence "Hereford" Donahue, Scott McAffee, Larry "Coon" Cloward, Marge Fulton, Evelyn Kahler, Ken Fisher, Barbara Ambrose, Mariann Ausich; in Pocatello by Robert McNealy, Edward Dorn, dawn stram, Mary Heckler, Zig Knoll, Dennis DeFoggi, Virginia Jo Bennett, Polly Abe, A. Wilbur Stevens, John Hoopes, Drew Wagnon, Gino Sky, Raymond Obermayr, Eric Obermayr, Gerald Grimmett, Jerry Johnson, Robert Serpa, Mary Miller, Berk Erbland, Clair Oursler, Gene Dawson, Jack Large, Phil Behymer, Geoffery Dunbar, Larry Rice, Herb Ruhm, Waller B. "Bud" Wiggington, Tomy Decker, Genie Arcano, Donald Johnson, Carl Dowd; in La Grande by mel buffington, Bill Merrill, Jo Merrill, Ron Bayes, Jan Kepley, David Hiatt, Robert Becker, Ben L. Hiatt, Nick Smith, Jolene Hiatt, Edy Kepley, Deanna Talbot, Robert Creeley; in Seattle by Edward Smith, Karen Waring, Elaine Smith, Louie Louie, Bill Bissett, Kym Snell, Oshune, Janice Porter, Barry McKinnon, Sy Turner, Crash Crosby, Spencer Hyde the Third, E. Roy Kaufman, Paul Sawyer, Paul Dorpat, Lorenzo Milam, Miriam Radar, Peggy McChesney, Steve Herrold at the ID Bookstore, Michael Murphy in Olympia at the Null Set Coffee House, Norm Sibum, Dirk Kortz, David Wagner, Boddie McClure, P. David Horton, David Tammer, Pete Winslow, Bobby Byrd, Paul Malanga, Chuck Carlson, Michael Wiater; in Portland by Dick Bakken, Carlos Reyes; in Berkeley, SF & LA, by Andy Clausen, Charles Bukowski, John Oliver Simon, Richard Krech, Robert Duncan, Philip Whalen, Charles Olson, David Gitin, Maria Gitin, Julia Newman of the Tenth Muse, the ghost of Charles Foster, Judith Foster, Pat Parker, Harold Adler, Sam Hardin at Shakespeare & Co. Books, John Martin, John Thomson, Peter Rutledge Koch, Joel Waldman, Darrell Kerr, Harry Smith, Len Fulton, Jerry Burns, Hugh Fox, Gene Fowler, Hilary Fowler, Al Young, Alta Bosserman, Paul Mariah, Paul Xavier, Scooter Woodruff, Jon Grubb, Herb DeGrasse, John Bennett, Richard Morris, Bruce Leary, Lenore Kandell, Stephen Vincent; in Salt Lake City by Velda Williams, Sherm Clow, Suzanne Clow, Karl Kempton, Kathy Green, Galen Green, C.S. Crowther, Greg Stewart, Sandy Anderson, Harris Lenowitz, Tamar Lenowitz, Dan Owen, Glenn F. "Zeke" Hiesler, Meredith Anderson, Nathan "Hezekiah" See, Nathanial Tarn, Claudia Jensen, Gary Jones, Michael Mayer, Harold Carr, Robbin Duncan, Lucky Luckenbach, Rex Barros, Doug Anderton, Edward Leuders, John Voight, Henry Taylor,

Nathaniel Tarn, Jerome Rothenberg, Charles Doria, Robert Mezey, Emma Lou Thayne, Bruce Roberts, Steve Jones at the Cosmic Aeroplane, Elaine Glenn, LaVerne Harrell Clark, Mary MacArthur, Gary Elder, Morty Sklar, Jim Mulac, Carl Weissner, Ellen Zweig, Michael Andre, Carol Aoki, Anita Davis, Sylvia Kempton, Joe Kirk, Cathy Gilbert, Charlie Freshman, Pat Parrish, Susu Knight, Pete Hollingsworth, John Christensen, Wayne Owens, Greg Floor, Victor Gordon, Mama Edy and her "Right On Beanery," Bruce Phillips, Betty Olson, Ken Hatch of Yarrow Books, Sherry Fix, David Wang, Gary Baker, Abelardo Delgado, Richardo Sánchez, Smokey Kelsch, Charlie Vermont, Charlie Walsh, Judson Crews, David Zeltzer, David Sorrells, Brent T. Leake, Sandy Anderson, Linda King, Dorothy De Prospero, Geraldine King, David Peterson, Randall Ackley, Nila NorthSun, Kirk Robertson, Lindy Hough, Richard Grossinger, Red Bird, Norm Rosenbaum, Brent Schonfeld, Henry Crow Dog, Malcolm Black Elk, Eugene Beyale, Paul Hartnett, Tom Montag, Rick Peabody, Paul Buhle, William J. Robson; in Boulder by Charley George, John Geirach, Kathi George, John Moulder, Jack Collom, Raven Books, Marc Campbell; on the road with John Thomson by Tony Scibella, Geoffrey Young, Laura Chester, Simon Ortiz, Larry Goodell, Lenore Goodell, Stephen Rodefer, Keith Wilson, John Rechy, John "Jinx" Jenkinson, Tony Sobin, Robert Head, Darlene Fife, Joe West, Terry Jacobus, T. L. Kryss, Jim at the Asphodel Bookshop, Charlie Borden, Jane Olinger, Larry Eigner, Fred Buck, Duncan McNaughton, Genie McNaughton, John Gill, Elaine Gill, Ken Milkowski, Ann Milkowski, Jon Reilly, Rich Mangelsdorff, Morris Edelson, Dave Wagner, Michael Finley, Thomas McGrath, Glenn Davis, George Mattingly, Anselm Hollo, Darrell Gray; and since back in Seattle by Stephen Thomas, Mike Kettner, Kathy McKettner, Trudy Mercer, Judith Roche, Paul Havas, Paul Hansen, Bob Redmond, Noel Franklin, Marion Kimes, Phoebe Bosché, Sam Hamill, Sue Pace, Charlie Rathbun, Madeline DeFreese, Peggy Nomura, Lou Stone; in Portland by Bill Shively, Bob Phillips, Carl Hanni, Rueben Nisenfeld, Melody Jordan, Dennis Stovall, Linny Stovall, Jeff Meyers, Walt Curtis, Rebecca Conant; in Idaho & Salt Lake, by Allan Minskoff, Rick Ardinger, Rosemary Ardinger, Scott Preston, Will Peterson, Ann Krielcamp, Tandy Sturgeon, John Wolffe, Stephen Jacobsen, Harald Wyndham, Bill Studebaker, Rosalie Sorrells, Penelope Reedy, Rex Widner, Judith Widner, Florence Blanchard, Tom Blanchard, Bruce Embree, Lorin Gaarder, Judith Klein Gaarder, Christy Austin, Bill Chisholm, LaReese Duke, Ann Jordan, Milt Jordan, Gary Hunt, Bob Moore, Max Pavesic, Kathy Pavesic, Lawrence Keith, Eric Wegner, Keith Browning, Bob Greene, Sue Armitage, Marc Jaffe, Terry

Bergmier, Mike Bowerly, Steve Carr, Lee Sharf, Alicia Harrad, Dennis Held, Claire Davis, Ron McFarland, Elsie McFarland, Jim Elmborg, Bob Holman, Marc Smith, Chris Varone, Karl Young, Craig Czury; in Elko by John Dofflemyer, Vess Quinlan, Rod McQueary, Trish O'Malley, Sue Wallis, Buck Ramsey, Sarah Sweetwater, Hank Real Bird, Linda Hasselstrom, Scott Mainwaring, E.T. Collingsworth, Bill Borneman, Ramblin' Jack Elliot; in Japan, China & Korea by Hisao Yamada, Toru Hasegawa, Masatoshi Yonenaga, Charlie Badenhop, Kim Long, Nick May, Nick Szasz, Jayne Geldart, John Liu, H.C. Tien, Chen Minzhang, Jason Hyland, Sameul Cheung, W.S. Chan, David Edwards, Ali M. El-Agraa, Beverly Jean Kawabe, Toyohiko Tamura, Guy Healy, Hideto Ohtsubo, Tomoki Takahashi, Akihiko Ikeda, Brian Burke-Gaffney, Dennis Florig, Chris Reese, Sheng Zhi; in NLP by Will MacDonald, Robert Dilts, Richard Bandler, Connirae Andreas, Steve Andreas, Charles Faulkner, Tim Halbom, Suzi Smith; on radio & TV by Larry Brill, Amanda Davis, Dave Lucas, Jane Karlen, Lorie Perez, Don Strickland, Bill Thompson, James T. Evans, Peter Thiele, Robert C. Anderson, Bill Christian, Steve Cramer, Robert Namer, Rick Barber, John MacDonald, Margaret Kriedler, Dale Harrison, Michael Broderick, Chip Morgan, John Marlow, Tom Prohaska, Carolyn Doughetry, Don Parker, Don Markell, John Quaintance, Bob Miller, Bob Quigley, Gene Pearsall, Joe Pasquali, Michael Calhoun, Dave Faneuf, Bridget Taylor, Eric Blumberg, Jim Walsh, P.J. O'Keefe, Mindy Jackson, Patrick Shelby; in Walla Walla by Ed Foy, Denis Mair, Yan Li, Meng Lang, Xue Di, Teri Zipf, Malinda Pankl, Pat Matthews, Anita Rebelo, Carolyn Kulog, Lani Schroeder, Dave Cortinas, Jeana Garske, Rob Robinson, David Reimer, Bryce Rugraff, Ted Stein, Sharon Doubiago, Neil Meitzler, Ken McIntosh, Mark Sanchez, Zhou Ming Fang, Jean McMenemy, Marc McGary, Jim Lavadour, Vic Randolph, Tracy Williams, Richard Denner, Norm Miller, Don Roff, Jodi Varone, David Axlerod, Phyllis Pulfer, Randall Son, Michael Kiefel, Zhou Min Fang, Paula McMinn, Richard Denner, W. R. "Bill" Wilkins, Joe Pjerrou, Bob Moore, Bob Farrell, Wini Farrell, Howard Young, Scott Forland, Donna Mustard, Eric Wegner, Brandon Follett, Allison Tait, Dan Lamberton, Clark Colahan, Sherry Zanger, Tom Cronin, Junius Rochester, Roger Robbenolt, Karen Yager, Molly Weatherill, Ray Bilderback, Vicki Lloid, Lou Renz, Kay Becker, Dorothy at the Gathering Grounds in Dayton. Undoubtedly, I've forgotten many who've helped me, whose names belong here. Know you are here in spirit. My records are spotty and my memory threadbare. We respond to the yearning to belong to a process that involves many persons, something more massive than ourselves. Thank you.

Contents

A Reason to Read, the Structure of the Spirit:
The Introduction to Pacific Northwestern Spiritual Poetry

I have been reading, writing and publishing poetry for thirty-five years. During this time I have kept my ears open for the sound of significance, for the exceptional poetry that is worth returning to. From the sum total of my life and literary experiences to this point, an esthetic has been distilled. Making this esthetic explicit will not only help to make clear to the assiduous reader the criteria the poetry in this anthology was selected by, but also perhaps to help form a touchstone and make a contribution to the esthetic of other readers. Poetry has a purpose: to elevate the state and feelings of the listener or reader. The purpose of language is disambiguation. Great poetry is disambiguation that stays put.

"A Reason to Read" consists of four main elements. Once presented, they can be considered from any angle and in any order as they make up the structure of spiritual access. Initially however, the first element will be an extract of prophecy as identified by the early 20th century novelist and critic, E.M. Forster in his work *Aspects of the Novel*. The second element, actually a system of measurement and evaluation, is the Buddhist concept of Mahamudra, as expressed by Garma C.C. Chang in his translation and annotation of *The Hundred Thousand Songs of Milarepa*. Poetry, like many other durable substances, can be created in response to pressure. Native American expressions of their faith and fate at the genocidal hands of the European Incursion provide a measurement of how high the human voice can soar under pressure, and are the third element. The fourth element is modern or contemporary psychological therapies that seek to reconnect people to their emotions or feelings primarily through the motion in emotion, ie bodies. Because these feelings are organically and physically related to prophecy, the therapies are tremendously useful. They include the neo-Reichian Radix Therapy of Chuck Kelly, Alexander Lowen's Bioenergetics, Fritz Perls' Concentration Therapy, and the more cerebral but still crucial, since it is the brain and nervous system that wires the human being and body together, Neuro Linguistic Programming of Richard Bandler.

Traditionally significant and leavened throughout, in addition to the four main elements, is a compendium of traditional concepts of how poetry can be created, presented, and evaluated. Among these would be Matthew Arnold's concepts of "high seriousness" and poetry as a religion; Frederico

Garcia-Lorca's elucidation of the gypsy aspects of *Duende*, or the irrational awareness of the presence of death; Samuel Taylor Coleridge's admonition to make a "willing suspension of disbelief" so that poetry may have its intended effect; and William Wordsworth's still contemporary concept of poetry as being the "spontaneous overflow of powerful feelings recollected in tranquillity." These and other traditional concepts of poetry help form an elastic bag with no known limits. It is also pertinent to mention that I have been the beneficiary of such American contributions to the poetic traditions as Ezra Pound's dicta to make it new, as in the *Duende* which can never repeat itself; the variable foot and resultant musicality of William Carlos Williams, our greatest poet; and the "Projective Verse" and "Composition by Field" contributions of Charles Olson. At least two poets in this anthology have consciously tried to make a theory out of their practice and the observable practice of others: Darrell Gray in his "Actualist" esthetic, and Bob Watt's "Inferior Poetry" concept. All of Watt and Gray are recommended reading.

The practice of poetry has a practical intent, namely its purpose to elevate the spiritual state of the listener or reader. Whatever is most apt to provide that elevation of the spirit will work. The only limits set upon poetry are the self imposed limits of the imagination. The elements set forth in "A Reason to Read" provide a structural platform rather than a set of limitations. Other people and poets may arrive at states of sublime spirituality through other methods. That is fine by me. The path and the destination are one. The way of going is referred to as style. Good style is invisible. The more styles we have and the more style we have, the higher we are apt to be able to get. The current state of social and political disintegration, brought about by forces one level of comprehension beyond conscious human control, has contributed to the identification of spirituality as the best permanent choice of coping behaviors. In Arnold Toynbee's terms, this universal state (what's left of the American Empire) has boiled our choices down to supporting the state, revolting against it, or elevating our spirituality. The equally practical matters of material, financial, mental, and physical well being make their contribution to a robust spirituality. We get better behavior from individuals in a spiritually elevated state.

In the quest for an elevated spirituality and a working esthetic for the evaluation of poetry, it is helpful to consult E.M. Forster's *Aspects of the Novel*. We are not concerned here with the individious distinction, occurring in English only about the middle of the 18th century, or barely 250 years ago, between poetry and imaginative prose. We want to know the structure of spiritual elevation. We are after the effect one human voice can have on the state of its hearer and are not in the least bound by the categories concocted by taxonomists seeking to make the disorder they perceive in the universe manageable.

Forster's critique, actually lectures delivered at Trinity College in 1927, has a chatty personable quality that makes it easy to absorb. A great novelist himself, Forster put his clear and compassionate mind to the differentiation of some aspects of novels. We are most concerned here with section VII, "Prophecy," which by placement and implication, Forster takes more seriously than other aspects. We are only peripherally concerned with the other aspects, such as plot, people, pattern, rhythm, and fantasy. The only four novelists that Forster could identify to illustrate the prophetic aspect are Emily Bronte, Fydor Dostoevsky, D.H. Lawrence, and Herman Melville. He is not, thank God, at all concerned with what he calls the narrow aspect of a prophetic foretelling of the future, but rather with an "accent" in the prophet's voice.

I've read many of the novelists he pares away while en route to identifying the four he selects and they are eliminated for cause and on internal evidence. I've also read, and in many cases re-read all of the work of the four in question, except Melville's novel *Mardi*. I have saved *Mardi*, in somewhat the same way a gourmet would hold back a bottle of vintage wine. I am going to need an impressive lift someday and when I do, I will finish reading Melville. Both Lawrence and Melville wrote poetry also, most of which is noticeably inferior to their prose. The works of Bronte, Dostoevsky, Lawrence and Melville are the most interesting in prose literature. Forster speaks of the accent in their voices, of their ability to sing, of the tone of their voices. Their stimulations are many and diverse, but their ear for song is what unites them and what relates them to poetry. Immersed too completely in some instances, in the poetic life of Pocatello, Idaho; Seattle, Washington; Berkeley, California; Salt Lake City, Utah; and now finally in Walla Walla, Washington, I have heard in the poets' voices this same tone and accent of prophetic voice. There can be no substitute of course, for the whole enchilada, and serious readers, whether skeptics or affirmators, will one day soon want to read not only the chapter on "Prophecy" but the entire *Aspects of the Novel*. It is a short book and the lift is vertical.

It is the voice of prophecy that extends us beyond our social containers and into the realm of human feeling. Bronte with the transcendent passion of Catherine and Heathcliffe, Lawrence irradiating especially our sacred erotic nature, and Dostoevsky's capacity to convey the sensations of extension and a translucent sinking, stimulate a transcendent spiritual elevation and release. In Forster's terms, it is ultimately Melville's undercurrent of depth, where we notice the stress and the intervals, but fail to catch the words of the song, that constitutes the most significant aspect of *Moby Dick or the White Whale*. We only know that someone has been singing. *Moby Dick* is a funereal poem, a dirge disguised as a eulogy for a rapacious economic system that will one day spit us all out. There is no better book. As Lawrence himself once said of Melville, he set out to write a metaphysical book and got deeper than metaphysics. The significance of artistic methodologies for releasing human emotions is not lost on us, for most of us are trained from birth to suppress our feelings and contain and otherwise thwart their expression. Unexpressed feelings result in the increase and buildup of negative emotional intensity. It is to getting rid of this angst and anguish that prophecy appeals.

There are more tidy methods for the release of feelings than the "intermittent realism" of the prophetic novelists, particularly the application of contemporary psychological processes, but alone they are absent the esthetic element which gives spirituality its transcendent qualities. We'll get to them shortly. In partial summation, Forster says: "Prophetic fiction, then, seems to have definite characteristics. It demands humility and the absence of the sense of humor. It reaches back–though we must not conclude from the example of Dostoevsky that it always reaches back to pity and love. It is spasmodically realistic. And it gives us the sensation of a song or of sound. It is unlike fantasy because its face is towards unity, whereas fantasy glances about. Its confusion is incidental, whereas fantasy's is fundamental...Also the prophet–one imagines–has gone 'off' more completely than the fantasist, he is in a remoter emotional state while he composes."

The "reaching back" that Forster refers to is related both in direction and intensity to what the psychologist Julian Jaynes called "The Bicameral Mind" which in his opinion was the state of human affairs prior to the acquisition of consciousness, circa the middle of the Second Millennium B.C. Jaynes' book, *The Origin of Consciousness in the Breakdown of the Bicameral Mind*," is worthy of everyone's attention. The condition of bicamerality, where old Jewish prophets heard the voice of God and transcribed it, where the voices of the Greek gods, acting like auditory admonitions, gave the Greeks their marching orders in the *Iliad*, has been replaced with the whining insistence of conscious thought where people have become their own gods. Bicamerality is also the condition that schizophrenics revert to when they hear voices. Old-time bicamerality is the source of both classic and contemporary poetry. Poets still hear these voices and simultaneously try to make sense out of them and link us all back up with or forward to, that reservoir of connectedness represented by the bicamerality. No wonder poets are dismissed by the majordomos of culture as representing a primitive, atavistic, and more or less mad aspect of humanity. Poetry will prevail.

Forster does not include James Joyce among the prophets, saying that "a prophet does not reflect. And he does not hammer away." Of Joyce he also says, "in spite of all his internal looseness he is too tight, he is never vague except after due deliberation: It is talk, talk, never song." And it is the song with which we are concerned. The song that will touch our emotions directly and, by stimulating the release of emotion, elevate our state so that we might be equal to the disambiguation of each succeeding moment with all the style at our command. It is possible of course to "talk" oneself or others a little higher, and at any given moment many are doing just that. The biosphere, or the infinitesimally tiny part of the universe in which we can live without life support, gives off sound. It is the ultimate responsibility of the poet to learn to hear and recognize these sounds that are the essence of existence and to get as many of them as possible across to other poets and people.

A surprising lot of misleading nonsense has been composed over the centuries concerning the visual and imagistic aspects of poetry. There can be no doubt of the primacy of the visual system among our five senses. Its hypnogogic aspect helps explain the commercial success of the techno-manipulators of everything from nickelodeons through movies to MTV and on to the Internet. It is just the primacy of the visual system which makes it so susceptible to being thrown into high relief by an exquisite appeal to first, the auditory system, and then to complete the triangulation with an overwhelming kinesthetic or physical sensation. The unifying sensations are as rapid as any neurotransmission and can occur in random order. We have perhaps been too enthralled for too long with the traditional romantic notion that our feelings are located or centered in the organ of the heart, or worse by the intellectuation of the feelings to the extent that we turn them into thoughts and locate them in the brain. Kinesthetic esthetics, or the art of motion, properly locates the feelings in the muscles (see the work cited above of Reich, Kelly, Lowen, Perls, and Bandler) where they have been stored and their expression thwarted by our traditional churchy and other fears. The tone or the accent in the voice is most crucial, for the tone is established by the attitude toward the subject. The typical prophet's attitude might be composed of different parts: humility, desperate seriousness, a fine eye for significant detail, a face toward unity, the ability to reach back from a remote state, and a sense of hearing that can make music or song out of language.

Prophetic novels have a "wreaked air" inside them and so too does prophetic poetry. It is, after all, the emotional jail of western civilization that we are trying to break out of. Other cultural troves approach human life with different esthetic equipment. I can't imagine for a moment that the felt reality of the Japanese culture, for example, where feelings are far less apt to be traditionally denied and the surface of things held in high regard, would find the prophetic esthetic remotely appealing. In the robust Buddhism of Milarepa, a Tibetan considered by his acolytes to be the Buddha reincarnate, however, there exists a way to evaluate language hierarchically to see how close it is getting to the elusive "song" qualities we seek. In "The Gray Rock Vajra Enclosure," a song to explain among other things, the four stages of Mahamudra, Milarepa sings, "A wandering thought is itself the essence of Wisdom." The four stages of Mahamudra are the stage of One-Pointedness, the stage of Away-from-Playwords, the stage of One-Taste, and the stage of Non-Practice. These stages correspond to levels of enlightenment. And we need to become aware of what is enlightenment and what merely resembles enlightenment. In terms of the composition of poetry, or prose, I am asking the four stages of Mahamudra to refer to levels of capacity reflecting insight into the human condition.

The first stage, that of One-Pointedness, could include practically all writing that succeeds in putting voice to paper by pen, or once of hitting typewriter keys, and now of the relentless electronic fingering click of the word processor. Regrettably, most poetry never gets beyond the first stage of enlightenment: "I think, therefore, I write and type and even without ever having passed through the requisite Cartesian doubt, imagine my work is full of wisdom and poetic virtues." Far too many poets and far too much poetry is stranded at the first stage on this level.

The second stage of Away-From-Playwords is a step in the direction of enlightenment. Playwords litter the poetic landscape like the bones of drought abandoned cattle. Puns, figures of speech, intrusive alliteration, rime, palindromes, decorative similes, poorly mixed metaphors and other bric-a-brac of language, are evidence the poet is aware that he or she is using words cleverly but not much else. The results are chiefly limited in appeal. Hard end-rime is the common cold of poetry in English; better poets get over it before it turns into something fatal. Mandarin

Chinese, a phonetically impoverished language with only approximately one-tenth the variety of sounds and syllables as English, is a simple language to find end-rimes in and still make sense. English, hopelessly imperial and hugely diverse, is not. Shakespeare knew to put his puns in the mouths of his most contemptible characters. Any poetry might have some of this bric-a-brac in it. It is when the bric-a-brac is displayed as the essence that it becomes most loathsome and necessary to avoid. While a step in the right direction, playing with words will result in word-play. It is rarely enlightening. The emphasis on hearing the song and the tone of voice suggests that many would be poets fail because they have no usefully engaging attitude, are tone deaf to boot in other words, and write with tin ears.

Transcending Away-From-Playwords to the level of One-Taste represents a mature stage of enlightenment and not a lot of what passes for literature gets this high or goes beyond. It is where, for essential contrast, the work of James Joyce stalls out. He gets so wrapped up in the punning potential of the 17 languages he wallowed around in that he fails to recognize what a small box cleverness finally is. If cleverness was all that counted, Joyce would truly be the greatest writer in English. Cleverness is worth something, but all that deliberate calculation makes the vagary suspect and the talk tedious. Talk gets in the way of song. The best "talk" in English is written by scholars and other focused writers considering objective subject matter one order of magnitude more pertinent than the clever poet focused on the intricacies of his own personality. That is the primary source of vicarious information not directly obtainable from experience. Any bright young man [or woman], as Kenneth Rexroth once said, can be taught to be arty but great works of art are nobly disheveled. The prophetic prose writers identified by Forster are as often clumsy as clever, because it is not the finished product that concerns them the most, but the motion in the forward rush of emotion that ultimately makes such a satisfying statement, far above the mess of all the contrivance of the merely clever.

The stage of Non-Practice, where the poet has achieved the level of prophecy, is indicative of the deep, serious, desperate circumstances that they write from, having recognized the entire human race to be on, as Eugene Lesser says, "the edge of a precipice." Evidence accumulated in my experience with poetry suggests that it is difficult and seldom if ever possible to rise more than one level above where the poet started. In other words, the "prophetic" poets collected in this anthology nearly all begin at the stage of One-Taste, and rarely, if ever, at the level of Away-from-

Playwords or down to One-Pointedness.

The greatest American Indian poet, Nezuacoyotyl, the Aztec philosopher king of Texcoco one generation prior to Cortez, whose name translates as the Starving Coyote, has prophetic elements, although he personally never suffered any depredations at the hands of the Spanish Incursion. Many examples of the wandering thought as the essence of both song and wisdom could be cited from the extant work of American Indians, since not only was their situation sad, deep and desperate, and much of it still squarely in a Neolithic bicamerality, their feelings were closer to the surface where their fate was sealed. Mangus Colorado the Navajo, after being allowed to return from Bosque Redondo said, "We were so happy, we felt like talking to the ground." Black Elk, the Lakota medicine man once observed, "Everything in the universe is trying to be round." Chief Joseph of the Nez Perce, when finally forced to surrender said, "From where the sun now stands, I will fight no more forever." Tatanka Yotanka or Sitting Bull once said, "I am here by the will of the Great Spirit, and by his will I am a chief. My heart is red and sweet, and I know it is sweet, because whatever passes near me puts out its tongue to me." It would be both wonderful and impossible to reproduce in these pages the utterly vertical sound of Sonny Mosquito's four octave range, over a drum on the Rosebud Reservation in Crowdog's Paradise, leading the singing of the AIM (American Indian Movement) song circa 1974. Many contemporary American Indian poets have such ready access to this stage of Non-Practice, that much of what they write is easily imbued with the aspects of song. Their compositional problems are of a wholly different order. They are in the nature of responsibility taking, a process that can be intensely painful, and in far more cases than just the American Indian one, systematically avoided. A work that is all song is finally as stultifying as one that is completely clever.

Responsibility avoidance is the national and perhaps even the international pastime. That is where the great psychiatrists and psychologists enter the picture with full force. There is more than a hint of truth in the application of the works cited by Reich, Kelly, Lowen, Perls and Bandler and their relationship to human feeling. Feeling is as likely to be stored in the muscles as it is in the traditional valentine heart. The literal heart, the genitals, the muscles around the eyes as erotic organs, the muscles of the feet and legs, which either ground you or leave you off balance, the arms with which you express the longing in the human breast, the way you hold on, these are the physical equipment of emotional spirituality. Mobilizing feelings held here is most rapidly done in Radix

Therapy with help. The Concentration Therapy of Perls can be applied individually to practically anything. Nothing will ground you quite as quickly as Bioenergetics. Lowen's books, *The Betrayal of the Body* and *The Physical Dynamics of Character Structure,* available in many languages, make the relationship between denied feelings and a crippled spirit clear. Lowen, a psychiatrist, cites Dostoevsky as often as he does Freud. The Neuro Linguistic Programming work of Richard Bandler, as in *Using Your Brain for a Change*, is indispensable help to get and keep you in the same place where the sound of prophetic poetry can take you. Motion and emotion move the song along.

There is a different type of fatality awaiting the contemporary inhabitants of North America (just as the Indians in their turn were done in by a bigger Spirit than the one they had in mind as being loyal to them–an utterly inadequate projection), and a related but different fate for the rest of the world's inhabitants. The premier American geographer, Carl O. Sauer, observed that it is accumulating divergence, rather than cyclical repetition easily charted by lazy observation, that requires attention. As we spiral into divergence at ever accelerating rates, the passionate need to stay connected to our deep feeling for ourselves and for the past has broken through many surfaces. Which may be why, that although Forster could only identify four major prose writers as being capable of "prophecy," there are many poets in this anthology who are. It is related to the increasingly desperate human situation. Only song will suffice; other writing and poetry stalled out in descending order at any of the three lower levels of Mahamudra might just as well be linoleum or wallpaper.

Prophecy is apparent in other art forms as well. In movies, the one that reaches back the furthest and includes more people with depth of feeling, is the Soviet film *Siberiade* by Andrei Mikhalkov Konchalovsky. Among traditional English poets, the most exemplary of "prophecy" are Wordsworth, Yeats, and of course Shakespeare with his fabulous objectivity. Much of Shakespeare's most prophetic utterances are directly cribbed from Golding's translation of Ovid's *Metamorphosis*. This is very germane, since the entire prophetic linking up with the past may be our efforts to reconnect with lost cultural roots, the bicamerality, of the pre-Christian and Celtic European past, the foundation of Ovid's great work. Modern Spanish poetry has it in abundance in many poets including Pablo Neruda, Octavio Paz, and Frederico Garcia-Lorca. The Japanese, having been wise enough to avoid Christian oppression in favor of their other domestic and imported brands, seem largely immune to prophecy. Aspects of it do however seem to be present in the best work of Miyazawa Kenji.

27

Coleridge's "willing suspension of dis-belief" is very straightforward and will always be germane. It is possible to refute Shakespeare, or any other lover babbling in your ear, entirely if done line by line. You must be willing to hear the prophets out if you are going to be able to hear their song. Wordsworth also is still hot news, although his appraisal that the best poetry is the "spontaneous overflow of powerful feelings recollected in tranquillity," is one of the most misunderstood and misapplied concepts available to us. All six elements in the appraisal have to be present or the process will reflect the results poorly. Far too many poets rush to open their mouths using only one of the six elements, or sometimes two, or even three. Many are spontaneous and simply gurgle without flowing. Others attempt to regale with their feelings, even though they are not powerful or strongly held. Many are incapable of re-collecting whatever feelings they may have had. Tranquillity is a rare state to get into, let alone maintain. If the feelings are not powerful, not spontaneous, and unrecollectable, stand by to be bored by any of several hundred thousand ways to be a bad romantic.

Going very far into *Duende* here could be counterproductive, for it has some resemblance to and may be the Celtic gypsy equivalent of the Tao–the longer you talk about it, the less of it you have. But looking up the full treatment in Garcia-Lorca is highly recommended in either *Deep Song and Other Prose,* "Play and Theory of the Duende" as translated by Christopher Maurer, or *Poet in New York* translated by Ben Belitt as "The Duende: Theory and Divertissement." The relationship between gypsies and spontaneous movement should be apparent, as they say it comes up to you from the soles of your feet, a sentiment Lowen would recognize instantly. They say life will kill you but they won't say when. Singing is the most convincing thing that will both reconnect you with and save you from your own death.

So, I am back to the beginning with a very unruly flower unfurled. Is poetry a bona fide religion, or can it or should it be, a la Matthew Arnold? What else besides the deep feeling of connectedness can be believed in for long? This is especially important for speakers of English, where our traditional emphasis on individualism and the rights of individuals, plus the psychological maturation process which attempts to turn us into self-responsible islands, isolates us one from another. I am sufficiently aware of the elaborate belief systems that pass for the world's major religions, belief systems that exist often without a shred of reproducible evidence, to realize that they purvey no spiritual relief. These religions are, in fact, the "evil" they incessantly warn us against.

28

Reawakened feelings are evidence of connectivity. Rejoice as you can. Not everyone will hear the songs of all the poets herein. But everyone will hear the songs of some. The more song you hear, the more connected you become. Nothing would give me any more pleasure than to know that a song or two here or even many might send you searching for the rest of that poet's songs (or imbue you with the courage to sing yourself), for that is the ultimate purpose of all theory and criticism: to lead you to the evidence itself. Learn to listen for the sounds of the universe in your own world. So many of these poets are already dead: Charles Foster, Darrell Gray, d.a. levy, David Sandberg, Charles Bukowski, Ricardo Sánchez, Bruce Embree, Zig Knoll.

This poetry was created in the second half of the 20th century, largely though not exclusively, in the Pacific Northwest. It is the work of independent poets, few of whom are or were acquainted with one another or even with one another's work. It does not represent the work of a school, no flying wedge of culture driven through the stout academic resistance of the university system where prophecy (other than explicit budget cuts) is about the last thing they want to hear. In Washington, the legislature explicitly meets to concoct policy that won't upset Christians with the truth. This anthology has nothing to do with nationalism, America, or any sociological hotboxes of cultural misrepresentation. There are several hundred poets, many of whom are friends and acquaintances of mine, whose work I have read and listened to, who aren't represented here. I don't love them any less for that; they compose in different ways for different ends. I mention this to make clear that the work has been chosen from a large expanse of possibilities.

These poets sing with a wide variety of voices. Among the very best of them, the prophetic elements are apparent throughout their work. Not all the poets in PNSP exhibit all the elements of prophecy all the time or to the same degree, though more of it is often displayed in longer work. If you have the knack organically, it is not something you can leave behind without distress. In other poets, many represented here by shorter works filled with epiphanic flashes, it seems to occur only occasionally. And as one disparate and highly distinctive voice, Bob Watt of Wisconsin says, "The best poetry is still in the air and has not been written yet." This anthology is intended to be the beginning of at least as many things as it is the culmination of. It is an instrument to tune your soul on, to answer the question: what is the structure of the spirit? You are responsible for the songs you sing.

PS: Just at the moment when it would have made sense to expand the range of PNSP, health considerations made it necessary to contract. Nevertheless there are many fine poets in the Pacific Northwest, let alone elsewhere, who aren't represented here and future anthologists will do well to consider the work of at least Janine Canan, Judith Arcana, Harald Wyndham, Judith Roche, Margaret Aho, James Bertolino, Ann Spiers, Bill Borneman, David Lloyd Whited, Paul Dresman, Sam Hamill, Noelle Sullivan, Paul Hunter, Michael Hood, Jesse Bernstein, Jeff Meyers, Reuben Nisenfeld, Charlie Burks, Martin Vest, Phoebe Bosche, Douglas Airmet, Belle Randall, Walt Curtis, Alex Kuo, Ron McFarland, Leanne Grabel and Doug Draime among many others. Anthologies are tests of the capacity to compromise. It would have been nice to have included Judy Grahn's "A Woman Is Talking to Death," and Stanley Crouch's "Slow Sea," and "Up on the Spoon" from his book *Ain't No Ambulances For No Niggers Tonight*. They are recommended reading. All the great poets of the Pacific Northwest not included here have my apologies. All the great poets included here have my thanks.

Sherman Alexie
(1966-)

Father Coming Home

THEN   Father coming home from work. Me, waiting on
        the front steps, watching him walk slowly and
        carefully, like half of a real Indian. The other half
stumbling, carrying the black metal lunch box with maybe half a
sandwich, maybe the last drink of good coffee out of the thermos,
maybe the last bite of a dream.

SPOKANE   Father coming home from work five days a week.
        Me, waiting every day until the day he doesn't
        come walking home, because he cut his knee in
half with a chainsaw. Me, visiting my father laying in bed in the
hospital in Spokane. Both of us, watching the color television until
my mother comes from shopping at Goodwill or Salvation Army,
until the nurses come in telling us we have to go.

CEREMONIES Father coming home from the hospital in a
        wheelchair. Me, waiting for him to stand up and
        teach me how to shoot free throws. Me, running
up to him one day and jumping hard into his lap, forgetting about
his knee. Father holding me tight against his chest, dark and muddy,
squeezing his pain into my thin ribs, his eyes staying clear.

AFTER   Father coming home from the mailbox, exercising
        his knee again and again. Me, looking up from
        the floor as he's shaking his head because there
is no check, no tiny miracles coming in the mail. Father bouncing
the basketball, shooting lay-in after lay-in, working the knee until
it bleeds along the scars. Father crying from the pain late at night,
watching television. Me, pretending to be asleep. All of us listening
to canned laughter.

INSOMNIA   Father coming home from another job interview,
        limping only a little but more than enough to

keep hearing no, no, no. Me, eating potatoes
again in the kitchen, my mother's face growing darker and darker
by halves. One half still mostly beautiful, still mostly Indian, the
other half something all-crazy and all hungry. Me, waking her up
in the middle of the night, telling her my stomach is empty. Her
throwing me outside in my underwear and locking the door. Me
trying anything to get back in.

HOMECOMING   Father coming home from drinking, after being
                  gone for weeks. Me, following him around all
                  the time. Him, never leaving my sight, going into
the bathroom. Me, sitting outside the door, waiting, knocking on
the wood every few seconds, asking him are you there. *Are you still
there?*

NOW   Father coming home finally from a part-time job,
                  driving a water truck for the BIA. Me, waiting
                  on the front steps, watching him come home
early every day. Him, telling my mother when they think I can't
hear, he doesn't know if he's strong enough. Father telling mother
he was driving the truck down Little Falls Hill, trying to downshift
but his knee not strong enough to keep holding the clutch in. Me,
holding my breath. Him, driving around the corner on two wheels,
tons and tons of water, half-insane. Me, closing my eyes. Him, balancing,
always ready to fall. Me, holding onto father with all my strength.

The Business of Fancydancing

After driving all night, trying to reach
Arlee in time for the fancydance
finals, a case of empty
beer bottles shaking our foundations, we
stop at a liquor store, count out money,
and would believe in the promise

of any man with a twenty, a promise
thin and wrinkled in his hand, reach-
ing into the window of our car. Money
is an Indian Boy who can fancydance
from powwow to powwow. We
got our boy, Vernon WildShoe, to fill our empty

wallets and stomachs, to fill our empty
cooler. Vernon is like some promise
to pay the light bill, a credit card we
Indians get to use. When he reach-
es his hands up, feathers held high, in a dance
that makes old women speak English, the money

for first place belongs to us, all in cash, money
we tuck in our shoes, leaving our wallets empty
in case we pass out. At the modern dance,
where Indians dance white, a twenty is a promise
that can last all night long, a promise reach-
ing into back pockets of unfamiliar Levis. We

get Vernon there in time for the finals and we
watch him like he was dancing on money,
which he is, watch the young girls reach-
ing for him like he was Elvis in braids and an empty
tipi, like Vernon could make a promise
with every step he took, like a fancydance

could change their lives. We watch him dance
and he never talks. It's all a business we
understand. Every drum beat is a promise
note written in the dust, measured exactly. Money
is a tool, putty to fill all the empty
spaces, a ladder so we can reach

for more. A promise is just like money.
Something we can hold, in twenties, a dream we reach.
It's business, a fancydance to fill where it's empty.

Diane Averill
(1946-)

Tour

So the rain in Monteverde
brushes faces with warm
powder   butterfly-wing dust,
as our Costa Rican guide
explains why
this particular species of caterpillar
developed orange dots on its back.

"A wasp will try to lay
its orange eggs
on top of a caterpillar.
If it succeeds,
the caterpillar will
still form a pupa, but what emerges
is
not
a butterfly. It's a wasp."

Through the pane,
a young woman has waited so long
in the abortion clinic, she's gone
into labor. An older woman stops
her tour group. Members complain that they
have only a limited amount of
time. They shift uneasily in Gortex
while the older woman helps
deliver the baby. A wet head emerges,
then a whole body. The young woman's
womb closes with a fast-forward shudder.
She smiles, begins to walk
away. "Aren't you going to take your baby?"
asks the older woman. The tour group crowds
are humming now,

going crazy, like frustrated sports
fans.

The young woman shakes
her red locks,
explains in the patient
voice of a guide,
"That wasn't my baby. That was a
parasite he put in me." She points to
a billboard politician, huge on
a nearby hill.
The older woman looks down at the
baby. It has dried into a tiny,
yet exact replica of the billboard man.

The wings in Monteverde bring
more rain, as the guide explains
that some species

protect themselves with bright
color. "Red, for example,
could warn away a predator who may
mistake its prey for poison.

Then again, it might not."

mel buffington
(1937-)

whats important is

whats important is
what gets done
& nothing is
getting done
&
nothing is important
& that is important

importance is
nothing getting done
as walls crumble
as buildings tumble
& lives snuff out
faster than one
can count: nothing
nothing, nothing
is light dying out
& when we see
the light the body
has already exploded
is done
& that is important
& nothing
is important
that gets done
its done
& now is never, nothing
getting done

stars moon sun earth
are not done & nothing
is important
getting done & coyote
howls the past

that is not done
not important
& when there is no
dope to smoke no
smoking gets done &
its not anything
not important
& waking up means
being asleep is
important & seeing
the entire day
ahead of you
is not important
not done
an abyss, really
impossible
& only important
after you get through it
& it is past tense
& not important
& nothing in this poem
is done & nothing
is important

whats important is
what gets done & u
can never have the last
word so dont look for
importance there
& here we are, going
not done going
& not important
until the going is done
& important no longer

& when you are no longer
confused confusion
is done & that is important &
u dont think about it
any longer & so
it is no longer important
& that is important
when you stop
,& think about it

code of the west

since we're neighbors

lets kill each other
its obvious

we dont see
eye to eye
over the fence

yr grass is greener

& yr barbecue smoke
stings my nose

yr guests are noisy
& keep staring at
my naked friends

yr dogs shit

on my rock garden
& bark at me at 3 a.m.

when I'm relaxing
under a full moon
w/ the stones singing sweet

across the cool night air

through the mysticism of
crickets in tall grass

& dancing worms
u have called the cops
on me, countless times

& i

have (not once) complained
about yr thick neck

yr poleyester clothes, yr
bestial children
yr materialism

i think it's time

for a showdown
(since we're neighbors)

u shoot first
i'll ask questions later
,code of the west

Multnomah Falls

at night
,spotlit,
it shines

cold, cold
my love drives
west, I hitch

east

the water
which fell

around us
falls
between us now

poets, poets, poets

o poets, poets, poets

everywhere singing
some damnfine songs, too

everywhere poets

hipdeep (poets)
in the streets

high in the mountains

poets, poems
flooding the sweet streams

out, in the desert

goosing indians
and gila monsters

pulling poems out

of thin air, poets
magicians, screwy

gurus

& LOOK (look!)
DISAPPEARING AROUND THAT CORNER

isn't that the foot

of a famous
poet

poets melting into crowds

poets lurking in alleys
poets joining hands

in common brotherhood, poets

joining the army
poets disguised as tourists

poets disguised as poets

o sniffing
through the garden, poets

under the beds

of vestal virgins
lying still, lying

still, stiff poets

stumbling along hallways
stoned, bombed, liquored up

out of sight poets

writing poems, writing
books of poems, poets

o, playing with children poets

chasing butterflies
in the wind poets

poets under glass

poets under fire
poets underground

high in the sky, low

in the saddle, deep
in the deep, blue sea

far from home

groping in darkness
blinded by the sun

searching for truth

lolling in the shade
of the old oak tree poets

yes poets, poets, poets

of rhyme and reason
of time and space and season

of love of hate

of war of peace of day
of night of loneliness

of greatness of smallness
of this, that
the other thing, poets

leading parades

of green angels of Erin
and flags of america

poets sinking ships

steering straight courses
by the stars

winning battles

losing wars, poets
of fuck

of dance and woo

of bob and weave
affairs of the heart poets

making it harder

making it easier
making it poets

poets of mystery

poets of sadness
gladness

virtue, vice

and everything nice
poets, poets

poets celebrating

life, lamenting
death

laughing, sighing, moaning

screaming, bellowing, cajoling
dancing and swaying,

singing, crying, groaning,

wallowing in sin, wallowing
in piety, wallowing in mud

wallowing in the murky waters

of all the seas
of all the world

high and mighty

low and earthy
poets, poets of despair

poets of academia

poets of just causes, poets
of poetry

poets of poets

schools of poets, bands
of poets

individual poets, all

bent and broken, straight
and proud, o, poets, all

humble men and women

tumbling through this thankful
thankless eye of time

scar on scar

they stack their poems up
on floors and tables

and on bookshelves

and in our minds
from day to year

we pull one out

(poet) (poem)
,and read it.

Charles Bukowski
(1922-1993)

The Hairy Hairy Fist, and Love Will Die

the dull haunches will sit in chairs and
fart   see
the paper
flowers   old women in
Lent   horse with broken
leg
        spider
taking it
in
        wrinkles under bedpan
            chins

acromegaly   diverticulitis   tabes
dorsalis

—your soul
        filled with
mud and bats and curses, and the hammers will
        go in
there will be the hairy
        hairy
        fists and
love will
die
love will stroke the balls of your worst
        enemy
and your neck with ache and toiletpaper will
stick in your
        crotch
and out the window: the same: pictures of
        torture & Murder & horror:
cats with
        birds
cats with
        mice
dogs with
        cats

blind men like ivory needing a
       shave
   and
the petulant and nasty children of the
        universe
stealing climbing planning
        cutting
    warring
always so healthy always so
    strong

ah, your soul will feel so
    bad
that the saliva will run from your
    mouth
      in cupfuls
patches of paint
    and sores
   will appear
on your face
      and under your
arms
and sleep will be the last thing they will let you
    have

men you could trust will fade like
     children's
      drawings
your wife will hate you
your child will
    ignore
     you
the police will jail you
     and
there will be no
   bottom

                            the soul will fall like a wounded
                            bird of Paradise
                    into
the most horrible stinking swill of
                    shit
and
still   no death
                    still no
                death
                    you will fail at
                death
                too
and there will not even be the
                    peace
                    of
                    isolation   the final
greyback cellar
                    just more
hammers
                    more saws more engines more bad
                    music more relaxed voices of
                    zero

you will be
            ripped
                    up and
                    down
until your clothing no longer fits
you
                you will be the
                        scarecrow
                    the
rag the smelling
                    rag of a
                thing

and

                    the enemy—which is
                    everyone—will
                    appear
beautifully clothed
                         calm
                         smiling
driving
                    smooth rolls of shining
                              steel
                              and
                    the sun
            will fall upon him like a
flower

your soul will feel so bad
that you know it will not every quite
live again and
there will be nothing you can
do—drink will not
patch it
prayer will not
save it
praise from the enemy will not
heal it

                    nothing will
                    work
                    nothing will be
                    nothing
like a harp with strings
broken
                    in somebody's corner
                    in somebody's misery garbage
while all around
                    like the 4th of July
                    like bedding with a virgin
                    like champagne over the head of
easy wildness
the force of other things and other ways will
                    celebrate the occasion   their
existence
without   you.

Casey Bush
(1953-)

Kiss of the Apocalypse

as the millennium descends religious fanatics drag the
rest of us into the total fallacy of this the last and
final war of words, that fiery collapse and total
destruction of great cities foretold by the Bible in a
world so plainly ours to invent pleasure and as often to
frighten ourselves with numerological superstitions,
Indoor outings, luridly sensational bitter personal feuds
raising tension breeding corruption, laziness and
stunning incompetence, demanding a demon of the unclean
bathing in a fountain of idolatrous water, baptism spawning
streets full of tumult whodunit fix-it-up soup kitchens
serving cool whip bird's nest, symbols and formulas, an idea
forgotten, comets filling the sky, iron bridges crashing
down from mountains, factory chimney collapsing into the
shop, hissing rows of windows waving fake ID in the face of
the fuzz like a nymph pissing on a tray of Christmas sweets
before the entire congregation of mermaids or gargoyles with
flippers and fins or the hooves of a cow and horns of a goat
and goblins whose lame bald headed leader is monstrously
endowed sprouting an unexpected seed that cannot easily
be eradicated nodding bloody lips in approval escalating
explanations of well financed premonitions upon a
precipice claiming eternal glory while decimating
recognizable subject matter as a necessary step in the
battle against the tainted materialism of our times.

Andy Clausen
(1943-)

J-E-E-E-E-E-E-E-E-E-E-E-E-E-E-E-S-U-S CHRIST

Extreme Unction
Part I

Root for Barrabas,
Root for Christ
Go Man Go

My United States of America died of a broken heart
    on the lonesome railroad tracks
    just outside San Miguel Allende, Old Mexico
My United States took ship to Europe
    and sends coded love messages from Istanbul
My United States is a pacifist archangel
    in exile hiding from the two-faced demons
    of the ten-sided asshole Mammon
My United States has been put on trial
    for uncontrollable dreams and
    living justice outside the law, just a man
My United States is as innocent as
    you, my friend, are innocent as the winos are innocent
And in your defense the birth wet infant howls
    as he enters the world with a resounding slap
    Ladies and Gentlemen of the jury your honor
I call you not judgers for fear I judge
I call you the soapy hands of Pontius Pilate
I call you an eagle with a broken wing
I call you thumbs down coliseum of Rome
I call you Salome the head-shrinking policeman's wife

We need no more religious we need more visions
We need not more politics but rather more crayons
It's all about God or fucking and it's a thin line
But if it sounds like something you
heard before it's because it is
and it's still all true, 0 my brothers

A pack of starved lions roared a bloody
Armageddon through
the crystal bell radio in his disintegrating
jalopy
He heard a Muzak machine perform the
Star Spangled Banner for the last time
He saw a bronze raven perched on the shoulder
of a black statue of William Jennings Bryan
And he waved good-bye to the marines
And stretched out his arms to our guardian angel
Flash a visionary I love you who handed him the
birth of the blues, a book to learn about birth
and the blues that follow
On the first page was a fifty year old
Photograph of a beer drinking party
which at first appeared to be just
some country folks celebrating the holiday
But the more he looked their faces grew uglier
smiling, smiling, smiling sinister
like jackals, like vultures like inhuman parasites
And there in the background almost
unnoticed was the ungodly reason for
this celebration
Hanging from an old oaken tree
A teenage Negro with a broken neck
Eli Eli Lamma Lamma Sabacthani his
ghost haunts the rat infested walls of
nigger town what is done is done
He fell to his knees and prayed sweating
for the second coming hoping to save his soul

When a rainbow did appear for a cunt hair
portion of a second
or was it just another hallucination
a blind man searching for his vision
inside his mother's womb
show me the way
show me the way
I think I've lost my way

She was a twenty year old who happy bounced
And laughed aloud when she wailed
Who threw her arms around him
When the spectre of his selfishness,
rendered him incapable
Yet still somehow for some unfathomable
reason she turned away repulsed by his
whiskied breath when he reached to
touch her leg and hold it against his face
Who sentenced him to the dungeon
Where he composed a booklet
of long ago abandoned poems
For her who am he recited Om
and a Catholic poem praying for mercy
hope, rebirth, salvation and enlightenment of Lucifer
and upon hearing the angels underground
chanted the ball and chain hymnodies of
the California Catacombs,
The please please please get it together
wails of impoverished America's cantos
aching for justice and love,
She for whom neon lights sparkled
Industry's illuminated alleluia
and unfolded amidst the iambic grunts of tractors
and the regimented pounding of jack hammers
the fulfillment of every prophetic
Lord have mercy cry of men imprisoned
inside a call
A blues good enough for me

A thousand tasks to perform
a million ways to tell the same story
three and a half billion tales to listen to
and make his own
Yet instead he got fucked up falling down
snotnose drunk
His sticky tokay stained orifice adhering
to the bewitched thirteenth rib
of the not so free Lady Of the Harbor
holding the key to a bank vault in one hand and a Playboy in
the other as he rolled over and murmured I thirst.
and was given a bottle of red vinegar to drink and expired
his last words "I'm going home to see Johanna," carry on
I buried him next to a mountain
that upon returning with
Wildflower bouquet in hand
had vanished
And in Its stead
Stood his ghost
Wearing a torn T-shirt
And faded blue jeans
Sweating, talking like crazy man
Feverishly clutching at his own body
Reliving before my eyes Paradise Lost
And countless wars that followed
the bitter tears of Cain's curse, a bent stick
and the look of a man who'd seen hell
in his eyes
as he spoke, "On one side of the mountain
Was a sign written in fool's gold
'No trespassers, violators will be persecuted'
And on the other, written in the blood of I am not
'Virgin Mary'"

Resisting the temptation to jump in the river and drown
he reappeared an California's Chicago water front
inside the body of a seventeen year old Japanese American
A reflection of flesh and bones

The miraculous substances that unleashed
martyred molecules in a sex savage
nuclear implosion of revolutionary energy harnessed
to momentarily halt a phantom train
of napalm exploding between the nerve
endings of his Nagasakied brain
which underwent a zipzap dimes worth
of wireless electric shock therapy
and awoke alongside a hookah
discussing Flatt and Scruggs and Ho Chi Minh
A gas station Marxist undermining
Standard Oil with contraband rocket fuel
And minted kilograms of disorienting dialectic
A cannonball cowboy planning a
Bloodless coup d'etat stampede in
the novocained hypothalamus of Wyoming
singing please won't you give me your heart
I want your heart beating close to mine
A self ordained deacon baptizing
his own heterodoxical body with the
precious turbid water
of the Ganges River miraculously
flowing out of an electric faucet
in the Santa Cruz mountains
D. H., Lawrence driving a Renault Dauphin
through a hail of radioactive brimstone
racing T. S. Eliot's Volkswagen to the
Saturday night barnyard dance
two eyes square dancing in Jonathan Edward's
tubercular mouth debating the most
    absurd paradox
to be or not to be/humanity or divinity
the electric harpsichord of theology
the three stringed banjo of eternity
neither relenting neither surrendering
until they both realized they were God
And ended man's trials and tribulations

only on a painful sacrificial level
Earthly purgatory considered normality
in the blasé neuter no vibe faceless
straight jacket psychotherapy of Agnew's
Mental Hospital
Then one mad crazy wonderful bold
defiant glorious day they escaped
to join up with a passing legion
of schizophrenics rumored to be
God damn it one of the lost tribes of Israel
The stammering strung out paranoids
Mind blown children of a masturbating deity
the uncoordinated kid who didn't
get picked for either team
the four-eyed smart alec who angered
his high school teachers by
refusing to recite the Pledge of Allegiance
as long as our farmers were paid
by the American government to burn wheat
while folks just like you or me starved
the frustrated athlete who used to
beat his meat every night thinking
there was nothing to be ashamed of
and there's nothing to be gained but love
and 4-F'ed for excessive paranoia
thinking there was nothing to fear
except the mention of fear itself
and gut busted for taking
an early morning stroll through the dawn
in adoration of the constellations in the sky
Busted by the greed of the liquor industry
Busted by the stormtroopers of the
thought control crew
Busted by the vigilante man gun in hand
an unholy epidemic spreading throughout the land
Busted for a few blades of grass
in the lining of his jacket

A Marijuana ontologist stranded in
the San Jose jail with an old spade tramp
for a cell mate to explain to him
where he'd gone wrong
seven cold months without a message or hopeful word
when one evening down on the street
a choir began to sing an ancient gospel song
We're gonna wait till the midnite hour
that's when my love comes tumbling down
Won't you sing me back home
    Hallelujah, Hallelujah, Hallelujah
to the song my mamma used to sing
Meanwhile back in Academic Limbo
stoned Stephen the believer wrote
a bloody mantra an the living room rug
cops is shitty, cups is fucked up
and was excommunicated for sacrilege and blasphemy
singing Hare Rama early in the morning
and Here Krishna late at night
smoke more shit, eat more God
to make you feel alright
Symphonic evolution of the blip-blop
rat-a-tat-tat drum rolls of yin and yang
and fell sick with clap, hep, pneumonia,
abscess and penicillin fever
a leering victim of crystal madness
foremost inventive craftsman of roach holders
greatest reefer roller in the world
crazed hero of crank transfiguration
Joan of Arc with a necktie
wrapped around her arm
sentenced to ninety-days on the Farm
where he dried out, got fat, was released, geezed
some speed, gut busted,
copped out, returned in his weakness wired for sound
changed his mind and flew a paper plane
thru the vacuum in space

and came out the other side
you'll hear from him sooner or later

A dozen petrified torsos boxing their shadow's shadow's
shadow's shadow night after night
until one day they were shaken by
a 20th Century gypsy terrified beyond restraint
by a tree growing inside his chest
saved only when his guitar bled to him
a poem which begins You are not alone
And with a revivification in faith
after pilgrimaging to Richard Farina's grave
pondered and explored the infinite pages
of both mythology and history
for words of evolution possessing magic
human enough to be heard over the
hungover junkie vibration of television
An immortal task delegated to a man
And decided to sail to New Zealand, Hawaii,
Yugoslavia, Iceland, Katmandu, New Orleans
And America's Bethlehem, Denver
All paths of travel eventually meeting at the cross roads
Where the seance attempting contact with
Neil Cassady's ghost will closely resemble a sex orgy
The last of the wandering auctioneers
giving his grandest verbose performance,
everyday trying to turn people on to
what they already know and accepting
a little piece of bread as a thank you
The ghost of Neal Cassady is the feeling you get
when you shake hands with an honest man
Whether in a mischief making street flash bag
or a wiseman connecting for Emmanuel in Los Angeles
A yea-saying positive poon-tang prana
traveling fuck circus.
where all performers, tightrope walkers and clowns alike
chance the hotrod Calvary highways

in order to spread their own bit of Karma
to all those who worship on the run
Escaping the motorcycle Gestapo dragoons
with the most honest dishonest real wide grin
ever seen on a chinny chin chin
Much later employed in San Francisco
keep on pushing now burlesque
disrobing in Golden Gate Park
for no apparent reason except
that he thought there would be
an earthquake if he didn't
and taking one last tote
repeated the striptease in
a crowded middleclass pie restaurant
and received no reaction
until he emptied his dinner on his head
at a Telegraph Avenue Mexican restaurant
and from our getaway car window
I saw a most beautiful naked girl
with hair flowing down her back
giggling as she rode
on top of a white horse
galloping with each electrical impulse
of the solar system
to the island universe of a million suns
warming the bottom of my spine
her WOW the most out of sight sound ever heard
soldier lay down your gun, help us! please! please! please!
tractors, tanks, factories, mortars,
Silence your loveless noise! please! please! please!
Molotov -cocktail, stick of dynamite
Hydrogen bomb, drunken thud on skull
no more explosions please please please!
I want to father a child
We want to have a son
Please, please please listen to the wind blow
We want the world and we want it now
demanded Elmer Gantry from the stage

Gain the world and lose your soul
cried back the beaten one in rage
Power is loving selfishness said Aynn Rand
the beat said power is thirst for sand
I posses no invincible power
I revere no deceiving power
I worship
no gun power
I ask only for your hand
I'll try to be clearer
so we can understand
He said we all must die
But I keep hearing this unborn baby cry
naked power is like a chain of men and women
forming electricity in the night
covered with a million billion trillion starholes
to let the light in

Part II
Francis Scott Key at the Last Supper
Don't just say ow say OW!!

Two saddle tramps picked and shook
their gitars in opposite corner of' the room
where in the center sat the redheaded one
rolling up the thirteenth amendment ,
into the biggest fattest nastiest looking bomber joint ever
and smoking it as a nation
we fell into a warp in time
where you know Lou engineered a ghost town tractor
well on second thought just a flatbed truck
hell bent for the open highway to transcendence
sing being invisible is like not living at all
we were all so proud of who we were
intoxicated with love crying out loud

as we cruised First Street waving and carrying an
I remember this wise old man of eighteen years
boldly releasing a stuttering ululation
    "N-N-N-oah's A-Ark"
    "We're gun-n-na b-b-ball
    a-a-anybody w-w-h-o gets in the way"
and re-entered from that manumissing dream
married and growing old in the chrome plated glare
of survival of the stickiest
Are there any among you
who have seen the slaves
running jackhammers?
I think slavery is a job
you hate and only do fur survival
Poet carpenters and acid head school teachers
Buddhist iron workers and long haired mailmen
singing with their shovels
pumping gasoline driving truck
handcuffed to their typewriters
hammering out the eight hour a day
Benzedrine anthem of the American assembly line
but alas the story doesn't end here
in through the door walks the son of Jesse James
(It was a dirty little coward
that shot Mr. Howard and send poor Jesse to his grave)
a 42 year old hobo out of Denver Los Gatos,
an angel sent heaven the son of a man
rapping and reaching out to shake my hand
42-61-87=38 promenade and doesy-doe
swing your partner let her go
around and around just wiggle your toe
where you land nobody knows
yet I couldn't resist the temptation
to stick my fingers in his side then
But now I believe more and more everyday
we might all be one great big soul
and we'll all be going home soon

The holy ghost, the son of the son of Jesse James
proving to Andy Clausen that no one
can win even the must spiritual of wars
A California Irishman fingerpicking
country licks on a sitar
beating a Conga Drum in the Negro afternoon
a message of St. Patrick's Day
the friendliest mantra I've ever heard in my life
It's all right, It's all right, It's all right with me
The time worn uniform of the Holy crusade
now a beads, buttons, posters, and
burn artist costume
But I still find splendor in the grass
and it was splendid while it ran
he wailed switching to the country music station
and a sung later to the voodoo rhythm and blues
with his left hand
his right hand piously accepting
a brass pipe full of opium passed to him
by a smiling Samaritan low rider amigo
who went to jail for a vision, it went like this
we would turn everybody inside out,
and turned out again honorary Mexicans
A high priest of the street
who attached no sermon to his turn on
An angry Boddidarmist philosopher student
Night Rider circumnavigating his
chopped Harley around
a totempole antenna receiving hemorrhoid vibrations
from the sado-plastic show factory
A renegade Commanche, the last of a proud tribe
moaning soliloquies of perfect contrition
absolving all his ancestors of guilt
and after digesting the crab of the imagination
grow sick and meanwhile wombed up on LSD
thinking America was just outside his window
tripped through a second story mirror
leaping on the hood of a Ford Mustang

raptancing a no where to go malaria
anguished beatitude into its hood
with a candle holder
coca-cola seven-up coca-cola
seven-up coca-cola seven-up
Vernon Cox Vernon Cox Vernon Cox
and was subsequently arrested
for indiscriminately handing pot
to every UFO that would stop for him
giving the welcome sing in the middle
of Highway One, Lime Kiln Creek, Big Sur, California,
ransomed and recharged with STP
he administered temporary self lobotomy
watching the devil vomit on the six o'clock news
machine gun ack-ack ripping unholy passage way
thru the flesh of Vietnamese peasants
shrapnel bombs bursting in air
mortars ordered to fire on its own army
flaming jellied gasoline defecated by bald iron eagles
modern warfare at its best
the war scares brought to you in living color
when like a flash in the nick of time
the screen exploded with zig zag lightening
and razz-a-ma-tazz thunder
a thick cloud of smoke thru which
after the last rifle shot was heard
He saw one rainbow flag waving
over the ruins of nationalism
and heard the fellaheen Ole! all the way from Old Mexico

Part III
Attila the Hun Prepares to Invade Los Angeles

The dadaist umpire nonpareil sees it
as he calls it strike one strike two strike strike three

you're out nothing nothing nothing absolutely happened
except that I seem to remember vaguely
this four foot man waving his flute in the air
proclaiming with child-like voice "I'm a Hobbit" "I'm a Hobbit"
But with a juxtaposition of dreams rearranging
an emissary arrived from outer space
the mystical head of a barbarian ecstasy
of nomads marching out of time
on a let's expend time together journey beatific
to the last dance hall in the United States of America
painting their mind maps on the ceilings
of cardboard apartments in suburb Golden State
returning to the University of Alabama
with two dozen August Blues
and a couple lids of grass
stashed in their suitcases
Dancing thru the icy San Fran streets
inhaling banana peals waving from
the tops of surviving Redwood Trees climbing
voices "I'm high, I'm high, I'm so high"
A dozen range riders out of the east west void
grande ole oprying the starry spangled regions of space
Tennessee Williams wrestling Geronimo
for Adam stuck an apple in my throat
Crazy Horse fucking in the sanctuary
of a Davenport cave, Cochise now or never
A resurrected nation of Indians fuck warpathing
in a circle around a brave and squaw
copulating in their intellect's flesh
on the floor of a lonely tenderloin
crowded one room apartment
a pagan resonance chanted
in the Catholic halo of nakedness
preternatural verse spitting forth natural cocks
weep inside cunctipotent cunts give a fuck
An insatiate passion for the continuance of the race
Every last one turned back at the artery

by the infallible Pope, the square root of Einstein
what goes in must come out
searched my whole life for a man
who looked exactly like me
yesterday he dragged his old man
to a bombshelter neath a Christmas tree
the remains of a generation
manhattaned and ulcered into submission
their childhood dreams mouthed
by manufactured mimics put on
inside a mahogany casket give away
your television and move to the mountains
paranoid concealment of anesthetized desires
hiding behind sheets of Newspeak
the dribblings of a talking fifth of Old Crow
Can you see him sitting inside a tin body
made in his own image his wallet
full of thin green paper fleshless passports to hell
upon which is printed the abominable blasphemy
    "In God We Trust"
Homesick teenagers trust in God
waiting for the lights to go out
in the book camp barracks to cry
Jet pilots kneel tongues pointed
receiving Eucharist before a bombing mission
Cardinal Spellman sprinkles holy water
on battle ribbons bound for Viet Nam
The mafia martinis the mayor
Pope Paul VI and LBJ break bread
End toleration of the Pope I deny Vatican power
let a 15 year old runaway
sit on Peter's throne (a couch to sleep on)
I curse the parasite vibration
that ate the proteins of memory from his brain
and point at his genitals wig-wagging catch as catch can
where the Pharisees of the Roman Rite
discreetly turn their backs

as he'd made to carry the weapon
of his own execution
yeach where the frightened trigger happy cops
pump him full of their leaden gisom
and on cue the deputy says he was only
following orders from above
and hurries home to sleep it off
The real reason for this senseless carnage
obscured by newspaper psychology
the 20th Century double cross double speak of Orwell's prophesy
geometrically growing out of blackmail journalism America
an IBM whitewashing of cold blooded murder
A priest masturbating at the foot
of a stone statue of a pregnant virgin
The whining staccato horn of John Coltrane
pierces the necrophyllic Berkeley fog
gone are Mark, Eve, Loren, Neal
across the bay spectral Shia of Troy
passionately clutches her rosary beads on Haight Street
Thru the Oakland rain the good thief
Dismas grins a battered smile from his cross
as I read a letter call it an epistle
from Tom Coffey who faces five to life
for attempting to smuggle 13 kilos
of marijuana across the border
I sing for Tom, I sing for Perry, I sing for Mark and Loren
Neal, God Bless America, land that I love
Stand beside her and guide her
Thru the perilous rain from above

Part IV
Benediction for the Bums

Can you dig Iwo Jima hill where the U.S. Marine
Indian Ira Hayes helped raise Old Glory?

Can you dig the ditch where drunken Ira died?
I brag and chant of the falsely accused Mr. Poe
John Doe the innocent standing trial for
vagrancy rap, petty theft, dope possession,
distributing literature, making love in public
for impersonating Jesus Christ
Blessed be his old man sitting in the park
Blessed be all the bums young and old
Blessed be Jesus Christ are you here again
Blessed be what's his name in Canadian exile
where he was heard to say,
I regret I have only one life to give
for this rag time tune I play on my guitar
Blessed be Billy the King who baptized me
with heart attack beer who opens and someone pours
Blessed be the daughter of a kingdom yet to come
a true Sioux princess who out of nothing
mothered a baby girl who is mine by a miracle of testimony
Blessed be the star over the one story adobe castle
of Montezuma bless his seven sons
Blessed be the real red stripe over Fort Chapultepec
Blessed be the empty holstered musketeer
commissioned to protect the regal light
in the farmhouse window
Blessed be the vortex where nothing came
thrice Jesus flash wow! flash O my God flash
Blessed be both David and Peter Reid
may their songs tickle their own souls
Blessed be the voices in your head
I got to have it everyday
Blessed be Benzedrine an appropriate name
for sure who brought his Falcon
to a halt upon seeing a burning bush
in the middle of the freeway
and detoured to the walnut arms of primeval Mexico
not uttering a single word for ninety days
returning to Oregon to buy in

on a certain poker game
Blessed be Mary Magdalene who has endured
the name whore long enough
smile when you say that
for she has loved much
Blessed be those escaping the world's
man belittling man enslaving-isms
I hope that hermitage
or mad house isn't the only avenue of escape
Blessed be the draft dodger and the army deserter
take this hammer to the captain
tell him I'm gone, but tell him I'm gone
just tell him I'm gone
Linda set two more places at the supper table
Blessed be Theresa of the Roses flower child
who screamed in ecstasy upon seeing the
fiery balls of Satan
You shake my nerves and rattle my brain
your kind of loves drives a man insane
you broke my will, but what a thrill
goodness gracious great balls of fire
Bless Bless kiss kiss kiss the terrific chalice
of consciousness overflowing with the embryonic wine
of a good women's cunt
Blessed be the garbage truck loaded
with 200 million shattered America dreams
Blessed be manifest destiny
Blessed be Divine intervention
Blessed be Abel's bones upon which Cain has built cathedrals
for his golden calf over which he has raised
his flag and under which he has buried his soul
A never ending supply of sanctifying grace
for the open air unnamed church of Baz
a Lebanese Sitting Bull answering only,
to the Aum humming inside his heart
Everlasting is the soul of Mike Saunders
murdered in Viet Nam by a demon

who walks, talks and looks like a man
His blood is not easily washed off the hands
Heavy is the chest of the AWOL soldier
in which his spirit is invited to live
Unbelievable is the superego
who hotrods in and out of this poem for me
I hereby nominate him for highest office
these words constituting the beginning
of a write-in there campaign
Blessed be the vote cast for your self in eternity
Blessed be the time come after eternity
Blessed be the overwhelming vote for heaven's sake
I'm here to boast and toast of
Perry, Dean, Pat, Neal
Don't look back whispers the wind
Move on steams the locomotive
Bless the blood violated
during the last Bonzai Wave
Holy the blood of Siddhartha
gunned down without a word
on an American street corner
Holy the figment of the imagination
Holy the lightbulbs clicked off
for a night of love
Holy the lightbulbs left burning
for a night of love .
I sing holy Linda wife
a woman created from the pages of *Genesis*
no idea what to expect but no reason not to do it
I want to tell you friends
if I was Adam
I'd make the same motherfucking mistake again
Mea Culpa, Mea Culpa, Mea Maxima Culpa

Part V
Ghost Writers in the Sky

Woe Woe Woe you War! Strife! Famine! Pestilence!
Woe Horsemen! Horsemen! Horsemen! Horsemen!
the time is resting on the palm of your Sunday hand
Gog and Magog Now the sun is as black as hair
Saddle up the voice in the void whispers your name
you must ride something calls for you
Put your swords in your mouths
(that's a hard one but it still goes in)
and sketch circles to plunge them into
I await the necessary fulfillment
of nothing's revelation
Ride on you nymphic anarchists
of my catechismal daydream fantasies
Ride on you rapists of America's sweating Buffalo
crazy man crazy man crazy man hey crazy man
let me see you do your unholy thing
Unzip your story exhibit your own Apocalypse
so all souls can learn from it
and have the chance to love it
Do not deny the greywalled ghettoes,
the bleached out suburbs, the penitentiary desks and machines
spread the legs of Delilah with a smile
the worst that can possibly happen is it won't be returned
I know who you are, no matter what front you hide behind
there is no use laying low-we grow old
So arise arise my untouchable brothers
strip naked in your loneliness so that
the Brahmin must either love you
or turn his back in shame
Ride on into the army barracks
no ride out of there ride into the banks
Dance Dance on Dance a dance nobody
ever danced before see the warmth it is not absolute Kelvin
Rise thermometer rise hard to get on hard on rise
go go go go girl go teach learn be speak the truth

as you know it love all as you feel it
we have nothing to be ashamed of
except pride which botches up our timing
stand on the shoulders of someone you've helped
Help him again let him stand on your shoulders
Babble on, confess, repent quickly reach out
drunk with God I won't attempt to define it
rest your belief in the golden unrule
without love you are just a sack of bones
a bag of but no better than the dung buried in the ground
Discovered yourselves rediscovering a way
to bring the armchair addicts
away from their televised thorazine
and thru the vanishing forests
across the polluted arteries and lakes
through the groaning tombstone factories
up to the white house door
and down the hall and show them
the pool of blood on the bedroom floor
Lady MacBeth you whisper like a crow
into Abraham Lincoln's dying ear
Die, Die, Die it is done now I am a queen
O Horsemen woe O Horsemen woe
can you hear me calling your name
charge seraphim calvary
cherubim bugler's blow
ride wahoo with drunk guitars
and stories beaten like drums in hard times
O myriad tongues rhythm in tune
with loping fuck gestures of crippled cosmos
with your renaissance hand gently milk
a warm flow of gizzum to inseminate
the geography that lies between
the Golden Gate Bridge and the Statue of Liberty
The Great Lakes and the Rio Grande
Sanctus Sanctus Sanctus
This is your body and
This is your Blood

Sanctus Texas Missouri, and Arkansas
Sanctus Vermont Georgia and Nebraska
America this is your heart beating
Sanctus lower east side New York junkies
Sanctus Southside Chicago misdemeanor outlaw street hood
Sanctus Larimer street-American Bum
Sanctus broken wine bottles in the gutter West Oakland
Sanctus Hollywood and Vine plastic matchbox
Sanctus Third and Howard and the end of the road
Sanctus San Miguel Allende
carve his tombstone out of no. 9 coal
America this is your soul perspiring
the four of us stare out the window empty and grey
maybe the last time shake hands with your best friend
naked scared silent fearing a fiery cloud
Lord Have Mercy I hear bombers roaring
like hungry lions overhead
I hear the bombs a toothless whistle
a light show so big gigantic magnanimous so big
I don't know whether to cry or laugh
Air raid sirens heard in the early morn
Police whistles ambulances fire trucks
Children crying in the night
The American mother weeps over the flag adorned wooden box
bringing home the remains of her sons
She weeps in wheat fields
She weeps in a trailer park,
She weeps in a Hanoi cemetery,
She weeps in Harlem
where tears are hard to come by
we hear the old wino moan as he's hustled
from the park into the paddy wagon
The last thing I remember is they put
this guy wearing the American flag as a robe
in the insane asylum
America, Mark, Loren and Eva are leaving you
Neal they won't come back
America your jails, your gas stations

your roadside cafes, your San Quentin,
your mountain roads, your highways
reek with the martyrdom of Neal Cassady
Women in heaven get ready Neal's coming home
And as long as you can tell the story
to someone who'll listen
Moriarty and Paradise live
and as long as you can utter
More Road, More Road, I want I need more road
yield yield Neal yield yield women aware
I dare to give you all of me
you love me you love me not
I am   I am not
finished yet   O hell
I love you I love you I love you
you you you you you
make me a prisoner
and only you can steer me back
On the road
Neal Cassady Dominus Vobiscum
Loren Fishman Et cum spiritu tuo
so long good-bye see you after a while
It's bound to happen within the next million years

Jack Collum
(1937)

4-6-77

As I walked down the street the will of God
began to rumple me from head to toe.
I stepped into a little Irish store
and there sought shelter from the rolling doom.
A man stepped out, his name it was O'Neal;
he seemed more nervous than a shopkeeper should.
To reach me he had passed through chains of beads.
We faced each other in that twilit store.
I told him I was sorely rumpled from
the will of God. Perhaps I spoke it wrong;
surely an Irish Catholic should have known
what sort of state I blurted out to him
and sympathetically adopted me
into his family, slight but thinly warm.
He only said, though, What you like to buy?
a question couched in standard terms of stuff.
Not everything is "buy;" I shook his gray
minimal style by beating on his table.
Stop, he said, you're drunk. I'll call
police because I do not care to carry
moods that you have brought into my shop
without considering that I might not be
a simple shopman, money on my mind
and nothing else, but maybe I have got
some touch of magic in my private life
that don't accord with yours. Think you it could
fall so? Och, faugh, he muttered, you would not
in probability have access to
the superorbital facts of shining life
that I have spent the last twelve years upon.
(His eye was filled with stable brightness then.)
At this I felt the set-to had reversed

itself. No longer did I wish to put
my troubled feelings re religion out
upon the counter of his little Irish store.
I felt romantic strength in prospect of
a walk alone through blocks and blocks of city.
I bought a marzipan shillelagh from
this alien blend of practical and strange
and, shucking off his fevered explanations,
stepped out into the light of Thirteenth Street,
or was it Fourteenth Street? I think, oh yes,
I felt the muscles of my legs rejoice,
but as a furtive glance fell back and through
his misty, dusty window, sure I saw,
for I am Irish too, of bastard sort,
him lay his finger on his nose and wink
and darkness checkerboard the place. My God.
Always unsure, I walked out to the left.

sept. 1968

the cherry tree is full of worms
she says, smoking a cigarette
as I drink Pikes Peak

a slice of pineapple "is" "like" a PICTURE of the sun, with hole

they talk about
how Jane talked about
giving 8 puppies away
"what are you afraid about
your face about?"

"you will see how beautiful that wound is"
"like a spring raspberry"

nothing to explain
the colors I face too
slight to indicate
pain, too dark to imitate the sun
the lines we come to
make, the habit of reality

& the red blood 'they' can
surprise the sky with upon exploding
out of that comfortable human look
keeps us
on our toes
dancing, the more indications that
it cd happen any moment
the more we like to talk

my cold & fever
realemon, water, orange ashtray

equation: <u>me</u> =   <u>clock as big as a house</u>
   bee   clock

people look like
clouds, that whole

clear weightless light
hiding essence. this is the luminous
quality of logic

I walked back
alone
in damp morning
lush
twinkly with light
& began to like it

living-room colors
strain apart
as bodies of any 2 people
are confused enough to do

to waltz among, on every day is Sunday
where Sunday is the bright penance
for reality, mon thru sat

the gray cat
so absolute in "coldness"
does her (his) dance
out of pure economy
I take
as a sign of life

the day settles in parentheses

this is the unity
of which I spoke – I take big cup
of coffee no. four
to get a little sick
see "MERRY-GO-ROUND" by accident
contemplate the crescents of scattered cars
edging the back fields, like shells
as if a wave of metal washed over
us, unnoticed, & subsided, leaving the cars
or the field, of earth
cast them up in
parked curls, on our visual shores
the mailman
walks out from the mental health center
& drives his truck away

"couch," no music
"playing" to cube my moments with
abstraction of somebody else's. no drinking
today, to not let loose
more meaning than the words can bear
the sea or railroad or highway sound
of my family
would disturb should it stop
building the air

there's a situation without light or dark

I piss
& passing the window see in the dazzle of light & grass
a focus of weight, a horse
"Trapper"

too formal to reflect, standing
out on that account. the meaning
of the head hung down
is eating

(Christopher
makes war with Franz, each
lamb & wolf in dazzling alteration
stink of peace an
irrelevant taste, like
olives, for their clean baby
evils)

the vacuum cleaner
fills the air
with the hum of Traudl's quest
the roar of her gray
desire
(cold scrambled eggs)

I go
piss, eyes flat
with noon

in the balance we may term
"the green meadows"

at last
my character albino

2 weeks ago Christopher said
if a giraffe
jumped on mybelly
I would go to the bathroom and puke

Abelardo Delgado
(1930-)

Totoncaxihuitl, a Laxative (1974)

totoncaxihuitl,
there are no others around me and yet i'm in the middle.
there is no doubt
          our world needs a laxative,
an enema would do better,
god can administer it with bullfighter accuracy,
sticking it right in our own hometown.
the flower girl with the soiled gown
walks her dog down the avenues...no flowers are around.
totoncaxihuitl
there are no others around me and yet i'm in the middle.
contemporary despair,
          contemporary hope.
               in need of vitamins.
albertson's at the westside
          reports no cash received
during the month of august...only food stamps.
we eat because big brother is around.
totoncaxihuitl,
there are no others around me and yet i'm in the middle.
potts peddles a poetry festival
with dimes and nickels donated
          for meter and rhyme and profound sound
for deaf ears.
          he smiles without the "i"
               and lives
waiting, like us, for death to bring him life.
totoncaxihuitl,
there are no others around me and yet i'm in the middle.
look at the judios,
          mira a los mormons, chicano
y aprende de los orientales.
ah, carnal, no me digas eso

                      they have evolved historically for centuries
While my raza esta todavia en su niñez,
we chicanos are taking our first steps.
totoncaxihuitl,
there are no others around me and yet i'm in the middle.
porno flicks...sex shops...sex...sex...sex...sex...yeah, yeah yeah.
3d movies, sperm flavored pop corn, i'm sure next they'll hand out
microscopes at the ticket counter to see the stars perform
at closer range. dildos can be found inside soap boxes
for the neglected wife.
one night stands...matinee quickies, infidelity around the clock
and prostitutes who give green stamps for economy minded dudes.
totoncaxihuitl,
there are no others around me and yet i'm in the middle.
carrasco kills himself with twenty nine bullets
and the alphabet bomber uses a chicano/greek alphabet,
the zebra killings, miss hearst, the zimbionese liberation army
and six get blown up in boulder colorado,
among them the great chicano bard...teran
and i keep hearing everywhere
                                we are at peace...paxem et terras...

totoncaxihuitl,
there are no others around me and yet i'm in the middle.
our chichesque society
                         inflated with silicone
                                   goes round and round,
dosie doe, grab your pardner...
migrant programs, head start, and o.e.o. is dead
now we have bilingual/bicultural, bisexual/bilingual.
tingo lilingo, tingo lilingo, tingo, lilingo.
totoncaxihuitl
there are no others around me and yet i'm in the middle.
there are some spots left

                    in which we are again
                                        tranquilos,
son nuestros lugares apropiados,
                            the center of the universe, our universe.
such spots are hills, chairs, beds, gutters, heaven.
totoncaxihuitl,
there are no others around me and yet i'm in the middle.
i no longer love you.
                        i want a divorce.
two by two those close to me are becoming one
y la angustia es mucha.
the children understand, they are the only ones who do.
there is an epidemic that hits the matrimonial intestines
as old greyhounds chase young rabbits around.
totoncaxihuitl,
there are no others around me and yet i'm in the middle.
the ugly word.
                    the ugly expression.
                                everybody is ugly. the sky is ugly.
the love experience is ugly,
                        even ugly is ugly
and an ugly blanket beautifully weaved
covers us with dark patterns of ugliness.
totoncaxihuitl,
there are no others around me and yet i'm in the middle.
...yet, there is a song,
                        there is a baby born,
there are some children playing who do not know or care
what time it is...there is a man carrying some groceries home.
totoncaxihuitl,
there are no others around me and yet i'm in the middle.

Richard Denner
(1941-)

thru this valley
where robbers roost

I strive with systems
to free myself from systems

easy to see the irony—
implementation's more severe

find a place where rent is low
gardens grow, mushrooms blow

•

in the end
it won't mater
we can settle on a small

farm in Berkeley—
just a radioactive cow
and a few chickens

Diamond Hanging I Blues

I mend the fences.
I tend the herd.

The shit is ten feet deep,
and the shitters play for keeps.
What are you after, they ask,
a hoof in the mouth?
The shit is ten feet deep,
and I can't eat or sleep.
Coyotes yap all night
below the blown moon.

The shit is ten feet deep.
Shine on, shine on.
Hold it down, you buggers,
or I'll rope your ass, I sing.
The shit is ten feet deep
and dear.
Hay has more than doubled in price.
There's no market for feeder steers.

The shit is ten feet deep
and clings like it's alive.
Pour on gas. Set those doggies afire.
Give those cows a kick.
The shit is ten feet deep
and thick.
Chew your cud, mama,
let those juices flow.

The shit is ten feet deep,
and sometimes it hums.
The shit is ten feet deep,
and here and there a head protrudes.

The Angus are black —
purgatorial beings.

The Herefords are red —
mythological monsters.

The Charolais are white —
easy to spot against the dung.

The shit is ten feet deep
and covers the fences.
The shit is eleven feet deep,
my shovel is hooked to steam.
The shit is beginning to climb,
making inroads through the hills.

O, the shit is infinitely deep
and running still—running.

Edward Dorn
(1930-)

La Máquina a Houston

The train has come to rest and ceased its creaking
We hear the heavy breathing of the máquina
A relic in its own time
Like all the manifestations of technical art
And without real gender
And hidden from direct appeal
By the particulates of the English language
Itself the agent of frag mentation
And lonely accuser of the generic lines
The heavy breathing of the lonely máquina
Stopped in its tracks waiting for the photograph.

The Apache are prodded out into the light
Remember, there are still dark places then
Even in the solar monopoly of Arizona and Tejas

We are with the man with the camera
They step off the train and wait among the weeds
They never take their eyes off of us, wise practice
We motioned the way with our shotguns
They are almost incredibly beautiful

We are struck and thrilled
With the completeness of their smell
To them we are weird while to us
They are not weird, to them we are undeniable
And they stop only before that, they are like us
Yet we are not like them
Since we dont recognize that. We say:
One cannot have a piece of what is indivisible
Is natural Apache policy
Where for us, that is a philosophical implication
We are alike, but we see things

From behind dis-simular costumes,
The first principle of warfare
Where *All of Us* is the Army, and they are the people
Precisely they step off the train
And this is an important terminal moment
In the Rush Hour begun in this hemisphere

This is the moment before the leg irons
They look Good. They look better than we do.
They will look better than we look forever
We will never really look very good
We are too far gone on thought, and its rejections
The two actions of a Noos

Natches sits alone in the center
Because he is the elegant one among them
Hereditary, proper as a dealer
He is inherent and most summary of themselves
Supple, graceful, flexible hands
Goodnatured, fond of women

As the train moves off at the first turn of the wheel
With its cargo of florida bound exiles
Most all of whom had been put bodily
Into the coaches, their 3000 dogs,
Who had followed them like a grand party
To the railhead at Holbrook
                              began to cry
When they saw the smoking creature resonate
with their masters,
And as the máquina acquired speed they howled and moaned
A frightening noise from their great mass
And some of them followed the cars
For forty miles
Before they fell away in exhaustion

Sharon Doubiago
(1941-)

Concert

You pull me across the sun to the stage
The eighty thousand in the thousand hills behind us
push me forward to the stage, the driving rockbeat pleas
of the musicians begging please back up you'll crush us
begging please come and fuck us

I dreamed I was blue and so I was opened
They drew out my heart and placed here instead
the martyred crowd, Bonnie crying *I'm blowing away*
and shadows
keep taking my love

to our feet, a miracle, we make room
a couple begging please take these chains, the beat of his ass
plunging her deeper into white trash, the deep
South, a boy turning his back on the guitars
to show us his face, colored scarves
of napalm, defoliated stone

Drums beat the blue skinscape of graves shelved above the town
the Purple Heart embroidered on his levi jacket
As we roar down the front wave of electricity, Breath
expiring from us seeds onto the hills, he stares
at me, he hums

> *what is it or was it*
> *and what will it ever be?*

for Bonnie Raitt
Stompin 76
Galax, Virginia

Letter to My Father on His Sixty-Fifth Birthday

Dear Daddy,

I'm watching a bald eagle.
He must have his nest in the bluff beneath this cabin
because Michael saw him about a month ago.
He perches on two snags that jut out over the water.

His eye is strange, black with a white stripe
circling. He has a huge, yellow hooked bill
for tearing his prey the book says. That rabbit
we found a month ago in our road,
the brain eaten out through the eyes.

My first eagle! And so, though this is Friday the Thirteenth
and I've lost two husbands on Friday the Thirteenth
and believe now in the superstition,
so far, this Friday is a lucky thirteen.

I'm living with Michael. (Have I told you, Daddy,
I count all my lovers as husbands?)
Our cabin is on the Strait of Juan de Fuca,
facing north, a little northwest. At night when it's clear
the horizon is lit with Victoria on Vancouver Island.
Earlier this week, after a rare all-day wind out of the Northwest
that brought snow the next day, it was so clear
we could see white skyscrapers.
And San Juan and Lopez Islands, the passage
called Haro Strait, the inland passage
to Alaska. To the east steaming Mt. Baker
and other snowcapped volcanoes I don't know the names of.
All together they make *The Ring of Fire.*
I hope you and Mama will visit, spend some time here.

Tomorrow is your birthday. Imagine
sixty-five years.
And I'll be forty this year. I always thought
you were twenty-six when I was born, until awhile ago
watching the eagle I realized you had to have been
twenty-five. Imagine, you, Daddy, twenty-five.
Makes my skin rush. I begin to feel
the years falling through me

like sand through a sieve. On each grain a picture:
I'm a girl in your arms. I'm the mother of a girl.
How strange and circling it all is, like the eagle's eyes. This Sunday
your father would be one hundred and three. I could remember
if I tried, you at twenty-five. You:
your father's thirty-eighth birthday present.
I wake so often at night not knowing
when it is, who's beside me, where
my parents and where my children are. I dream
of getting home. I've been toying with the idea
of giving myself the gift
of turning thirty-six for my fortieth birthday.

In my bar I remember Johnny's. Waiting
lonely and strange in the dark car while Mama goes in for you.
Once or twice I got to go in. I ate Bit-0-Honeys
displayed behind the bar. Still, when I bite into those little bits:
the smell, the neon, the men
of the forties.
Once I had a Shirley Temple. Now
when I make them for kids
I'm sitting on the barstool with my father,
the most handsome man in Johnny's.

As when I watch a man roll his cigarette
I'm sitting on a granite boulder
on Mt. Wilson as you roll the tobacco in your thick fingers,
all the sky and the Los Angeles basin
enormous behind you. *Biggest land city
in the world*, you say, blowing out over it.

My job. Lately it's not good.
I like my customers, they are only rarely
difficult. It's my bosses, the company
I grow to hate. Wednesday, for the first time
in eight months I cut two men off.
It was near midnight, they were the only ones left in the place,
drinking double whiskeys since eight. It's true
they'd spent almost eighty dollars, but now they were raving
about raping women and shooting whales
for the fun of it. About
raping me. I went to the back
told my boss to get rid of them. Instead he walked out,
poured them two more doubles, joked about women bartenders
not being able to take it. He wanted the rest of their money.
I've taken a lot from my boss, I'm patient

and I was inexperienced, but now it happened.
I exploded in a rage that blew him and the two men
out of the place, a rage for which
when I can think of it without getting upset, I am quite proud.
I learned to fight from you, Daddy.
I'm glad our fights are over, I couldn't take them now,
but I learned. Jobs. When I was a girl
and you worked at Douglas you'd come home so angry, so bent
in bitter fatigue, I knew the worst fate in the world
is to be stuck in a job you hate. I was glad
Mama told me of your job, what you thought
was right and what you thought was wrong,
the time Nixon, running for his first office
by calling that woman a Communist, came through your plant.
When he held out his hand to you
you turned your back on him.

I must have been very young, still the forties,
when you hit the back of that stopped car in the fog
and your license was taken away.
Your anger terrified me, how it filled your body, the house,
the whole world, *the injustice! The crooked courts!*
The lawyers for the rich and I vowed
I would never forget this. They say a girl
gets her sense of right and wrong from her father.
There are those now, including you at times, who say
my sense of right and wrong is too strong
but I'm glad, Daddy, you made me
this fighter.

So often I see a bridge across the Los Angeles River
you built. I loved to drive over it
but I could never figure how a bridge is built over deep water.
On our Sunday rides I'd sit in the backseat for miles
contemplating this. My father knows.
And those Julys in the fifties we fished from Fisherman's Bridge
in Yellowstone. We caught so many we had to give them away
not because of the law but because of our bounty.
Mama fried them in egg and corn, served with grits, how often
I've tried to cook that same meal again, fish my son and I caught,
while you tell me again what happened to the Indians,
how it was wrong. Then the forest ranger, his teeth
through the woods, the first man I looked back at. And I saw
that you saw. When you designed and built Edens' Drive-In
I wanted to be a carpenter. I saw
the construction out of those redwood trees

was like my construction of the red dress
to meet the sailor home from Yokohama
who became the father of my children.

As now I know—it has taken me all my life to know –
the construction of a poem: how my book, Daddy,
is dedicated first *For My Parents Who Taught Me The Land*,
the richest heritage of all, those Sunday rides,
though I always wanted to go to the ocean,
and Mama always wanted to go to the desert,
and Clarke always wanted to go to the mountains,
and Donna always wanted to drive the new freeways.
And those vacations across the continent, Mama figured out
how all five of us could sleep two weeks in a forty-nine Ford.
Now I keep remembering last year. I'm in the backseat
of the Chrysler you keep though it is several years old
because it is the last car they made large enough
to pull your mobile home. You are driving me and Mama down
a weedy forgotten path
out over the largest natural lake in Northern California
Clear Lake
looking for a lot you bought sight unseen
at a tax auction, the fancy *New Yorker* tipping down
and nearly off the steep dusty side of the cliff
right past the *No Trespassing!* signs. I'm holding on
squealing in the backseat, *Oh! this
is just like me! I don't know anyone else
who'd drive here!*

These images shape me, Daddy, that you were born
on Valentine's Day, the day
birds choose their mates for the year, the day
before your father's birthday.
Maybe the eagle made herself visible today
because she is looking for him. Or, coyly,
trying to be seen. Ever since Hollydale
I've wanted to be home again
when Mama makes the chocolate heart cake
decorated in redhot candy bars. These days
I come to appreciate what a good father
you have been to me as an adult woman,
even if you did change your mind about right and wrong,
vote, to be our president, Richard Nixon.
I hope I learn to become as fine a parent to my grown children.
There are so few lasting ties, thank heaven

for family. Daddy
I would write you a birthday letter
saying everything a daughter would say to her father.
All the unspeakable things.
This year, for Danny and Shawn's birthdays, I wrote them
of the day they were born. Right now as I write you –
excuse the messy typing, we don't have electricity
and I found this rusty Navy field typewriter under the cabin,
it sticks and I'm not used to a manual – Dave Brubeck
is being interviewed on the jazz station from Vancouver.
One of my first classes in college, when I was pregnant with Danny,
was with Howard Brubeck, Dave's brother. It's funny,
Dave is telling the same family stories his brother told
over twenty years ago. I remember now
how Howard became a musician.
Someone told him his father had died
and in that moment he heard music
unlike any music he had ever heard.
Even so, he said, he was sure that music is commonly heard
when someone tells you
your father has died. He became a musician
to find that music again. Daddy, I know
we are going to be old folks together
just as now we are middle-aged folks together,
but even so, from somewhere in me,
when I think of you and how I became a poet
I hear that music, *how you always called me
Lu*, it's the music of the love
of one's father.

Happy Birthday, my Valentine,

Sharon Lura

Photograph of the Two of Us

I never liked this picture.
Yet here are two.
Two sizes, two shades, blue and grey.

Your hand is on my leg
    and here again your hand is on my leg

and blue you hold my hand in your lap
    and grey you hold my hand in your lap

Our leggy forms and the sand glow peach
our bodies so naturally married
our legs around
even the last day
when the car came to take you away
we were making love

These familiar but long-forgotten clothes
    these funny clothes we threw away so long ago
the mountains though unchanged running blue layers to the sea
    the mountains though unchanged fading grey to the sky
and the pier you wanted to live with me on
    and once in a storm the pier we fucked on

It must be our child who is taking this picture
    Oh it is our child years ago, see her shadow on the sand
I gaze at her to see her then, you look out to sea, I seem
to be a sea myself, sweet fathoms young   and open
I look at her so small to tell her yes I love him   faith
on my face, like mountains, as she takes
two of us, one for me
and one for her

Men have always said to me
you don't realize how beautiful you are
In this picture I never liked
I see they are right
a heart pulsing so large the sand still quivers
gold beneath our feet
but I also see

a small blue being
trudging the deep sand behind us
    a grey sexless thing she caught
      bent naked, walking the quicksand behind us

as you say again
I only stay with you
because you fuck so well
and faith on my face like a mountain
I answer
that's as holy a reason as any

But only now in this bad picture of us
do I see how well
I fucked you.
I made myself into your image, years
it took you gazing out at sea, your astonishing face
aglow before you knew ·
you didn't know who I was

and so you were gone that morning before coming
    as always you were gone before coming

Danny Boy

Today I drove you over the mountain to the airport,
the glens and meadows shadowy green with the coming summer
when you will leave for good.
Baby lambs wandered free into the road
through the broken slabs of old fences
their nervous moms helplessly watching,
too fat to follow.

At the Philo Mill your large body
moved into the window
to the workers crossing in front of us.
Suddenly you've come
upon the weighted world beyond games, curious
like a lamb, and afraid, for your place in it.
Do you know that Philo means love?
My last lessons just like my first, geography, language,
story, heart. Last night
you were studying the Senior page
of your Freshman yearbook
realizing only now
who they were.
You called to me from your room,
where are they now?

as I found the lyrics to the song
I sang you at my breasts
Oh, Danny Boy
it's you
it's you must go
and I must bide
and learned it is the world's oldest recorded tune,
learned for the first time
the original words

my love is such
I will
leap from the grave
when you walk by

We crested the mountain and looked down on the clouds
into which you will fly.
"Why you look just like a kid yourself,"
the young man at the airport said
searching for the mother in my face.
The plane was late
so we hung-out together, me in my purple shirt and boots,
you in your striped t-shirt and adidas
going off to be some school's
famous athlete.

We ate crab in the car, played rock 'n' roll.
I read to you about a coach in New Mexico
who wears gold, silver, turquoise.
I followed beneath your tall body
all the way out the airstrip
to the small cockpit beneath the fluttering wings,
reading to you over the windy motor, still
reading to you, both of us giggling, enjoying
the outrageous sight we made,
we've always made,
you, finally, after all these years
enjoying your outrageous Mom.

      The plane lifted. Your golden silhouette
between the scowling pilot and the worried businessman
rose into the sky

and I sit here, on a curb,
watching you go,
humming the world's oldest tune
into the warm ancient Ukiah,
dyslexic *haiku*,
feeling left
just like a kid.

Bruce Embree
(1949-1996)

Beneath the Chickenshit Mormon Sun

It turned out worse than I thought
The champion defended his title
then Eldridge Cleaver came on
to talk about his reasons for becoming a member
of the Church of Jesus Christ of Latter Day Saints
Grandma and I damn near fell out of our chairs
Went to town and got crazy drunk
Came back home, called you long distance
after cruising and drooling Mainstreet again

This is my last wish and love poem
It is as follows
Want to hold the wake at noon with plenty of acid and rum
No friends or relatives
Ghost music by Hendrix and Byrds
drowning all sound
as you fuck me to dust
beneath the chickenshit Mormon sun.

Stick Together

I was drunk when we met
but she let me stay anyway

Close to five years
and we're still together
in spite of
drunk driving tickets
snow up to the top wire
screaming chainsaws and buried
rejected stories
middle age
jobs that come and go
ship that never comes in

She snores at night
and I never cut my toenails
Our roof leaks
cars are all junkers
Chickens eat the dogfood
dog gets the eggs
and we just got busted
for growing pot

Days, years go by
sometimes looks
like everything is shot in the ass
Yes, but we're made for each other
We stick together
like Vibram soles and dogshit.

American Hero

Jeany and I went out to dinner last night
the food was good
We overheard a man who had really been up
against it and had somehow come out to the good
"The ball was almost completely covered in sand
but I played a wedge and came out
six feet from the pin"
He slouched back in his chair like the old vet
recalling the Jap machine gun he took out

I was splitting firewood this morning
when Brigham the pup got run over
He just looked at me with his busted jaw
eyes already going funny
The animal doctor
will call if he don't come out of shock

The mad old ayatollah
sends kids up against mines and tanks

The silent millions die
cutting timber, digging ditches in Siberia

You can drive along the freeway in El Paso
look across the border to shack town
where kids die for lack of water
in the hundred degree sun

These kind of bad movies
are without end
list goes on and on
but don't you think there is something magnificent
uniquely American
Yes in a man standing alone
against it all
with his sand wedge?

Michael Finley
(1950-)

This Poem Is a Public Service

Listen when I talk you little nothings
Little zinc-heads in the cupboards
By the rattling plates
And the nutpicks and the mallets
And the napkins and the forks —
When it comes it will come
As a surprise.

Inconspicuously they are laying tracks
Up every porch of every home in this city.
Into each room and every squeamish store.
Through the backdoors of slaughterhouses
Where sides of nothings, rubber carpets
Hang on hooks
Circling the sour and bloodstained floors
Like pedestrians.

Stop doing what you're doing.
Stop tapping your feet.
Stop asking can you be excused.
And what are you going to do about it,
For your lusterless bodies?
And your partners? And the children?

By now you have noticed no one signs on
For the detail of love anymore.
They say get yourself another stooge.
Let this one have the dirty job. Am I
Your slave?

It was called cooperation.

At the depot boxes and boxes of kits of lives
Pile up on the loading dock
Squealing for hands.
You can't count on the help
To lift a single finger.
We expect a little something
A special extra some kind of bonus
For his type operation.
You're better off dead
The rich get richer.

At night freight trains cross state lines
So no one can see the lines of giant zeroes
On their backs, three to a flat.
Each one weighs tons and enemy agents
Are snapping them up,
They think they're our replacements.

The other tracks they let decay
Like rows of teeth a thousand miles long.
The enamel starts to chip, the sugar
Does its work.
Between the lean and rotting ties
Grown dogs howl
Like flapping cloth.

You blind little ninnies cry for sweets.
You ten ton babies kick at your baskets.
You've outgrown your usefulness,
Why don't you go home?
Who can take care of you in times like these?
Who can put up with the things that you do?
If you knew a trade —
If you worked with your hands —
There must be someplace else?

Monday they stuffed my secretary in the outgoing file.
Followed by a cut in pay.
Thursday my office turned up missing.

I miss my memoranda.
Now they're asking for my shoes back.
It has just been announced, we have
Run out of weekends.

I am lifted on a stretcher and carried
Out of court.
A paper airplane where my eye should be.
I had taken my complaint to the top of the top.
For a judge he struck me as immature.

Plain and simply we caught up too far too fast.
Now no one is safe in his own suit of clothes.
No one is secure for a second.
The machines have started to nag
They say
Well
We bitches are hard to satisfy.

What we have in mind is a generation
Of animals.

Desperate losers mechanical slapstick
You dumb seamsters you have snipped
Your antennae.
What happened to your sense of humor?
You've been trapped for days
Between floors on an escalator.
Think. Everything
You see you make gauze.

Businessmen walk the streets
Wet with expressions of loss.
They stop and speak with everyone they see.
Where are all the buildings,
They want to know.
There used to be buildings.
Hold my hand, I couldn't bear

To jump from a tree.
Good sir can you direct me
To the nearest revolution?

Listen you dumb nothings brown nettles
Red gristle dumb people.
The housewives in our city are
Grinding their arms into sausage.
All our shops are boarded up.
Newspapers lick our streets and broken glass
Makes pretty sparkles.
The president has taken to wearing his shirts backwards,
He's taken to giggling.
You can beat this thing, he says,
And explodes.

What nonsense, this town
Is crawling with reptiles and pimps
And you know it.
Each one of them busies himself through the night
Plotting your underground surprise.
Your luggage was sent on ahead.
A list of patrons is circulating,
People you spoke with only this morning
Have signed up for double
Triple hitches.

At night mechanics rub burnt cork on their cheeks
And drum till dawn on the hoods of junked autos
With hammers and socket wrenches.
Children all around the world have
Stopped falling down. Their nails are clean.
They've stopped hurting themselves
And stopped needing you.
In your company they have started
Crossing their legs.

If you hadn't realized
If this comes as a shock

If you didn't know by now
Things are coming to a head.
The lonely beast you keep in the cellar
That wails and wails
Only last night pulled all the red pins from his map.
All your lovers have written your name
A dozen times and torn it up again.
Every stone in every field takes careful aim
And flies. Things are getting
Sticky everywhere.

What can you do, you want to know,
To help yourself through this difficult transition.
How to defend yourself or explain yourself
When what has been heading your way all your life
Arrives with its vengeance.
Are you prepared, the trains are pulling out
Everywhere, bound for unknown destinations.
Fuses are lighting in every bedroom.
There has not been a successful suicide
In weeks, and you sit
Playing with your hands in your lap.

What is it oh what is it, oh,
The name of the song, our song
That's been stuck in your head like a rusty needle
For what seems like years.
Are you coming? Are you going?
You pitiful people you
Tiny nothings your fractured lives
You can't rise up from, can't speak out of,
Can't pierce the membrane that you
Call home, can't break
The quiet that's killing all that you love.

This poem is a public service.
When it speaks to you
Listen.

The Brood

I don't want to share anything with you,
I want to be alone late at night,
I want to drink until I'm dry
I want to make secret journeys down the dank streets
where married men don't venture,
I want rooms of clinking crystal
and appreciative smiles,
jokes tumbling from my lips
like silvery grunions
slapping in the moonlight.
I don't want to help carry groceries in from the car,
groceries I will never eat,
go for endless walks that take us nowhere,
rub your back when mine is killing me,
I want sleep forever under sparkling snows
and dreams of ballgames and girlfriends
and the years of goodtimes before
this dagger snaked its way into my breast,
I am afraid of waters and doctors
and the look on your face
when you are in trouble.
I want to undo everything, erase my assent,
irradiate my sperm, runoff
to a nation that is beaches only,
that welcomes heels and celebrates
desertion and whose official flower
is the beget-me-not.

And yet, to be father
of this melon thing in you
with all its sweet red stuff, and seeds and rind,
is a grand endeavor, and I see plainly in your eyes
that this is your wish and because I am your slave by heart
I accept the full penalty, let them come, let them swarm on me
like ticks, I will bounce them and change them
and wipe them clean as if they were my own
and all the while knowing where once there was life
is now only children, and the windblown fluff
that was once my hide is all that remains
of a boy who loved
to play.

The Lord God Has Words with the Choir

All ye who are weak and puff up yourselves with words,
hear me now.
All ye who achieve with the arch of an eyebrow
what ye will not do with honest toil.
Who are persuaded that your sordidness lifts you above
these other my creatures,
who imagine that I harbor special grace and store
for the masturbators and malingerers
of this my world.
Ye who imagine that an inability to speak simply and without design
are signs of my special favor.
Blow trumpets, howl winds, swirl gyres of ocean and cyclone and rage.
I break with the poets of the field and the air,
I deny the poets of the heather and hearth,
I forswear the poets of water and land
who get it wrong more consistently
than idiots quaking in the square
or misbegotten monsters who live but an hour
goggle eyed in their mothers' maws.
Break thunder, break cataracts, break trees at the knees,
break promises not to destroy you again
in a boat, in a fire, in a meteor blast.
While you amuse yourselves that I send muses to each of you
to draw out the milk of your beauty,
as if legions of angels had nothing better to do
than attend to the daydreams of lazy vanity,
pet preference of the I-Am,
O do not play footsie with the whirlwind,
do not make nice with death-in-life,
Crush granite, crush planet, strike heaven with one swipe,
curse me as a jealous god that I am harried by these gnats,
will no one relieve me of their pretense?
I've grown tired of the customary acts of faith,
widow women turning on spits, infidels lighting
the streets into town, I want a special cut of meat from my subjects,
the hearts of their poets pierced en brochette,
the best minds of their generations
sautéed.
Down with the poets, commence the crusade.
Line them up and start shooting, mow them down in my name.
Begin with the successful ones in the same towns as you,
the men and women in salons who know that if they

were in any real place and not some jerkwater parish
far from Rome
they would be nobody at all.
The people who get endlessly recycled in anthologies,
panels, talk shows, the works,
them who have started to take it for granted
that they are the spokesmen for nature's community,
the voice of the flowers, the agent of the wood,
and talk and mince like boneless politicians.
Get them.
And then get the street poets who might have amounted to something if only
they'd set aside being mad
at people who've done them no harm
but that would mean losing the attitude
that is their weapon of choice
in the unworthy world so forget it.
You would not know an apocalypse if one bit you on the ass.
The pagan poets — find them, tell them the Lord God says
booga booga!
The surrealists — find them! Tell them they are all crazy.
Hamstring their minds, let them be prisoners
of syllogistic logic, unable to associate
or make the leaps that make them feel superior.
The solipsists — let every reality be real except theirs, let their imaginations fail
them, let them be wishy-washy yeah unto death.
The suicides — dig them up and reshape their mouths into smiles, set them to
work doing community service for the people
they shucked off.
The myth poets who walk in the shadows of shadows,
drive them out into the light, invite them as guests
to our poem pogrom.
And the introspects who do not get out of bed until every dream
is chronicled, rouse them and bring them to me.
The botanical poets and the bird poets, who wander
through the fields —
naming things and reporting on their noises and smells,
imagining this what I do with you —
find them, mulch them, return them to their nature.
The social poets who don't write much but never miss a party,
tell them they won't miss my party, I've got them on my list.
The alcoholic poets with the hair-trigger responses
and faltering follow-up,

who sought refuge in the weak stuff, spirits of grain,
their flame will be smokeless and clean.
Tell the writers of confessional poems their penance
shall be infinite fire throughout infinite time.
Tell the poets of rhymed verse my favorite poet is Whitman,
because of the resemblance.
Tell the feminists about my long white beard.
Tell the writers of love poems I hate them.
Tell the poets obsessed with rhyme and meter that a clock is ticking
in their asses, and their hour of glory is nearly come.
Light ovens, start fires, pitch boil till blackness fills my nostrils
like perfume.
The smoke of a thousand poets in residence, who communicate
in surreptitious form the lack of respect extended them
in departmental meetings
because they don't know anything anyone with a brain
lodged inside a skull would pay $100 an hour to learn.
Torch their jackets with the patches on the elbows,
string up and disembowel their large white dogs,
bring me the beating heart of the ceremonial poet
assigned the dedications of new gymnasiums
and alumni center parking ramps,
flay the chancered workshop poets who labor with laser
and page the world with simultaneous submissions
of the same thick verse a hundred times over,
a backbreak of postmen, a slaughter of spruce
and for what, some pointless exercise in imitability
that gives pleasure to neither reader nor editor nor language
nor world, slack stillborn refraction of art, a bag of vomit
from an unclean mouth, vanity everywhere, top to bottom,
fetch matches, fetch torches, fetch fire.
My prophecy is pain, my prediction the mass graves
of a suitable population,
nutritious to the earth beyond all reckoning,
they that held such store with their words instead bequeath calcium,
nitrogen, zinc as their gifts, their limbs interwoven
in a tapestry that puts the lie to individuality,
O, that one there, row four hundred, two hundred sixty-fifth
from the right, did you know he was a genius,
a genius, a genius, a genius.
My geniuses will be cloth.
Rage, quake, pestle, shout,
all my pretty ones blotted out,

Women poets ploughed with lime, men poets enriched with manure,
And please invite the editors to join you in the earth
those who have learned to say everything kindly
and are yet without kindness, who say "some nice things here,"
and grin as the blood spurts from an open wound between the eyes,
invite them to our feast.
Invite every glad spirit who puts down the words,
the terribly timid, who confide the only truths they know
to incomprehensible lines that no one will read,
O, their fragile courage moves me so,
how could I attend to the business of keeping the bodies
in motion and the atoms charged
knowing they are having a bad day in a dormitory
somewhere in New Jersey,
heap them high like hosannas of unexercised flesh.
Death to the clay-faced outdoorsman who writes in a cabin
deep in the woods by the light of a candle and trust fund.
Death to the radical poets who assailed the princes
that I myself had installed,
making their jobs even more impossible and unpleasant
than I had made them to begin with
You who make life difficult but sleep in till ten o'clock,
draw tenure, clink glasses late into the night, Good night.
Feed to the reaper the kids who bus into town to depict
the painted horrors of the street in verse.
Feed to the incinerator the kids who hitchhike out of town
to bless the state park campgrounds
and mouth the names of dead Indians, whom I personally know,
and who if they saw you standing there, spiral notebooks at the ready,
would split you down the middle
in disgust with an adze, or an atlatl,
they were good honest people don't you know.
Come to my supper and sit at my table, ye troubled souls.
You are fit and right and meat.
I turn all your water to wine, all your bread to cake.
Come inside the abode I have prepared for you for a trillion
churning years.
As you are creators and as I am creator let us now be as one, alive
in the lava of language.

Charles Foster
(1922-1967)

How everything
was in the end resolved
in California

it
wasn't
san
andreas
fault
it
wasn't
mine
things
just
started
sliding.

9-1957

Victoria Mundi

for W.B. Yeats & Judith

now i walk thru the bodies
of twenty creatures, men
& centaurs, the solid flesh
torn or altered
by the manifest velocities
of doom foredoomed, doom foreknown
& aimed into, as a goal, a
salvation!
        twenty lives
of the creatures
           quickened
              thru this passage
              thru desert and pasturage
              a whole life on foot
                wrapped against the sand storm
                in a mulberry-dyed robe
                reading the book of life
                out of dust motes
                the sun of our passage
                the song of man feet
                sandals of cowleather
                & unclean hoofs
                of the ungulates
                our beasts
these i could then boast as my lot
as tho the dust of life, my life
had been thrown up by a wind machine
simply a prop, the mere slipstream
  at the edge of the terrace
    and the god, whether in the machine.
    the angry eye of the whirring lens
      lighting up all, making all glow
        in the savage light of its reborn
          energy - penetrating the loomsong;

and now, after the twenty
fathers of creatures
and the dryads, in the crystalline magic
of the single centered eye
the gate of horn between
unicorn eyes
where, canted, equiposed, lies
the universe
of nails vinegar & wood
splinters, especially tho,
the crowd
.   blind street
animal
yakking yakking pretending
to be there, here, to be
even slightly aware
where here is
& there was -
a hero?
no.

simply say that the weather worsened
and that some of the onlookers became physically ill and
that others, still yakking in the old language of the tower
were heedlessly working thru the vomit.
you should bear in mind,
also, as the day grew on it became hot. The stench of the
crowd rose up to mix with its already overpowering stupidity;
and these smells mixed with THE BLOOD, which had mostly
dried nicely, even caked, but still, in spots, in the deeper
shadows of my WOUNDS, it was moist red and salt. the flies
came, emerald-green, and for a time i found distraction
in their terrible beauty, in the planting of white eggs
of new life at the exact points were the torn lanced
flesh would fester
where, father, where
is my unicorn's eye?

   – but why, even after they had eaten
wheat cakes & tarts bought out
of peddlers' sacks the talk concerning
   market conditions, the wise cracks
    of the whores to the soldiers
     – & even after the full moon rose
    & began to eclipse the afternoon sun
     over & over again
     after the mere orgy of flesh
     began and took all things into itself
      until the thunder opened and the lightning
       fell crackling loud breaking the branches
      over the fucking multiple bodies in
     joint, on the hillside
      even after all that they persisted
      little knots of old men
       elbowing their way thru the women
       kids, foreign soldiery
       fiercely agreeing not
       to name that feast

     for they had that day passed
     thru the shadow of the. rain forest
     where eater eats always & only

      the self, old million
      mile eyes. sadly

        passing as panther
        eating boa constrictor
        who is turning into vine
        who is the bursting grape
        in the hard bruised hand
        of my self my strange
        self, no more than eye
        away from this drying out
        this 999th selfsame.
        happenings: i eat.

hurry, for
my tongue is cracked
a wasp is dying
in the sun, on the floor;
hurry
    confess & condemn
    with cracked black & split
      nightbirds tongue
      the felon dismas &
        his equal; hurry
            take flight

as your own mudballs
formed wing, eye, and soared
over galilee

      go & love them
      go & love the daughters
      the high-breasted
      girls who have waited
      their lives for you
      go, quickly & love
      my waiting daughters!

how could i deny her?
how could i ever
    deny her anything her
    heart wanted?

i went back to live where
    i had once been a
    prisoner, a visitor
    only just passing now
    living
      with the afternoon
      dry scorch in my
      shoulder tendons i
      passed naked into the twenty
virgin christmas bodies/ EMERGING

spent, not wasted
as one of us
who are one
    i return at the last
    point of the flickering eye
    a blue-black bird
       with a curved iridescent beak
       sitting on my sundown skin

       my mother
       the split throat of my dream
       passing from among the other women
          passing between the sentries
          taking my dried, puckered flesh
          away from the copper brash cuirasses
          the argument about the birds
          pecking away eyes
              with no age

          caught in them, or
          the wolves, cracking
       the fear, the tumult the
       unrest the unrest growing, to
       put it to rest
          even with wolves
       as she passes calmly between them
       cracking faceless legion
          taking my lifeless body
       taking her own, her sacred
       golden grasshopper
             out of their midst
          holding my deadcold dry corpse
          back to her breast
             where i had eaten
             of her substance
             she joined us
             we joined as one.

then, my mother, for i
was dead, spoke to the faithful
concerning the disposal of my
remains

then for a night and a day
forever

i waited for the north wind
bearing its death
of wand & cauldron
the stiff may prick
of my father the oakseed;

bound, fettered, in a five-
fold flower offered
to summer lightning
to the scorched
soot-stained white
midnight lips of
dancers, merry
fools. holy
malignant
eaters of
my heart, those
members of
my body

each one
undivided
of that light!

. . . but to continue
in an age of sacrifice
in a period of superficial flagellation
the breaks in the skin, wounds and marks
as the beast fights off its boredom
the lassitude of its envy, and much worse
            the deep sickness
            up from the stale lungs
            into the stale morning air
            the lovers trapped in a valley
            of slaughter, the sounds of the
            f east with no name
            which does not end
            with the coming of the dawn

            it is no hurried nativity
            – a morning of birth pangs
            and visitors from far places
            coming after the long midnight
            the labor of coming out, under
            star light to a straw basket
            and the chanting of the camelboys
            beyond the edge of the light
            and at the borders of the dawn's
            garden coming in the rage
            of the moon, new red crescent
            rage & the agony, flesh & spirit
            sung, scratched & roared
            out of the hairy grey wolves
            throat!
                        i remember, while i was
            present, everyone was very calm
            even the words, spoken or unspoken,
            seemed a part of that holy silence
            as if the Child Himself had opened
            a hole in the Word
            filling the room with it

so that, later, in the
sed the west desert
         where the sun
     smelts bronze
there is no water
but there is a secret
a sacred stolen moment
a garment, sanctified
gathered to the flesh being
worn around the heart
or, flung to the dirt
making a night's haven
under clouds

the world star
under the stars in clouds
we as the thief
at our right hand
weave into the passage
of light currents, vehicles,
dust clouds:

it is dry here
it is dead here
where there is no water
flesh dries, shrinks,
as leather
from clinging to
the light
     the dark
from holding fast
  into the main
  where new birth
  is only
  natural
     miracle . . .

. . .but the spasms of birth
subside
as the new-born suckles
the comet
river of ether
light launched

without ending or beginning
holding, holding
together
hands linked
hearts linked
lovers connected
eyes coupled

the ten thousand things, man souls
beyond number
holding together

performing again in the
eternal eye of love
the constant
never recurrent
miracle of
all
one
undivided
thing!

1966

Hugh Fox
(1932-)

Jurassic Seas

This is something about a house and a sense of permanence.
Grandma and Grandpa and Aunt maple and their middle
daughter, Morty, live there. Then Aunt Maple dies at 94, and
the following year Grandpa dies at 66 and Morty gets married
and Grandma moves in with Morty and the house gets
sold and the neighborhood's been changing anyhow, no one
they grew up with lives there any more and what'll happen
to my wife's head, where did the first thirty-eight Christmases
in her life take place, and where were the rabbits out back of
where and you drive by twenty years later (with thirty-two
more years to live) and the house is still there only they've
painted the red brick white and there's a hurricane steel fence
around the front yard but you will want to go up snowy front
steps, open the storm door, turn the brass knob on the wood
door, open up and find your crabbyass father smoking a non-
filter Raleigh (for the coupons) in a cigarette holder watching
basketball on the color TV, past the tree with the two ornaments
on it you made when you were a kid, into the kitchen
where Mom's making mincemeat and pumpkin pies and oyster
dressing for Christmas dinner, and Aunt Maple's there
making her special spice and citron cookies and you might as
well add your own Grandma (dead 25 years) into the scene,
sitting there with one hand on the head of her cane telling
Maple, "Don't use up all the sugar now, there won't be any
left for coffee or anything else tomorrow, you do it (the word
'every' lost in an echo-chamber) year..."

Will the Real You Stand Up, Please!

"You've gotta get rid of all
these fictive selves,
that's the real problem,"
he says as the metal walls
slide open and out
I go into Chinatown
again,
beginning with the
Imitation of Christ,
no bones about
THAT,
eat and become the
Godhead,
I.D. with The Word
through which the universe was
created,
carry Him through your
days being
formed...by Him...

as the Chicano woman across
from me on BART
on my way to North Berkeley,
first looks at
scads of her-defining
pictures,
her white lycra lace pantyhose
defining her,
doing her defining
makeup,
all clothes,
everyone,
all religions,
slots, notches

taking the undefined and
defining it,
as if it were real,
cutting, defining, classifying,
you do your report,
get your paycheck,
pass your test,
you must be a pathologist
passing barely visible
through the landscape of the
lab,
I write these words,
send them in,
editors and audience
define me,
and if they don't
the old definitions of
my childhood DO,
my mother with her
"You're a good-looking
boy, keep your shoes
shined, you'll be a
movie star,"

my father with his
"You're the young Doctor
Fox, my medical heir,
we'll open a clinic
and clean up,"
my grandmother with her
wordless, admonitionless
acceptance amid
rituals of toast and
jam, purple cabbage and
caraway seeds,
my church with
its engulfment in

The-Kingdom-yet-
To-Come Christ,
my middle-class
neighborhoodness,
adoration of
Toscannini,
Sir Thomas Beecham,
Mahler, Bruckner,
Shostokovitch,
Hopkins and Virginia
Woolf,
all tossed together
into a fictive
tossed salad of a
personality,
would probably
keep me painting the
canvas in the
otherwise meaningless
field in
Arles.

[When Hugh Fox read this poem
at the 1990 Walla Walla Poetry Party,
he introduced it with a reference to a book
entitled *Who Am I This Time*. Ed]

Ed Foy
(1967-)

A Homecoming

Old clatterteeth
to clench together
And shoulders up to here
Fall asleep to the closing
of the door & drift along
Okay okay Okay
They use the voices of
schizophrenics as a broadcast
medium for the rest of us
"And here the city
lights and there it falls
apart — didja take a warm
jacket?
The door to your life is
closing, kid, better get out
while you can..."
I keep falling asleep
in this damned closed circle
And all I want to do
Is spit and scream
And turn this bus leonine and send it scattered down the street
The CIA uses several
different secondary
broadcast channels
And if I turn just so
I'm catching them all
The ego Of it all
It's talking to me
It's talking about me
They're telling you about
my dreams

"...The mirror girl marries
and has a four-legged baby...
Over there, by the newspaper
house
did you catch it
The metallic skin tall
as every building
Your eyes have turned
to ice, goodlooking, but
the thaw is close behind"
My throat is raw from
Your shouting at me
"Hey, Pal, Hey, Pal, Hey, Pal"
Give it up, I'm locking
myself out and you're
gonna have to break something
to get ... back...in.
"He's disturbing the
passengers.
He's harassing the passengers
They're killing the hostages
They're killing, the hostages"
Better turn those radios
off
And let me turn this headache
off
And let me turn this head off
Before I become your voice
Before I take your face
HeyPalHeyPalHeyPal
I'm your voice
I'm your face
I'm your paranoid dream
at 2 am
Out of the bus and
into the street
Close the Mannequin
Moments away
I'm home again

James Grabill
(1949-)

Sandbagging the Banks

Sandbagging the banks of oblivion,
using our best science and historical data,
summoning up explorers of distant survival
and the strongest thick-trunked cottonwoods
full of river rains and luminous August dust
vibrating how the winds breathe in subatomics,
pulsing with bulldozers through flattened canyons
of news talk, we were doing our level best
in spite of the predictions that everything
we know and everyone we love will vanish
in crystalline outer-space midnight eventually.

That ought to be enough, you'd think, to bring
back the desire to live in the only hour
we have here, but still many work against
neighbors, trying to carve some sheer trophy
out of the money radios flooding our houses
with suggestions demanding material form.
Nobody wants to vanish, no people or dogs,
no houses or fir trees, and so the sandbagging
with neon signs and pleasure crafts traveling
rivers of personal intrigue have continued
rising out of the mud into the landscapes,
and lace has been held out against the candlelight,
workboots have followed their iron stairways,
instruction books have blown open like car doors,
as dogs have been barking and no one wants to vanish.

Clearly, no one wants to swell and explode into sky
and rain, and no one wants to fall out of body
into star-swirled ditches of a billion miles forever

curving back around what it was signaling,
and no one wants to be mud on the feet of the dog
or glowing paint on the side of a lost bridge.
No one wants to walk out in a body and never return.
No one wants to see what they've worked toward
swept up in a broth of tonnage and continuum,
the sparking wires traveling behind the theater
sliding down the collapsing cliff into the muddy river,
the plutonium burning floors and walls from inside
molecules, the river inside the molecules
overflowing with thick nothing, with absence
of whatever this was, and nobody knows
what to expect really, past a certain point.

Darrell Gray
(1945-1986)

To the Reader

The reason you have been placed at the edge of this
ocean is to increase you in directions hitherto not known.
There are many things for you to learn. As April is closing
in on an ancient heel, sparks fly off, and these rudimentary
passions will lead you to a new discovery, buried and
smiling — a knowledge which in the total energy of its cities
distracts from love as love distracts from savagery its
balanced thunder. The grass, for instance, has begun to grow
more quickly now that the sea has expanded its base of
reference — doors in the cities appear to be opened less
often. Everything now participates in how even the birds
suspend their resistance, and the landscape projects its
original metallic cry.
　　This cry is heard in three distinct and coexistent
aspects: *coming*, *going*, and their hybrid which prevents our
extended notice, as on a trajectory one can say "Hi" to
whatever form approaches — perhaps a girl coming down to
the beach for a swim, separate from the sun, in the amazing
context that has formed to contain her, merging at last
with the white ambiance of the waves.
　　So you see, though the scene includes a great many
automatic and penetratingly shaky elements, it cannot be
reduced beyond the assumptions that give it birth, even as
you yourself cannot choose not to be there, cloud-like,
poised in a process completing itself at a distant point you
call your *life*; sloping stones down to the water; thunder
inside; light some years away.

Planets

for Cindy

Our bodies are like the shadows of unborn planets.
Sometimes, when we are alone, they are all we have.

Prongs

The prongs of graphite and leather.
The prongs of shoes reflecting the moon.
The prongs of watermelons at a picnic.
The delicate prongs of icicles.

The prongs of justice and the prongs of lice.
American prongs and the prongs on incubators.
The prongs asleep in the eyes of turtles.
The prongs that shiver like hair.

Black prongs.
Red prongs.
The prongs of arthritic barbers.
The prongs beneath seats at cheap theaters.

The prongs of feminine recognition.

Robot Hash

language will always be fucked
by Outer Space   Here, on this planet,

   in a plate
my brain will sleep: i wish
it were in the dream of a girl
like Mayakofsky
         chain-smoking his way
            to Heaven.
Yesterday I wrote: "a tiny trap-door is all we know
      of the Epics . . ."
Living inside a brain—the brain-wheels turning,
   a humming of gears filling the room
is not my idea of "poetry."
                  Better to go out & rob a bank
            than read in the newspaper
         how even mathematics grows like some alien fungi
   in the shadow of Ezra Pound's house outside of Venice.

And over & beyond all this, its hard
to wake up every morning among the Greats,
knowing your poems are secretly writing themselves
in the dresses of the passing girls.

And so we all go to the movies.
"Hi there!" . . . (things like potential people) . . .

   and
      "coming back"
         knowing
at the end of History there will be some shoe sales, crumbling
apartments, and lots of robots
standing around in the haze.

For the Future Occupants

Having shortened the space between our fingers,
and felt the walls pull finally apart,
we are no longer ourselves

on edges, nor care to be.
breaking the surface of the formal past
we discover endless cups of coffee,

paper-weights containing tiny oceans,
and old shoes emitting a slow
blue light.

Our neighbors in the bone stand close together.
Their children draw on our doors
mountains and rivers,

and below them, in bold letters:
IF THOSE THINGS IN THE DISTANCE ARE STARS
THEY'LL HAVE TO BE TAKEN AWAY

No one listens to the shafts of sunlight
arriving continually to take our place.
At the moment, we are not here. The moment is

shortening, taking us
in. But we come back on the sand,
on lawns. We look around.

We are on an archery range that extends forever
like a photo of arrows caught in mid-flight.
Some of us have glimpsed the dart-games of ruminant angels,

and some, touching the delicate curves
of clavicles, have forgotten their names.
We are going back to where we had no name,

back through the grass, through the groves
of pianos. We are approaching woodlarks, crickets,
and bridges long covered with water.

In the distance, transparent tractors
climb the terraced hills, and into the fields of dark poppies
whose seeds contain old photos of the Civil War.

Colorado Space Sonnet 3

Up all night again, where space is singing, here
in Boulder in my head & tongue. "In the mountains
there you feel free." T.S. Eliot said that. He
knew a lot about things, I guess, tho I have always
secretly hated THE WASTE LAND. What point is there
in telling everyone how shitty things are? They must
find this out for themselves, no? Actually, things
are totally great! The ground is flowing through
the night, with plant-like ornaments, and stars. I read
poems by Samuel Beckett (POEMS IN ENGLISH), Ted's
SONNETS, and *Elm Fuck Poem* by Ed Sanders. I know
what he means. "A whistle blows shrilly." Outside
the window the street ends in a (pill). I take that pill
& am gone. Birds fly because they have more imagination.

136

The Stamp Act

I remember the day nothing changed except the cows.
I was standing in an abandoned pasture with my friend Minnie,
who had taken too long with her hair. She had been combing
it in the rear-view mirror for about eight minutes when
this cow came up to us and began to paw at the ground. Minnie
was thin for her age, and followed strange instincts more
often than not. Anyway, this cow was looking into the fore-
ground—its ears were up in the air. Minnie took off her
t-shirt and offered it to the cow. When the cow opened his
mouth, she stared in. The cow stared at Minnie's bare breasts.
I found the papers and tickets and kicked the engine over.
The cow got small as we headed away for Detroit.
Years went by like short paragraphs as we sat and
watched men go into plants in search of vacation. Some came
out, their expressions greatly cowed. They said things like
"Use is too deep a friction" and "Concepts are robbed graves."
It was then that we realized the rear-view mirror was
inexorably caught within history.
A couple of heifers came out one weekend and did a
little stamp act in the dust.

with **George Mattingly**

The Exit

You are now approaching
the exit. The door
is marked by a green

light saying itself,
but the door may be small,
may be a flame

running up a wall, or
fall at your feet,
flashing. Things change

so often here that no
one knows how to breathe
in the proper manner,

but you, in your bombproof
skintight pants, living
as it were, on the edge

look cool and at ease.
But when you get to the door
it gets to you. You see

yourself out there
surrounded, thinking
Flame, cool Flame, oh flashing.

The Dream Wedding

Pressure gets in the eye.
Its pain is round.
During the lapse of several years
Would you care to smuggle this strange little plant?
By the small unbearable noiseless sleeve
Just after the porch those lovers visit —
I dig persistent holes in the leeway
To improve their seasonal drift.
Out of that wind, tho, flashlights keep us awake.
You get up and swell the oysters with a lovely color,
Say of the sky, or that dangerous beach-colored breeze
Falling expensively over the wedding
Of dreams. So soon they assume
That even penmanship outlives them,
There in the imprecision of their huts
Reflected like a drawing on the water.
A lampshade covers the feet and ankles of the swimmer
Tho, in a potentially emblematic disaster,
While you and I play on the smuggled guitar
As if nothing happened. Steam rises,
Which is really a hurt form of water,
Into the air that is really
Rising to cloud. And I wonder who,
In all these relationships flickering on and off
Will find our tears grown shiny and strange with pressure
Here in the only world we know or love.

Adam Hammer
(1949-1984)

Fun With Death

I want your Senate seat!
said Muriel, politically.
A Pale sauce oozed slowly down the meat
of Hubert's final dinner.
But Muriel! he gasped.
Remember how in love we are, according to People magazine?
Remember how we used to lie around and light practice matches,
and throw them at each other?
Think of the children.
Think of the adults.
Think of the fans of the Minnesota Vikings,
and of their sadness, to be without a first-rate quarterback!
Muriel went out to mow the ice,
and to give herself some time,
to think about justice, and to think about
how huge and misshapen Hubert had gotten,
what with all the life-sustaining drugs he had been given, like reds.
Thick, dark, wet, sticky, happy, murky, stocky, lactose tears
began to fall from her eye-hair.
Fuck Hubert!
She thought.
I will indeed take that Senate seat
so long desired by me, but never attained,
due to my funny name, Muriel!
How I wish my name were Martha!

Martha!
Come in quick!
It's me, Hubert, and I'm probably about to say
some of my famous last words. Quick, write them down!

I want a Senate office building named after me,
I want to be on a postage stamp, I want
lots of neat books written about me, and I want
some chocolate pudding, right now!
Martha was quick to sense that yes, Hubert was just
about dead already, for he had grown even more small,
and was now sitting inside
the pocket of his yellowing pajama top,
waving sadly goodbye.
O Martha, one last think—tell the reporters
that I go forth on my final journey sans fear,
and that I am looking forward to it,
and tell that checker down at the A & P that she's a real strudel!
What a piece!

Muriel lifted Hubert from his pajamas
and held him in her left hand.
How pale and unpresidential he appeared!
In her right hand a single corn flake lay,
an identical image.
Here's your dinner, Huey! If you can handle it!
And at that Hubert began to grow very large again, and round,
and then he hacked up Muriel with the lawnmower
blade that he had hidden in the bed, inside his stiff pajamas.
TAKE THAT, JACKIE O!
said Hubert, confuse, and then he climbed back
into the Muriel costume, and flew off to Washington
to take his Senate seat.

Carl Hanni
(1952-)

Final Solution

I want to marry a white witch goddess
and move to an organic broccoli farm.
She'll have long, ropy dreads
a checkered past and an old Studebaker
named Shelia or Wilsun or Frank.
We'll never bathe
because we don't have to
and we like the smell of sex
sweat and dirt--
they're all natural.
We'll live in some pungent rural backwater
in Missouri, Arkansas or Oregon
in a ramshackle old farmhouse
with five or six other
grinning idiot refugee pranksters.
The redneck locals will lust
after our beautiful goddess women
and think that we're all fucking each other
and they'll be right!
for the first time since 1973.
We'll have kids, and figure out
who they belong to when we see
who they look like. If it's a boy
we'll name him Penis, and if it's a girl
we'll name her Vagina, and they'll never
go to school, but stay at home and learn
the ways and means of benevolent anarchy
group love, dirt farming and organic revolution
filling their young souls to the bursting point

with the music of Captain Beefheart,
Sun Ra, Funkadelic and Psychic TV
and the writings of Terence McKenna
William Blake, Hakim Bey and Robert Crumb.
We'll be armed to the teeth
stoned most of the time
always wear our Lil' Abner shit-kicker boots
and, because it's the end of the millennium
keep an e-mail box on the
Industrial Mystical Now Age Internet.
Once a year on the solstice
we'll throw a week long
pagan psychedelic hoedown
and crash worship into the new year.
Eventually the locals will come gunning for us
with search warrants, German shepherds
and the god-fearing moral perversity
endemic to the rural south
but we'll already have
wired the bridge over the creek
with homemade, all organic explosives
taken all the good drugs
and be hightailing it out the back forty
in our customized army surplus land rover
on our way to a new dawn
on a new horizon
with the nuclear wind at our back
and the lights of forty million suns
burning in our eyes.

Robert Head
(1943-)

I Dont Wanna Go Back to Jail But

dear doug (blazek)
yr letter came this morning
& it cheered me up
i'd just gotten bailed out
the night before
$25 to the fascists
& i was down

disturbing the peace
whose peace?
by fighting
i never swung a punch
i was too scared
it takes guts to swing a punch
3-4-5-6 to 1
cum to think of it
it takes guts not to swing a punch
3-4-5-6 to 1

this young biznessman
iron rod in hand
(the kind they reinforce concrete with)
circled around behind maloney
while these other things in white shirts
stood in front of him
& took turns
niggerluvver! whap!
niggerluvver! whap!

i wanted to get away   from there
but i was afraid
this bastard with the iron rod
wd split john's skull

& i at least wanted to be a witness
so dumb me
i try & stay between em

me in between a racist and a militant pacifist
wow!

compounded my mistake &
tried to talk
my way out of it
"i'm no fighter
but i don't
go for this iron rod bit"

"head if you're no fighter you're in
the wrong place"

you can say that again

meanwhile this young biznessman is startin to
twitch &
foam at the mouth
as if thats not enuf
he rips his shirt open
"get out of my way
or i'll haf to hit you too"

my thumb got in the way
oh well
better a broke thumb
than a broke head

john maloney
he was beautiful
not a word
until the thing in the white shirt
calld him a gutless son of a bitch
& then he said TALK TO ME MAN

two brothers
one of em goes to yale
& reads heidegger
& the other carries the iron rod
this is not a parable

up against the wall
move a muscle i dare you

sumbody said that i had
a big long knife
& dave he was so astonished to
hear it
that he turned his head around
without thinking
& thats when they hit him
without thinking

the fuzz stood there behind us
you dont believe me turn around

john maloney did it
even if me & dave had run
& there hadnt been no witnesses
he'd have done it
i can say that for a certainty

you can only back up so far
i'm sure if yud hav
left it wd hov gone much harder on me
& for that i thank you
but i'd hav stayd anyhow
you can only back up so for

they told us to get in the paddy wagon
maloney cd still talk
he askt em are we under arrest
& the cop said yes
& he sat down
& they began to drag him
by the heels
dragd him across the concrete
bareback

the fuzz sd
is he yr friend?
i said yes
the fuzz said
you're sure he's crazy
i sd i'm sure he's not crazy

9:00 monday morning
1st municipal court
fuzz didnt show
par for the course
done their duty to segregation
thats an interesting word segregation
implies white apart from black
not white over black the way it is

10:40 PM
for Dr. Van Spruiell

i hav 20 minits left
no i'm not a captured VC
i'm a white southerner a goddamn degenerate worker
11:00 is bedtime i haf to punch in at 8
if i didnt get my 8 hrs sleep i mite fall down on the job
             god forbid
sleep is a need our corpses impose upon us
labor is a need their corporations superimpose upon us

freedom given the hypothesis of it
in order to gain it
do away with one of two things sleep or slavery

if i cd see the psyche
that got me thru highschool (& into college)
i'd ask him about this

doc my heart hurts it hurts horribly
it hurts for heaven it wants
it wants for freetime
you got a pill so's to set me free
free from sleep the lack of it
no but i got a pill
so's to set you free from sleep the want of it
so's your heart won't want

thanks doc thanks
giv my regards to the company
yours i'll giv to ed clark

ed clark that vulgar marxist
he never went so for as to say we shd do away with sleep
fond as he is of it
but he did say we mite, it's only an idea you understand,
                            do away with

the profit economy
that makes me labor
8 hrs a day
for a millionaire
(110 million to be precise
Swig his name is
(you neednt remember it / i will))

that's more than you my doctor ever did
three years i saw you
three years & never once did you say
that highschool you go to (had to go to) shd be done
                                    away with
no it was me shd hav been done away with
what'd i do in my freetime the hour i already hav
the liberated territory i already hold
the hour that a boot in the TV tube (RCA Victor's) won for me
well you see doc it's hard times
they hav an army
& I dont
an army
that takes its orders
from the top down
if you plan, as i do, it's a hangup i hav,
to free the privates & the sargents
& forge another army
an army
that takes its orders
from the bottom up
that takes some deep thinking
a good hour a nite's worth

11:00: bedtime

i've spent
my last 20 minits
writing this
it's nothing new
good thing for them it isnt if it was it'd blow up /
                                    Port Chicago

Mary Heckler
(1946-)

my sorrow is greater
         than the hills
it lives in this valley
        i
    shall never be able to leave them
anymore
     than i could leave these years
  out in an autobiography
if any present friend
thinks I shall have forgotten him
  when my words are spoken
         on a different continent
let that friend come to me at that time
  to find the truth of the word by which
       i now call him
and should i live in this valley
       the rest of my life
    i will love it always
  for
of these years it can be said
i come and go with the seasons
  and take these
notes on a natural happening.

Dennis Held
(1958-)

Charismatic Hacky-Sackers

Implacable, bereft of even the trace of ambition
and impeccably dressed in rare buffoon pantaloons
here they come, feet free-wheeling the bean-filled
scrotum, dreadlocked white guys from Sheol,
incubi of pure pachydermal insouciance drunk
on testosterone and heisted microbrew, eyes
a bit greazy from Idaho ditch weed and lack
of sleep, numb from the knees up and grinning
the gap-toothed leer of adolescent fascists,
hootenanny masochists elastic in their convictions
and damn glad to be here, coiling down Main Street
in packs of six, spilling off the sidewalks
and placidly tying up traffic for miles,
grateful as always for deadlock—kick, kick,
the nervous flickering inflections of ankles
and a hip-glancing pok, then past, Beelzebub's
bad clowns caterwauling on out of town,
content this time to scare the curtains
off your windows, behind which, trembling,
the thunderstruck daughters won't get along
with their business, thrilled to the toes
by the graceful, hateful spectacle of change.

Night Cats at the Grain Elevator

Not one black: they don't need it,
these slinks of the dark who wear
their own shadows, eat light

like a cave. Of sound there is
none, each footfall a padded
measure of silence. Their eyes

shine pure and lethal,
a feral purposeful blank stare
that holds no malice, no ruth,

just a simple prophecy:
I alone shall survive.
They eat their ill-formed newborns

spine and all with poisonous teeth
and jaws that crush skulls like candy.
Their tom ears are tuned

to the minute clicks of vole claws,
a packrat's clatter and rasp,
the damp pantings of a buried

skink. After years, these cats grow
through their ninth life and become
luminous to each other, levitate

to tread pathways of air, snag
pigeons out of their battering flight,
commute with their dead

and drift without season, saintly,
to where there are no more
filicides, no hunger or abandonment,

where day may not follow,
to the perfect feline dark.

Ode to My Scrotum

Old man of the pubis, apple-
faced and glum as Jehovah, plum
bob of my trunk, snout
of my groin, altar of the first

scratch of morning. adorable
cahone holder extraordinaire,
stone boat, snood-like sackful
of my worst and best moments,

I apologize, for twice I have defiled
you with painstaking razor and soap:
once at a casual request, for lust.
once for the doctor of vast indifference,

snick snick, a quartet of bristling
black stitches and oh how you did
dilate, wrinkles distended to an eight-ball
smooth and size, you were made to swell.

fellow. host of the thistly nubbins that chafe,
O totem, O glorious shifting seedbag,
unself-conscious sachem of the gonads,
treasure trove, most tender

and vulnerable storehouse: hurt
me there and I stay injured.
a bruise like a heart wound. an evening sky.
dark blue that by morning will yellow.

David Hiatt
(1946-)

Vicegrips

i'll paint my room
a deeper blue
and paint the stars
and smog in too
my five by twelve
with the roof coming in
like a wooden shoe

my last hold
out to the world
in half a ten
by twelve i stand
up all the way
on one side
while the other
bends my head
in sitting

here i am
caught in a fuckin city
with no where
to watch the sun
come up from the night
i don't know what to do
without

my hexagram says all
i need to hear
about the love
i have to bear
for you and here

the fire does
not linger long
upon the mountain
passes rapidly along

5/68
berkeley

Daniel Jacobs
(1963-)

Baby Blue

Intro: I was a premature baby and, as it turns out, that was
the only event to date I have ever been early for.

Dr. Compeau was making his rounds
through the maternity ward
when he found that a baby-blue hue
had leaked throughout my premature body.
Cells screaming,
blood stale with oxygen-empty hemoglobin,
He tucked my suffocating shell
Into the incubator
which pushed air into my new lungs.

"You looked so pitiful, there," my father tells me.
"So full of tubes, more tubes than baby."

I have seen the picture;
he's right.
More tubes than baby
wrinkled red lines on skin
that sings the blues
pop out from what could be a space suit
or a baby-shaped Hoover vacuum-cleaner
in a small glass box.

In the 1960's, a Preemie's life paths
split off
toward blindness,
toward brain damage,
toward death.

What we have now,
and each second of our life
is bonus time.

Our first experience in this world
is to be held hostage
by our inadequacies,
by our immaturities,
so full of tubes
we can't even cry.

Lying suspended between
the womb and the world
waiting again for birth
behind impenetrable glass windows:

Sometimes I find myself
again in a small glass box,
suffocating
more tubes than baby.
Sometimes still, I jump into things
a little early:
the contractions come
and I can't resist the push
to stick my head out
and try to breathe new air
with equipment that's just not yet up to speed.

I lie suspended between worlds,
waiting to be born
once more

And at first I panic
I kick and thrash
with those pathetic
bent-up excuses babies have for limbs.

But cell by cell
pink leaks over the blue
tube by tube
I am uncovered

And when I fly in dreams
the sky is blue
and I am pink
and my baby body paints the breeze
and gives the wind its oxygen
and last night I seized some bonus time,
pushed my head out of the stagnant atmosphere
of my bedroom
and into the night
and thanked Dr. Compeau...
for the cool, fresh air.

[Dr. Compeau, I raise this glass of wine
and drink to you.]   8/2/94

Peter Rutledge Koch
(1942-)

I Smile With My Teeth But Not With My Purty Eyes

O long and constant determination
find for me a pleasant definition
for this life I'm continually living.

Long passages
in an unframed wilderness
wildflowers blossom
beneath glacial surfaces,
and the Pilgrim maps only
unfamiliar landmarks.

The gate lies abandoned
the wall remains unclimbed
all the doings are yet undone
while the Pilgrim awaits no one
and no one can outwait the Pilgrim.

Our Sun rises over the familiar
the unknown is ever further
the journey is never over
and the familiar has never known
the sight of any other Sun.

While not far away—the sea
is washing the coastline clear
the sound is like the droning
in a deaf man's ear.

—and upon entering—
I see Troll men
gruff goatkillers and
defenders of the bridge

I see Stone men
transfixed by the light of day

I see Ice men
prophets of our coming age

I see Strangers with familiar faces
crowding in the photographs
of class matriculation

While the great Grey Goddess
with eyes of crystalline blue bile
attacks the denticular rectus
forcing an unlubricated entry
into the gastric sanctum
of the privatest organism.

"Come in me Come in me"
she cries in constant disintegration
of the factual body
that lies within.

Deep within my cells machine
the mitochondria dance
just like that

No transistors missing
there ain't no message
the electric light is dimming
the machine is only passage
    to a lonely island
    in a sweltering swamp
filled with extinct crustaceans
forming geometric progressions
of empty halls and
headless historic processions

I'm a day trader
and the market has exploded,
the garbage man has retired
and the rubbish leaves
no room for improvement.

The baseball diamond
has etched its pattern
into the windowpane
of my mind

O America
you send me reeling
your culture delights
the sports fan in me.

I suspect the
MAGNUS ANNUS
is coming soon
but i am not prepared
for total interruption
I am not all here . . . yet—
something is missing.

I am trying not to be impatient
but it's hard
knowing that somewhere
something is hidden.

Yet I am naked
underneath my clothes
I conceal nothing

I am a mirror
you can see yourself in me
for ritual cleanliness

is godlikeness in
our habitual
though uninhabited spaces.

"I can't go on"
I say, going on
with what I am saying.

I am making a pilgrimage
a journey to the point of departure
and I may even catch up with myself
on the way

But don't think that my
symbols mean anything
or my gestures describe anything

Just brown bellied boredom
directing enigmatic expectorations
to pass the time of day.

there is no greater
compliment I can play
than falling in love . . .
someone might ask how
but it's such a simple matter
rubbing two sticks to make fire
and fire is a joiner
and I am a plumber
capable of lifting 200 pounds
without breaking
and truth is a matter of fact
in tensile strength.

I smile with my teeth
but not with my purty eyes
because the thought appalls me
that today may last
forty more years.

The glass-walled cafes
and a hundred tabletop skies
of conglomerate marble

And all the strangers
with familiar faces
scratching their names
on the city's walls.

The same song is playing
that I have been
forever listening to...

A circle with an arrow
circumnavigates my periphery
"Symbolic salutations
circle in the sky
I greet thee with
fountains of pleasure"

The entire cosmic lie
floats before my eyes

I cannot see where
the essential difference lies
between you and me.

The Queen collects around her
all that cannot resist her
she grows fat with pies
she grows

Her son rises earlier
the day gets a little longer.

The alchemist lives again
and my search gains momentum
I am looking for the
philosopher's drug

Flesh dream disc
veiled orb of
distended vision
I eat a microcosm
with each sacerdotal meal.

Mothers cooking
indiscriminately eating
coconut macaroons
sold in grocery stores
sometimes
I get a little worried
about the high price of . . .

While over there on the other side
the grass is not yet mown

     moan
Should I deliver my own son
into the hands of strangers?
there is no home
there is no place
there are only names

The flesh has disappeared

The graveyard is full
I am the last hole to be dug
my hole is never deep enough

I cannot reach the other side of here
    hear
Hear the sound of
metabolic transmutation
that sings in the
deaf man's ear

A song piercing every fiber

A razor cannot reach in here
but to destroy.

    Heavy Heavy
The ship sinks beneath the sea
the boilermen scream
I cannot hear
I am not there
the fire goes out
the waterfall mushrooms
here I am
I am here
I inhabit your universe
can you hear me breathing?

El Greco's Christface
stares unblinking
while Judas Iscariot
a thousand times betrayed
repeats a familiar pattern.

I feel that I am
going to be here
forty more years

This day has just begun.

Zig Knoll
(1940-1997)

Rabbit Drive

A burly truck driver in a cartoon t-shirt stood up
to leave the Idaho Falls Cafe. Printed on the back of
his shirt was the question, "Where's Mud Lake?"
On the front was a caricature of a jack rabbit on
crutches with a bandage around its head and ears.
Above the rabbit were the words "Beats the hell
out of me." Penny was both amazed and dis-
gusted at the thought of a souvenir t-shirt from an
animal slaughter. She witnessed her first and only
rabbit drive near her grandparents farm just two
months shy of her thirteenth birthday.

Nine Minidoka County families helped
build the rabbit corrals that summer. A notice in
the hardware store offered a bounty of fifteen cents
an ear. The previous year's total was posted and
1953's participants were urged to try and top it.

Not counting children, at least two
hundred people showed up the morning of the
drive. After all, it was a sporting event and, like a
barn raising, people from all over the valley were
expected to help. Besides, the potluck in the
evening was legendary.

Everyone had a specific job to do. Anyone
who could swing a gunny sack or pound on a
washboard formed into lines of beaters and
herded rabbits toward the appointed slaughter
sites. Only the fittest men and older boys worked
the killing pens. Oral communication was im-
possible and in the frenzy there was danger that a
smaller or slower person could accidentally get hit
with a club.

The killing went on all day as rabbits
rounded up by the beaters arrived in irregular

gray waves. Smaller boys became so excited with each new surge, they would use their beater-sticks as spears and hammers gouging or stabbing rabbits before they reached the enclosure. Early casualties lined the trails and a thick dust pinpointed the herd.

Penny watched the slaughter outside the lath enclosures with the boys who cut and tallied ears. As her grandfather Warren had predicted, animals hurled themselves into fences and trampled each other in an attempt to escape; but the majority of them darted into the funnel shaped corrals with the club wielding farmers. Thousands met their deaths. Dust, noise and confusion created a gruesome bedlam, although Penny's mind recorded the event as a kind of incessant, slow motion dance.

Merciful blows between the eyes sent teeth and brains flying, but that was rare. There was no time for aiming. Instead, the clubs struck without accuracy. Stomachs split and scattered. Spines, skulls and hindquarters tore apart. With eyeballs dislodged or intestines dangling from a sloppy hit, a rabbit might run several yards before it fell and died slowly from shock or loss of blood. A second attempt to stop a maimed animal was unheard of. One vague swing ending with a familiar thud was what the men wanted. They knew if they got a piece of wood on it, the rabbit would die sooner or later.

And always the clobbers waited for the next wave. They blew their noses with their hands and wiped pieces of bloody debris from their clothes and skin. The men's shoulders shot with pain. Their hands were bruised and their backs ached. There was a rhythm and a passionate energy in the action. No real joy in the carnage, but righteous satisfaction when it ended. They thought of little but their own discomfort; looking forward, at the end of the hunt, to a naked group ritual in which they would burn or bury every piece of saturated clothing.

Penny shuddered, cold with goose flesh and nausea. She crouched down gripping her knees, stifling her excitement for the kill like a hungry cougar. Adrenaline exaggerated her heartbeat. She watched the clobbers' carp mouths opening and closing as the men's profanities receded into the red tide beyond the fence.

Seconds later she scratched the prickly heat on her arms. Her hands trembled as she thrust them deep into her pockets.

Piling carcasses was the oldest boys' job. Their pitchforks helped flatten the swell in the center of the corral. Small mountains of bloody flesh were formed at every corner of the wood and wire enclosures as the young men and their companions fought to keep debris out of the way of the clobbers. Shoveling the layers of guts and liquid tissue which collected near the shoots became a tiresome responsibility. The boys slipped in the slick red muck, sometimes falling, or filling their shoes with it. They laughed at the sight of one another. "Nothing multiplies faster than rabbits," a blood soaked, young man near the gate shouted. "They're such lusty breeders."

Searing death whines went on long after the men had quit pounding. Wounded rabbits wailed eerily into the night and their bodies continued the motions of escape even after death. It was as though the distant foothills created shrill echoes that came back to strafe the flatlands. The pervasive smell, the awful death odor, didn't wash off with the guts and blood of the drive either. Instead it lingered and putrefied in the Idaho sunshine.

Ironically the frenzy, the gruesome madness of the dance yielded only futility. It was as if the rabbits were permitted the final blows. When the farmers took down their fences early the next morning, a new supply of jack rabbits would be grazing among the carcasses.

Mary, Penny's grandmother, hated the drive and did nothing to encourage her family's participation in it. She refused to cook for the big get-together afterwards and usually went to bed before the others got home. This time, at her husband's insistence, she agreed to fry some of the meat for supper.

Carefully eviscerating several rabbits, Warren skinned the carcasses and washed his hands. He finished cutting up the meat for the skillet while Penny tracked down the lid for the iron fry pan, oiled it and left it on the counter by the stove. Fryer pieces filled the skillet twice over, but the lid went on in spite of the crowding.

The meat sizzled in the covered pan as grease crackled and splattered against the heavy lid. A half burning sweet smell wafted through the kitchen when the flesh began to sear. Mary peeled and chopped potatoes and onions to cook with the rabbit.

Penny set the table and poured milk before she went to the stove to watch her grandmother finish up the cooking. The food in the black pan smoked lightly. As Mary removed the lid to turn the meat, she stood very still staring into the pan in disbelief. From deep in her throat came a gasp like canvas ripping. In horror she dropped the fork and covered her eyes with her hands. Penny stared at the cancerous looking blue black lesions that oozed from the rabbit pieces. By now the entire house smelled scorched and rotten. Mary gagged as she wrapped her apron around the handle of the pan and carried it outside.

Warren kept his thumbs attached to his bib overalls, "Tularemia, the whole goddamned bunch of 'em had tularemia. Those critters have had the fever off and on for their whole existence on earth. We have these drives every few years and sometimes twice a year when it's bad enough. What makes you think people will get sick this time? We'll be all right, just as long as we didn't get the germs in a cut or something." Mary was in no mood to argue or joke about the danger. She smiled bleakly and rolled her arms in her apron.

Through the summer Penny was pre-occupied with novenas to the Virgin Mary, her grandmother's namesake. She promised hundreds of prayers if the Virgin would keep her grandparents safe from rabbit fever. The miracle happened; no one got sick.

As the nights grew longer, a fire in the wood stove burned to stave off the chill and late one afternoon screeching peacocks and guinea fowl announced the arrival of the gypsy field hands for harvest.

Penny and a young gypsy girl, Ione, had spent every summer together during harvest for three consecutive seasons. Penny could hardly wait for camp to set up. To her the gypsy wagons were like elegant train cars. Saturday afternoon, while Ione's father and brothers played music in town, the girls would have their chance to visit.

Ione rolled back the flap so Penny could climb into the wagon. The gypsy girl's mother was nursing her baby in a rocking chair under apricot trees a few yards away. Her high pitched song blew into the wind as she rocked back and forth. The singing caused goose flesh on Penny's shoulders. She wanted to stop and watch, but thought better of it. She was fascinated by the infant's tug on its mother's dark nipple. The woman sang in Spanish, a language Penny recognized but didn't understand. Ione always spoke Spanish with her family when no outsiders were around, but it was a point of honor to speak English whenever they were among strangers.

The wagon was a wooden structure with rounded canvas sides that rolled up in the summer. To keep it warm double thick curtains, which looked like they had been made from old clothes and fabric scraps, hung in front of the canvas walls. It smelled of spices and ripe fruit. The floors were covered with sheepskins. Half of the floor was a sleeping area softened with blankets and a feather comforter. Huge pillows lined the edge of one wall. There were trunks and baskets and knickknacks everywhere, even hanging from the overhead struts. On a shelf at the back of the wagon stood a small shrine to Saint Anne. Candles and wild flowers and a thimble of brandy greeted her each sunrise.

In actual age the girls were a year apart, but the dark skinned girl seemed much older. Ione handed Penny a pomegranate as they sat down on the featherbed in the back of the wagon.

"See what I brought you? Bush rubies."

Penny broke the pomegranate skin open with the tip of a spoon. Their first summer together the girls made up a game which forbade them to break the fragile particles as they prepared the fruit. From then on it became Penny's job to peel away the rough outer layer and break the ruby bunches apart. It was Ione's task to pick the individual seeds from the clusters. Another rule of the game prevented either one of them from sampling any of the seeds until the whole pomegranate was ready to eat. Then they would spoon the tart fruit into their mouths with real silver teaspoons. The brown eyed girl was proud of her mother's silverware.

For a moment the bowl of blood-red fruit reminded Penny of the crimson boot prints in the corral at the rabbit drive. She unbuttoned her sweater and pulled her blond ponytail out of her collar as she leaned back against the pillows on the floor behind her.

Ione took off her shoes. She wore boys' oxfords with baling twine for shoelaces. Her slender legs were bare with a dust of brown hair.

"Have you ever kissed a boy?" Ione's question was answered with bewildered head shaking.

"Who would I kiss? There aren't any boys at boarding school. Why, have you?"

"Yes, but it wasn't romantic or anything. Once my cousin held me down and kissed me."

"What did you do?"

"I just puckered up and kissed back. He let go of me real fast," Ione laughed.

"Would you do it if he was serious?"

"Oh, probably, as long as he didn't stick his tongue down my throat."

Penny was horrified but she didn't want Ione to know. She put a spoonful of pomegranate seeds into her mouth and crushed them with her teeth imagining a mouthful of miniature tongues. She sucked the juice from them and chewed the nutty centers.

"You should see your mouth. Your lips and teeth are bright red. Stick your tongue out and let me see." The girls compared stains and tongues.

"Show me how you kiss, Ione. Pretend your hand is a boy. Kiss the back of your hand just like you would for real," Penny begged.

Ione pulled her sweater off over her head leaving a purple and orange blouse held together across her breasts with a safety pin. She positioned herself before Penny with her brown hand in front of her mouth.

"No wait, kiss my hand, I want to see what it feels like."

Penny moved closer and thrust the back of her hand into Ione's face. She jerked her hand back when she felt Ione's lips on her fingers. Her first impulse was that the gypsy girl might bite her.

"Kiss like you are kissing a boy. Do it again."

Hesitating for a moment Ione took a deep

breath and tried again, opening her mouth a bit. Penny watched and imitated her friend's mouth on her own hand.

"What does that feel like? Do you think it's right?"

"I don't know. It's too embarrassing. Here, I'll do it to you. Hold up your fingers."

They scooted around on the mattress until their thighs touched. Ione swept her wavy black hair out of her eyes. She smelled spicy sweet. Often, she chewed cloves to hide the smell of garlic on her breath. Ione's mother cooked with great quantities of garlic and sometimes during the winter insisted that her children wear eight or ten cloves on a string around their necks to keep them from getting colds.

"Open up. Are you chicken?"

Penny opened her mouth slightly. The gypsy girl thrust her fingers between her friend's teeth, "That's how French kissing feels."

The fairer of the two shrieked and blushed. Ione clamped her hand over Penny's mouth and held her still. "Be quiet or my mother will hear us." The girls fell together into the pillows and tried to keep from laughing.

Penny stiffened and pulled her arms tight against her sides to prevent Ione from loosening her undershirt. Her heart throbbed in her temples and she knew her skin was bight red. She felt out of control but slowly she lifted her elbows away from her torso and embraced Ione on the feather comforter. Tongues and mouths began a damp search for ears, eyes, nipples, buttocks and bare clefts. The magnetized bodies bumped St. Anne's shelf toppling the statue face forward into Indian paintbrush and pink, wild roses. Ione was breathless, not laughing as Penny had imagined. Penny smelled spilled brandy and the yeasty odor of her own body. Her stomach muscles contracted as if to control what felt like a gray wave of rabbits thundering over her. Thousands of animal feet drummed her skull. Her head was about to burst from the noise. In desperation she opened her eyes to stop the pounding. A white visceral ache obliterated all sensation. The clamor of their rush to trample her had stopped. Outside, the baby started to cry, and the Spanish lullaby began again.

Ronald Koertge
(1940-)

The Day Alvero Pineda Was Killed

It was almost post time, the horses were
lining up. Pineda's was spooking so he
stepped off, outguessing trouble, and stood
on a little shelf in the stall of the
Puett Starting Gate.

Nobody knows what happened, but people
with binoculars saw the sudden blood. They
stared as if he had removed his helmet
to reveal a fall of thick, red hair.

The siren faded, the race went off, somebody
won. Then the announcement that he was
dead. "Boots And Saddles," a moment
of silence.

For the rest of the day we worked
the bartenders numb and heaved our money
through the windows, making everything
the favorite.

After the ninth we went home
38,000 of us
all sick
all broke

feeling lucky.

Two from *The Jockey Poems*

William Shoemaker has a Valium behind. He is
able to console more horses into the winner's circle
than 10 Tall Men could batter there in a month.
Other jocks draw their whips like D'Artagnan. William
is more liable to extend his into his mare's field
of vision and say, "I know you're capable of better.
Why not give yourself to me completely." He allows
animals to slide back through the trauma of lettuce-
fed soreheads who have jumped her since the age of
two. Back then, she wanted to run. William
Shoemaker stands thoroughbreds out of their way.

Racing is something primitive, shrunk and
codified. The concept of men astride beasts
is dazzling. Man always feared other animals.
Now with flight channeled into an oval, we
have an enormous compression with mammals mounted
on other beasts riding like the devil to finish
where they began. At the moment of highest frenzy,
would anyone be shocked at the sight of prognathous
fans fighting over bones?

Fucking Other People

is fun. It is flattering and makes
you a little tired like a day
at Sexland on the Vag-O-Slide
and in the Womb Room.

Fucking at home is more serious,
darker. One does not proceed
like a salesman, "Do you like
this? Do you like that?"

Everybody knows what everybody
likes. Now to do it harder, deeper,
now to draw blood.

Otherwise one is always fucking
other people, standing in line,
ticket in hand, knowing it is all
going to be over in a minute.

It Got To Be Almost A Hundred In Pasadena Today

and I started thinking about this girl I knew a couple
of years ago. She was young, 20 or something incredible
like that, with amazing breasts which she kept shrouded

because she was a Christian: church every Sunday, Prayer
Meeting on Wednesday, Young Adult Bible Class, that
kind of thing. Also she has a husband who was very sensitive
about them.

Lynn and I sat in a little park one night. She had a clean,
pink cat's mouth and she kissed like I was about to go
to war. I got one breast out from under all those clothes.
I could not see, but it was heavy as a can of honey.
We agreed that parks were too vast. We needed
walls.

It turned into a regular thing. "I'm somebody's mistress,"
she'd say. Or "I'm a concubine. King David had 300 of us."

She said she did not want me to get tired of her. "Show me
where to put my mouth." And "If there's anything you want
just tell me." And "It's alright. I don't care if
it hurts."

Finally it got to be too much, every sermon covered her
like canvas, every other word in every other chapter
and verse harlot, whore, adulteress.

But if we could get married.

I thought of the parents who clung to her like shipwreck
victims. I thought of the nights she would lie awake
waiting for the Second Coming. I thought of her husband
and his guns.

Today when it got to be almost a hundred I remembered how
she liked to sweat when we screwed and I thought of those
long, eelly afternoons.

"Better," says my wife, "now that the sun's down."
I nod, take a drink in total
disagreement.

Richard Krech
(1946-)

Sgt. Pepper. Where

Sgt. Pepper. Where
are your soldiers now? – they've been seen
                                    wandering
down crystal shattered lanes
the fragments converging
on one point. the end

of a needle
puncturing a paraffin vein,
the days going in . . .

hours,
spent getting
the exact sensation.

"It's pretty much the same" he said,
"More money passes through your hands,
but you're in the same position."
                        his words fading

as he spins into another nightmare/

                        Old Sailors
stumble into the afternoon dust
of a cob-web,
the corners of the room
going faint.

Rip Van Winkle sleeping. The corner
of his laugh
turned-in. His volume boosted
by amplifiers.
In Turn

boosted from record stores. The whole world
a big burn.

Acid Salesmen
carrying guns
to keep from being robbed. The whole scene

going down Your drain.
Heroin;
getting fat
off the skinny bodies

the way you make them
crawl/

October, 1967

Barbara La Morticella

(1942-)

The Underground Economy

1.

Twenty-five years we lived in the woods
in a house with no locks
while the trees breathed and grew.
We thought they were giants, our mysterious companions,
but all the while they were really money.

Now they've been extracted like teeth
and the bare hills gape.
And if the land comes back green
it'll come back without giants
for the new world is crafted by cash
and cash is a low thing.

Don't get me wrong—
I like snakes and worms.

But in the language of cash
everything is abstracted to "zero"—
eyes, hair and skin, fins, wings and seeds—
even the sun in the sky grows hollow
as a sucked egg,
and the earth itself becomes zeroed
on the spindle of some dark star.

2.

I cried when I saw the picture of the onion man
draped in his pungent necklaces, riding his
bicycle through the streets of Normandy,
calling:

"Onions! Onions!"

Maybe it was simply the onions,
or knowing how far the onion man needs to ride
peddling like crazy

to get out of the sea of red ink
Where we owe each other so many millions
that we can pay only by breaking the earth into dust,
and the dust into atoms,
and the atoms into zeroes,
nothing at all.

3.
An onion is a zero
that has put on flesh,
a wedding where the sky and sun
have lain down together in the dirt.

They were married in an underground cathedral
all flames and transparencies
walls of glass that open for bicycles
and little horses of tears.

The economy of trillions
is a divorce decree:
The faces of the families are rubbed out,
the furniture is thrown onto the sidewalk,
and the children are scattered,
and sent wandering, homeless.

But the economy of onions
marries us to the whole earth.
The wedding guests offer up their gifts
without shyness:

Globes of white flowers,
Bulbs fiery with juices,
The big bang of vegetables—

Creation that keeps happening
again and again.

A Liturgy for Trinity

Our fathers of the atomic industry
thought there was a chance
New Mexico might be destroyed
when they exploded Trinity,

or even that the entire earth
would flash. They took the chance:

stationed soldiers in bunkers and foxholes
close to the blast to see...

I was driving my sister home, and we were
about 20 miles away, when she looked out the
window and shouted, "What's that light?" The thing
is, my sister is blind.

Oh immense light boiling out of the ground:
iridescent colors—red, purple, orange:
pistons and wheels like ten suns moving across the sky.

We were in this big desert when the bomb went off,
and suddenly the desert looked tiny and the
    mountains looked
tiny. I've never seen things the same since.

Petals of light falling on the backs of the animals in the fields,
spokes of light spinning in the genes of the unborn,
saucers of light landing on the platelets of the blood,
coins of light across the eyes of the now dead.

Our mute mother of this atomic age,
we need to see things never the same again also.

Never again only two eyes with their left and their right
separated as fast as they're named.

Never again, please, this third eye with its blindness:
this eyes of the Trinity waving a green goodbye.

There needs to be more than a fourth eye that shrinks like a
violet from the light of the blaze.

For even five eyes aren't enough to help us see over the top
of this huge pile of bodies—

So we've opened the sixth eye of smoke
and the seventh of darkness.

2.

Seeking perfect security, the world in 1980 spent
a million dollars a minute on defense.

The fathers turn away from each other, but are
joined at the waist by the hinge of their darkness.

In the last days of the Piscean age,
perfect materialism snorts uranium like cocaine;
perfect spiritualism builds a nuclear submarine called
Corpus Christi, watches the seas boil.

Without telling them,
Russia uses people of the Urals like mops
to wipe up nuclear accidents.

When today's army talks about an integrated battlefield,
it means a field where the soldiers are nuked & gassed & shot
all at once. The Ayatollahs say death is preferable
to an imperfect world.

In the last days of the Piscean age,
CIA agents passed out LSD on Haight St.

The President ordered opium stockpiled outside the cities
for after the blast.

No matter what happens,
Corpus Christi is secure—

The rights of the bodies of Christ
to form a huge pile reaching all the way into the sky.

3.

Light a candle for Thomas O'Dell
Portland lawyer who died of leukemia at 45
20 years after he was a soldier
at Yucca flats.

He didn't ask to have X-ray vision,
but after he'd stood with his back to the blast,
shielding his eyes as he'd been told,
and saw—clearly—his hands with the blood in them,
and the bones white, cuneiform, startling—

he was never the same again. Some unknown
line of defense breached. All the mute bones
articulate:

his hand like mountains trembling in the sky,
his hands a puzzle heaped on his wife's thigh,
his hands two piles of coins.

———————

Sometimes when it's nearing dusk
there's a sheen on old boards
and on the surface of the dark soil

as if the sky had come to nestle in things,
meeting them on their own terms for a change,
with a blue that's neither melancholy nor cold.

In the course of this kiss, this delicate exchange,
the light is ineluctably drawn into the cut grain
    of things,
and the darkness has stars folded up into it
like blossoms of light...

Eugene Lesser
(1936-)

On Listening to Mozart's
Piano Concerto No. 24 in C Minor
Behind Illegal Drugs

Mozart, I've neglected you.
The truth is, inside, I've always put you down.
I guess it was that silly
Picture of you in profile.
It made you look like an asshole,
On top of this, I thought you were aloof,
I was suspicious because Shaw dug you so hard
But my ear is up against the speaker tonight
And we're friends for the first time.
Mozart, can you hear me ?
I'm sorry.

Mozart, I'm not fooled
By your trills and your prancing.
You didn't intend to fool me, I know,
It's just the way you are.
Still I used to be fooled
But now I see what you mean.
The trouble with being precocious
Is that no one takes you seriously.
That's the trouble with being good, too.

It's been almost 200 years (think
of it) and tonight
I've finally decoded you, tonight
You're saying something to me
That I *know* is true. For example:
One does not have to be stoned
To be where you are. This
Will always be a revelation.

As long as there is dope and a record player
Musicologico-Esthetico-Socio-Ethico
Historiographicianismists
Will always be amazed to realize
That the straightest person
Can be making it at a level
At which it takes 2–3 joints for guys like me
Just to get close to the neighborhood
Of what you're laying down, just
To begin to apprehend the truth of it.
Another amazing thing: What did those people
In powdered wigs hear when they heard you?
Here's what you're saying to me:
The right way is better than the wrong way.
You wish your heart could do all the talking but it can't.
All our trappings are transparent,
There are more important things than being happy in love
But you have trouble expressing them clearly.
We are all on the edge of a precipice.

Music is my mentor.
I've discovered this through dope.
I'll get to the others one at a time but
Mozart, I just wanted you to know.
I always knew you were good
But I never knew you were that good.

Alchemy

I.

at 5AM
market st is finally sincere (though
market st and every st and every
thing is sincere all the time always
being no other thing than what it is
        I mean then
that market st at 5AM is subject matter
which is the experience of the poet
and the only experience of the poet
and that is all I mean) at 5AM
market st says the following:
I am not what you made me
        but *you* are/period
market st insists on being sincere
and not my subject matter and this
is the struggle of my poetry
        two definitions:
a)myth is the rendering of someone
else's experience into subject matter
b)art is the rendering of one's
own experience into subject matter

myth making is a public service
performed by the poet (poet is 'maker' in
greek) and this is not a matter
of predilection but of survival
        the poet (me) cannot
allow market st its sincerity/believe
(me) thus while it's true that I
        personally
never broke my ass for gold
a hundred years ago/I break my ass
transmuting my own historic dross
into something I can experience
and so when it comes to the gold rush
I do know what I'm talking about
        to some extent
and in fact it is fair to say that:
I am america and america is me

which (by
means of a desperate logic) is
a kind of proof that market st is wrong
    base metals into gold
    market st into myth
    my life into art
I've had enough gold for one lifetime

                    II.

greed is very poor subject matter (as
are all the sins) but if we take lust
for gold/manifest destiny/the general
metaphoric possibilities of the wild-
erness (the hard-line jeffersonian
        craperoo is what I
mean) if we put all this together
we have what I call subject matter:
me you the prospectors this poem
market st all of this/subject matter
        but if you
are also desperate (and we must both
be desperate or else it won't
happen) we may yet have/out of
this/something to experience and
if we can do that:the poet
promises never to bother you again

III.

a hundred years ago america thrust its
market st stake through the heart of san
francisco and the body politic dropped
dead and has been a corpse ever since
        the poison ran
under the rockies/through the quilted
farms of my fifth-grade geography
book/cold peristaltic spasms triggering
the black Oklahoma jissom (like the
jissom that shoots out of the hanging
man) tributaries twisting through dixie
subways under my birthplace bronx
        before greed

found me panning gold on my own
ground/my own gold rush and
                        at 5AM
lusting for the ancient resources
I watch the nuggets/the ones the earth
a hundred years ago would not part with
struggle through cement:and from the
        bronx
I made a great rumbling sound across
        america
to pluck the wealth of subject matter
something for me to experience/for you
to experience too for we share this
same   debronxification

IV.

I was going to say
we are all
tourists.

V.

we share the bounty of a wilderness
that was maybe murdered maybe dead
of natural causes but I'm no hart
crane (nor ts eliot nor would I be
unless you paid me a lot of money)
the air glittered in my bronx but
I would trade it and all of my
                        subject matter
if there were anything to trade it
for/settlers coaxing new cities/places
caked on their shoes:if the story
only ended in the fifth-grade
        but we poets
never graduate from grammar school

I watch the gross century of the
emporium pennys woolworths/this
stolid top of the sarcophagus
and it is enough to bruise
        a poet's heart/valentine shaped

VI.

pigeons
sniff the pickings with such arch
has-been dignity/down one end
behind the ferry clock
                                tugs
  gargle in the harbor:here
around fifth/the dinosaur buildings
feet stuck in the tar
          blink and stumble
toward my children's laughter
glassing intimations of grace/great
squares of fire as I turn toward

morning
          and see the sky
inoculated
          with one more vision of cathay
pyrite paradises
          bursting over mountains
      that the city had
      completely forgotten

light rushes down the market st sluice

d.a. levy
1943-1968)

new year

when i was
six years old
we dipped
apple slices
& bread
in honey
touched small glasses
of wine
& sed 'to life'
    'to life'
that was the only time
my father ever hit me
his eyes were very sad
& he just sort of walked away
knowing he was wrong
or that he couldnt reach me
i dont think he knew who i was
perhaps even asking if i was really his son
that was 1948 – it is now 1968 and i know
he is watching a football game on television
in another city – his grey hair
        his sad eyes
and he is probably still wondering if i
am really his son
what father wants to admit that his
son really is a 'poet'

i think i was ten when i asked the difference
between christians & jews
and his reply was
'the jews believe jesus was a bastard'
he was wrong again
the jews believe in living, the christians
believe in jesus and have formed a death cult
around his image

a cult dedicated to suffering & love as a
means of liberation
the jews know, that one becomes liberated
thru living not *only* thru programmed acts
of masochism or blindness

it was sometime afterward
my father and i
went to a temple to hear
the services
       sat down in time
       to hear that haunting
       language for just a moment
when someone told us we had to stand in the
back – we had chosen 'reserved seats'
seats that were paid for
we left & it was thus i completed
my external jewish education

My father was right
we never visited another temple
& now i wonder how many jews are
destroyed in this country each year
my father with his lonely eyes
trying to return home
only to have the american god of money
slapped in his face
when we left it was as if
he passed the message on to me
'there are no jews left in this place'

and i spent years
trying to fill in that
hungry space denied me

on holidays i did not
know about i found myself
thinking of the old man
and later trying to remember
what i dreamt when i was
a child

i kept discovering his quietness
when did the first images
appear in my head?
'a place with sand where it was
warm – the blue sky – strange
trees'   my fathers eye
had never turned from israel
i dont even know if he knew
what was inside his own head

once visiting hillel house
i was told about keeping
traditions alive
         lighting candles

the secrets i learned from my father?
how does one pass them on?
         my fathers terrible eyes
         the loneliness
         flash phrases like
         'genetic memory'
this poem?
that i remember once
being free to walk
through all secret doors

to walk with a free people

where did i learn that?

when i think of my father
i wonder if he can hear me

this poem?
for my father
who will someday be reborn in israel

& this poem
for my father
that i may once again be his son

         & the name we carry
         was once a name to be proud of

now it is new years 1968
in a barbarian country
that has always *felt*
alien to me

while blind men struggle
to keep traditions alive
my father watches football
games on television
to pass time
& i dream of his dad eyes
and i wonder about those blind men
do they ever wonder who wrote
their fucking traditions for them?

what songs will be sung
in israel for the young jews
beaten or murdered in the south
trying to keep alive
the internal spirit

what songs will be sung
in israel
to remember the young jews
who took drugs into eternity
trying to find the Spirit
they couldnt find in america

what songs will be sung
in israel to commemorate
the subtle murders
while rabbis danced the hora
ate dates & figs
& looked the other way
to keep traditions alive

my father watched football
on television
his eye did not lose sight
of israel for even a moment –

and at least once a year
i break bread with him
quietly in my mind

i found it at the movies (or)

hummmmed-off in a laundro-mat
(for Franklin Rosemont)

a great place
to get it or just to dream
about it because no one does
get it except in european
movies
     —a long legged broad
with silver gears & wheels &
springs tattooed on her
amphetamine skin —
pulls you off with black lips
in the mens room while the
washer hummms & the dryer oms
yr clothes
     in a dream
     waiting with nordic
     precision
     30 minutes for wash
     10 minutes to dry
     students know - it
was never like this at home
No Mens Room — stroke the
Pepsi machine
     push a dime
into the slot — uhh —
it hurts — a little tight
accidentally get ACTION—clarion bleach
which means i shoudnt drink before
entering
     have to drop another dime
     for Fab if yr a right winger
     or All if yr a left winger
     & wonder about the bleach

Its Magic
      after washing white shirts &
      dark shirts together for years
      i guess thats why the same gray color as
      my face in the morning
chlorine bleach! i guess there are
people who can afford to use two
machines – & they probably dont dream
about getting it in the slot
the dream lady with silver tattoos &
black lips
      they watch the clock & read
      U.S. & World News Report

it is 12:45 – Madison Wisc –
i wanted a quiet laundromat
where i could write a poem &
maybe jam a machine or two –
instead, there are 3 people here
& their brains are sending out
all kinds of 'creep thoughts' like
English 202 – History, renaissance
politics – translate U.S. & World News
into Sanskrit – etc
meanwhile i cant sleep at night
my friends in jail haunt me
my friends in jail because some
asshole politician tried to make
a name for himself by getting someone
else arrested
      & everyone pretends its
      all right
      everyone thinks the people
in jail belong there
i will hate America for the rest
of my life
      because of some cheap
politician with his secret links

in the Kiwanas or Masons or
the Universities or The Knights of
Columbus or the Rosicrucians or some
other dream inquisition
disguised with the flag of humanity
or God, or education or 'save our
children from' reality by putting
everyone who disagrees with us
in jail

they are all murderers in the establishment
and we will not learn the lesson

i drink some R.C. Cola
pretend it is soma - liquified hash
give them new names
new laundro-mats for the students
& drunken poets with fantasies
trying to forget
friends in jail

after all this country is
better than any other
esp if you cant afford to leave it
& find out otherwise
R.C. Cola . . .
the lady with
black lips

                    oct. 14th 1968
                    madison, wisc.

Lyn Lifshin
(1949-)

The Way He Is With Women: Or
It's Always Show And Tell With Him

if he does some
thing he wants every
one to see it   the

way he leaves stuff
in his pants   he'll
bring the girl with

4 black lovers home
he only wants some
one already taken

slobbers on my best
friend   sniffing her
pants   but he hates

his penis   wants a
woman who can make
it do what it cant

some pretty slut to
give up all cocks
for him   what he'd

really like is a
woman with long
black hair   her wet

slit open on his
fender like a
dead deer

Nice

floating thru chairs
then opening
your hand
snakes in thru corduroy
my slip rides up the sun
makes the rug into a wool beach
sand   assapples   a wave of
thighs opening
skin prints a v on the rug your
knees go there
opening
and mouths suddenly too a
crack touch the pink smell
the sleek breathing flesh moans
a taste is nipples
bumping and your sail of blood
shove of bone tongue
traveling into this moist
lips opening the first bang of
hair and clothes rise from bodies
tremble the warm buttons rubbing
scratch of your month there
the damp nylon crotch
petals dissolving in a water my silk
hips you open and your fingers
under plunge so are pressing lips there
and your flesh
root shining

rocks your heat to my belly and my
legs spread so wide
greedy for the whole boat of you
in me your lovejuice dipping these
sloppy hills of cunt and you
put your good
hardness up me opening
skin rooms pounding
and circles slide your raw stem
my nails pull you
tighter
in and the slap of licked flesh oil
waves lunging and teeth
that eat everywhere ramming
the slit wet
opening and spread so
wide and splitting bite the sweet hot ache swell
your bomb breaking
too sucks the whole room up
fur zippersbeercans
and the sweat hair of groaning and sperm
till your cock bud throbs more
to ball me over and
again   better than summer
deep and nice
bringing everything
home

Gerald Locklin
(1941-)

No Love, Please; We're Americans

i get my daughter to her ballet class
ten minutes early. she has never been
early for her lessons before. she cuddles
up next to me on the waiting bench.
all the other little girls are comparing
their hairdos. they have a professional
knowledge of "perms" and "crinkles"
and conditioner and shampoos.

the other little girls and their mothers
look at me and my little girl as if we
must be a little weird to be locked in
this silent embrace, waiting for the
ballet class to come between us.

Friday: 3 p.m.

"It rests me to be among beautiful women" – Ezra Pound

All the sad young coeds sleepwalk
on the sands of time, no time on their hands,
but unawake they walk in lovely like
the day and talk in nonsense like the night.

I have seen the sad young coeds dreaming
through dull classes and on sunny sundays
driving young men mad by seeming not to
care for sports cars, not to crave pastels of one

day's unreality. They are real
as short red skirts, red polished nails, crossed
legs, espresso hair, a generation lost
and found as new as new year's eve, they feel

the surf at Santa Monica is sacred,
sex does not excite them, fond
of fate, they pay lip service to dead gods
and in eternity discern a grain of sand.

All the sad young coeds arabesque
across the granite campus, high with
dissonance and dying with the risk of
living high. Let me share their joy.

we almost had twins

at *gandhi*, in orange county,
i think I see her.

she is with a man a little older,
a little fatter, a lot richer than i,
but, like me, an over-the-hill jock.

i remember that she used to like my arms.

she's aged. graying. rounding.
i haven't seen her since 1967.
i have to calculate whether she,
or her mother,
would look as she does now.
i have to remind myself that i
am even grayer, and that i was only
a little older than she.

i could make positive identification
if i could see her toes or knees or nipples.
she had unusually long feet, bony knees,
abnormally long nipples.
yet she was as stylish in appearance
as any woman i ever was allowed to sleep with.

long after we'd begun to hate each other,
we couldn't keep out of bed.

but once we finally broke for real,
we stayed out of each other's sight
for fifteen years.

my kids are with me,
but i stare enough to let her know
i think i know her.
she looks at me the same way.

when we used to park because
we had no place to go,
and i had brought her off,
all she had to do was touch me with
a fingernail to fill her handkerchief
with my young sperm.

i've written about her elsewhere:
her father was in law enforcement.
she'd already given up one kid.

she got pregnant by me
and the abortion was twins.

this is not *the umbrellas of cherbourg*.

kids

i've fathered five, been father to none of them.
they all look like me, more's the pity.
i had a girl aborted once, and it was twins.
an irony: i've always wanted twins.

my youngest son is one-year-old
and now i want another.
i didn't realize that this was bugging me
until i analyzed last night's dream:

my wife had had a child,
a boy with the potential of an einstein-chamberlain.
she claimed it was by the holy ghost,
and i insisted it was mine.

i do not think this is a case
for some conditioned analyst.
i think it is a case for the stork.
bird, bring me another son, soon.

i don't care if it is my wife's
or borne by the girl that i am living with.
it may be someone i will only meet that once.
i want another son, somewhere in the world.

i know this is a crime against society.
my son
is more important
than society.

i dedicate my thing against The Pill,
natural hormones against synthetics.
no, pope paul, i'm not on your side.
i'm going to raise my kid a manichaean.
i saw *true grit* the other night
and rooster cogburn had a son somewhere
but mattie ross would never marry.
i wouldn't mind a kid with kim darby.

what a great movie anyway
after months of italian self-indulgence.
fellini, antonioni, visconti,
what is the point of your posing and panning?
you have too much money now, that's your trouble.
your films have run to fat.
rooster cogburn was old and fat,
but he had grit.

europeans just don't have it;
it's lucky that they only fight each other.
some blacks have it.
i'd like a black child.

the mexicans are too concerned with *machismo*
and the russians stand up too straight.
i realize this racist approach is unfashionable,
but it's fun to bug people.

"no grit rooster cogburn — not much!"
exclaimed mattie, as john wayne moved on out,
the best film since *midnight cowboy*, or
right up there in a class with *shane*!

"remarks," said gertrude stein, "do not make literature,"
but how much literature did she make?
all anyone remembers are her remarks.
i'd rather have a dozen kids with deborah kerr.

where were we — yes,
they'll never make kids a dirty word for me.
let the misguided liberals assign me a role
as id-in-residence.

o chestnut tree, great-rooted blossomer,
are you the leaf, the blossom, or the bole?
o body swayed to music, o brightening glance,
i want to get into your pants.

Lucky Luckenbach
(1942-)

Juli II

& who's carrying my child of tomorrow mutant freak
monster baby who
might even be 1 or 2 years old polka-dot   prison-striped
                            telepath   psychopath
                                        who knows

    you don't and care less but dig soft dope
    ice cream   being dumb
    grocery stores   windowpanes ceilings at night   Nembutal
    and cryptic messages tacked to our door from old suitors
    of your sexy yesterdays
    selling your stinking ass for a shot a throw

but maybe that's not being fair
        Juli you had more class than that even then
    bleaching your mind blond with Clairol & goofers to
    freakout all over giggling paranoid   hysterical &
    running off with Holsworth to have a suspicious and
    very timely car wreck with my dope
        Damn funny you sonofabitch

but after all
        home wasn't my cat you hated
        and the antique shop we lived under
        no

        home wasn't the supercheap hole-in-the-ether
        motel on Aurora   we
        so often went mad in together
gibbering supernatural phantoms at nite & backwindow bogeymen
weird early morning visits from Curly and George
who talked through an electric mega-throat
& shot up all my tintrite of opium your eyes
wide and speechless

not even a cardboard sandwich sometimes hiding from
the landlord miserable paupers with over 3 grand in narcotics
stashed all over
while the dead-man's suitcase of defunct clothes in the corner
stunk the whole place all to hell

        beautiful
not even 15 cents to buy some sandlewood incense
but cameras   guns   swiss cheese
getting moldy and overexposed by our wild excesses
passing out on the bed
and waking with hamburger all over my face
bed   the walls everywhere
you assaulted me while I slept
        getting horny & trying to revive me with frozen lunchmeat

        home wasn't Harry's living room we lived & roomed in awhile
with all my poetry, paintings, ENTIRE LIFEWORK EVERYTHING
in his basement to this day
        shooting deadly wax Nu Morphane suppositories
rusty spike maggotminded explaining to you I was going to die
any day now as you schemed on how we could afford
a 15 cent ice cream bar I was in no shape to boost

you nagged and really cried when I shot up all the heroin and didn't
believe it was medicine for my swollen leg bullet wound

        home was really you moving back with your folks
carrying sad suitcases
goldfish   puppydog   cardboard boxes of mismatched shoes underwear
& my raggedy copy of *Existentialism and Human Emotions*
you promised to treat like your baby
also at your people's place
        you waved a sighing goodbye   we drove off to Montana
thinking to yourself tomorrow
– Thank God he's gone – I can turn a quick trick
and get that ice cream bar – "Be sure and write!"

Denis Mair
(1952-)

On the Olympic Coast

Part I

Walking in the burnt-over woods near Shi-shi Beach,
I see gutted trees growing in knobby shapes

They have been half-dead since the Forties,
but strips of bark are still taking sap to live branches

Behind me the old conifers stand like cathedral pillars

But in the huge trunks only the inner bark has live, multiplying cells

The wood is made of cells that grew stiff with fibers and plugged
   up with resin.
They died and became support elements for the plan of the tree

The bark is layers of corky, plugged-up cells that built up in
   furrowed patterns

The trunks of these monsters are mostly cellulose

Standing there in columnar form, or down on the forest floor,
   they are uninvolved

There is more living matter in this rain forest than if the
land were simply covered in green slime

Nature taught itself to stack layers of leaf, and thus give room for
   more life

The whole point seems to have been: get as much matter as possible
   into the web

But most of the matter that made it is only half-involved

Dead logs littering the seashore

old stalks of beached kelp, studded with barnacle knobs

Dried sea confetti stinking to the sky

Shampoo bottle from New Zealand, used by someone on a
   container ship

Glass globes that floated fishnets miles wide

Wood nubs and coke-bottle beads, smoothed in gem tumbler
   of sand and wave

A deer jawbone with only one tooth: the tooth was deposited
like a diatom's calcareous shell in the chalk cliff of the body

oddments thrown from nowhere where things were in the thick
   of being made

All this matter was coaxed into the dance for a while

But the moves were hard to follow, and the stuff got *buttslammed*
   to the side

Most of the dancers at any time are forced to be wallflowers,
   uninvolved

Like most of the contents of my mind

Snags and deadwood, all bundled away

So much is not allowed into my heart at any one time

And this trickle of thoughts is me, what is allowed to be alive

But even this much of me is only walking

Just an uninspired two-legged creature walking on the puncheon
trail, in relation to the uninvolved trees, uninvolved

What can I do to be more alive?

Something morbid, intriguing, slightly repelling?

Dostoyevskian convoluted moral retch trip?

Or go to galleries and see people's spirits lodged in paintings?

or read some thorny book and get a furrowed brow?

Everything will get subsumed under the Uninvolved

No use smoking Marijane if your sense of wonder's gone

Any communication repeated loses meaning

While an auctioneer with light-up necktie raises funds for
the Chamber of Commerce

And legal messengers streak across town carrying Hanford payoffs

You are just parked there, clueless

When you are off on your trip to be active in the Democratic Party

The Rush Limbaugh audience thinks you are badly painted scenery

Even screaming crowds are frozen in their screaming

Judgments are flying thick and fast; people get stymied deep inside

If you can't keep up with the green edge, you will have to be wood

Part II

I've got to get this stupid preoccupation with matter out of my head.
It is the malady of analytical man.

By seeing the tree as a column of cellulose, it's easy to be helpless
when others are cutting it down

In a **good dance** there is no strict boundary between the quick and
the dead

I even look for materiality in the social sphere; that is sure to get me
nowhere

Suppose the arms-merchant economy is the provider of some people's
"needs"

If it's just a structure that deals out resources,
why is it so alive in its reproductive functions?

You may think it's just part of the scenery but to IT, **you** are just
part of the scenery

What a mess being the green edge and the left-behind stuff for
each other!

The trees are blessed, if we can only spare them

Their column of wood never fails to hold the green growth high

But our materiality has spines and turrets that come piercing
through tender bark

The green edge spreads wide and dangerous into other hearts

Singers join to make slow-floating circles in the mind's sky

Singers, join to make slow-floating circles in the mind's sky!

David Memmott
(1948-)

Too Many Windows; Not Enough Doors
for Art

I dreamed someone was knocking on my door.
Looking out the window I saw no one there
so turned away, going back to work.
Again I heard insistent rapping
so looked out the window and saw no one.
I have no time for this. There's too much to be done.
Yet again I heard the knocking
and this time pulled the door open, saw my dead father
standing on the front porch.

This man taught me to breathe in the dark.
I followed him down dragging handtools into basements
and cellars. We crawled on mud-wet bellies under houses
strapping up lengths of galvanized pipe to broad beams,
poking our heads into fiery mouths of furnaces,
the sound of our hammers ringing up registers
into rooms of strangers shivering for need of heat.
I followed him down day after day
until I could fall asleep in dank or dust
curled up in spiderwebs and mouse droppings,
pulling the darkness in around me,
knowing the darkness as my friend.
What better place to forget yourself,
to become nothing — and everything?

Perhaps I've been looking through too many windows
without opening enough doors, windows to the world,
windows to websites, windows to streets to risky business
wrapped up in deadlines and commitments
without fear of too much exposure. I understand, father,
why you do not step across my threshold,
why we do not embrace but stand regarding each other
in this new light. I understand the way is open to us now;
we are free to come and go. Just as you once eased me down
into darkness and taught me to breathe,
you help me now to stand in this light.

The Storm That Put the Phones on Hold

In the afternoon deluge
the power failed.
We put the phones on hold.
In my cubicle I did not see
the sky darken, protected
from the fickle variable of weather
by the temperate mean of air conditioning
and a stable, artificial light.
I'd grown blind to the numbing legato daze
in the care, custody and supervision of the State,
crapulent and secure accruing vacation time and sick leave.

So when the power failed, for a moment the old spell
was broken; it held no power over me.
A smoking caldera
opened up beneath my chair and the musk
of wet fur permeated the sulphurous air.
The mindless interface of brain and computer – with prolific
phosphor tracks scurrying across a black void,
a white noise of repetitive tasks,
opening and closing narratives
lost to memory like bad dreams still leaving
a feeling that some intruder has broken into your house –
was severed by a midday storm.

Unchained from our desks,
we ran outside through double doors.
The low clouds roiled just beyond our fingertips;
rain pelted our uplifted faces,
tongues tasting a timeless power
causing even new buildings to shudder.
Silver needles electrify, explode on my skin,
breaking the somnambular embrace of convenience,
the mutual masturbation of work for pay.
Such utter delight in a pure physical world!
Then the lights came on.
We straightened our ties, confessed our bodies
brushing the dark was simply coincidental.
Stop this staring off into space, my friends.
The phones, once more, are ringing.

Jo Merrill
(1932-)

Cinnabar Is What I'll Say to My Husband
If I Should Leave Awhile

It's as though I thought
I held that bridge up
with my eyes and if I
turned my back it would
collapse and make that crash
because *my* ears were there
to hear it.

And along the freeway
seeing shooting stars
I *know* they blow because
I'm here all big eyed
and sighed up with
the look of it.

Vanity,O Granny
you have got it. Go
off to the city where
the air is so full
of things you can't focus,
the locus is nowhere, the point
is to let your eyes wander.

Like your son says,
"My mother's attention
span is so short she
reads the dictionary so
she won't hang up on the plot."

It's not that sonny, although
you're only put on intermittently,
let me disagree, just
for the record.

There is one word I've
heard more years than I
can accurately remember
It has a round round sound
I come back to as in
treadmill, ball bearings
money, maypole, the moon, moon

and "cinnabar," there you are
again. That means red, means
metal, is part Mercury—
cynopar, cinabre, cinobre,
cinnabaris, kinnabair, zinjafre,
zinjifrah, sinoble, sinople,
sinope—in all tongues defies
my intent to describe it.

And were I to close that
book for the bit in the
city, you'd bug me. Knowing
I'm only half there when
you're half here. Having
only half said it: Cinnabar
              You are.

Les Fleurs

1.
We hum by halves
uncertain of the source
but certain
in our ears a madness
makes it inadequate
or tame.

If there could be
a clarity, a song
consistent with the heart
and timed to sound
music in our alternate mood;
then as flowers
in their season we
could shine,
constant
to all we look to
and for each perform
that music
as only love allows.

2.
I hate flowers
to wilt
an hour to,

You
held me once
lightly
below a storm
you said was gathering.

Now
you're nowhere in this rain
or in the wake or
in the words

that coil around us;
philosophies that shed
our skin.

I
don't know what's meant
by "win."
We
share one
medal, mirrored
in that
sudden blossomed
hour
in a storm's eye.

3.
Do you remember then, that lighthouse,
the rock, the curved sand, how the poppies
spread out in a field before it, how
they were so gold, how that blue was behind
them, the white tower, the red roofs?
Poppies. The gold of September.
But we are too old to remember.
  The painter Wishart would remember,
  writing to her:
    "You were still very young and you
    really could not bear the end of
    anything ever. Some weeks later
    you had filled my cabin with roses
    which made it harder to realize
    that we should not meet again   until
    we had both completely changed. Perhaps
    this is the moment
    to thank you for them."

translating to canvas
"Roses on a Blue Cloth"
"Water Flowers"
"Garden for the Child Mozart"
"Rose ......
                a stem, a petal, the mists
                that surround them
                impressions
                past time a florescence
                the rose, life everlasting
                look!
                he has left off the thorns

In Idaho, Morning Glory
is a dirty word.
Morninglory Morninglory
why do you wind round
the wheat so
cover gold with blue
why do you
Morning Glory?

Do you remember then, that Botany was not a bore:
There were the flowers, always; the names committed
to memory, the drawings to he done, the cellular structure
a form of beauty, an inner order.
To learn
we learn to dismember.
                And we are too young to remember.

Mary Mary quite contrary
I'm stealing again
from a nursery rhyme
and a world filled
with macadam.

And yet they are everywhere
the flowers

Edelweiss
Anemone
and at all varying heights
a reminder of us
breathed past   Pleistocene
                November
                        but we are
                        too old to remember.

4.
The answer to a Koan, a zen riddle, he
has made an answer to a zen riddle they
won't tell me. It is that old game—I tell
you an answer for a question, now you must
make the question, I do not know the question.
Dante Gabriel Rosetti, his name a flower,
has made an answer to a zen riddle, not hearing,
does not know he has made an answer, writing of
a man in a field of flowers, in a field where!
the man has run, his hair streamed

in the grass, his naked ears, he says, hear
the day pass, hear the day pass in that
nameless grief we know, has run into the
field, throwing himself to the ground
hearing the day pass, reaches out, touching
a flower, woodspurge, its name is woodspurge.
I know this riddle, live it, hear with my
naked ears the days pass, Dante Gabriel
                Rosetti writing:
                        "From Perfect Grief there need not be
                        wisdom or even memory.
                        One thing learnt remains to me—
                        The woodspurge has a cup of three."

Dante Gabriel Rosetti, his name a flower,
and I would sing of flowers, how they grow,
how they are themselves, always
only themselves, how when I was 12 in

another time, how when I was too old at 12
in another time, I crawled under the neighbor's
fence because it was forbidden, lay under it
and looked up through the green leaves.
There among the leaves, the pale yellow in
profusion, the tightly closed buds as candles glowing
into the fade damp, how as the day dimmed they began
to open, how I watched mindlessly, transfixed,
how they opened petal by petal of pale yellow
perfect flowers.

"Evening Primrose," my father said later, forgiving
my trespasses as now they have changed it to "debts"
we said then,
"forgive us our trespasses."

And I would tell you as Dr. Williams does
of the thorns, why they have their place.
What does he say, where is their place.
where is their place? I have lent my books
again, now I need them, they're gone, now
I have no Asphodel, now the words are gone.
What words did he use, how did he say,
"I come, my love, to speak to you of Asphodel,"
did he say there were flowers even in hell?
I have lent my books again, now I need them,

Dante Gabriel Rosetti, his name a flower, not lying
"as I have, saying truthfully it *was* a weed
the woodspurge was a weed in a field, crawling
under fences in nameless grief
my naked ears
hear the world, the days pass, I,
Rosetti
       myself
       my friend
       the day he died
       saying,
              "I can no longer do with weed clutching."

5.
I will leave this room
we have made of resemblances
If you are
still
here I *will* leave
not calling you.
A strangeness has come upon
our room, the flowers bent from
us, longing for a lost light, crossed
from our window.

Doves have flown here, the sea
has touched andmuch
that was graceful
laced branch on
that grace of us.

I will leave
Lost
The five steps to the door, foreign to me!
un
deux
trois
quatre
les fleurs
The Flowers!

Ray Obermayr
(1922-)

Fort Sheridan, Illinois

It's to be closed,
The President announces,
For reasons Of economy.
I could give him a thousand reasons
To close that fucking place.
It was never economical.
It was never
In the interest of any American
For that place to exist.
It served no one,
Not even those who sent us to War,
For we who did time
In Sheridan's guard house
Learned things that were not in Their interest
For us to know.
It stripped us of the Warrior Myth,
Our uniform,
Never to be worn again.

Except for a few,
Who would have been in jail
Anywhere,
Without a "P"
We were not criminal.
We were penned in yellow-grey brick
For violating lock-step idiotic
Military bureaucracy.
We came to Sheridan, naively thinking
Hitler's morality was confined to Germany,
We left understanding that immorality

Has no location.
The question was
Were they, the instrument of our government,
Us? Were we a part of that?
Later we fought the War alongside those
Who didn't know
Another enemy lived unconquered
In Fort Sheridan, Illinois,
Resistant, unsubdued,
Still with us, a clear and present danger.
We know, and retain the memory
Of living locked in a cage with the Gorilla,
And are wary, even today,
Of his every move.

The policy at Sheridan
Was
Economy.
They wasted no time instructing us
With deeds, what life was like with the Gorilla.
The building was dingy brick,
A work of art,
Architecture expressing the very essence
Of the viciousness inside.
One story, but tall.
The entrance, a bank of open doors
To the lobby, large, like that of a high school gym,
Flanked by offices with glass-windowed doors.

What way is there
To express the frustrated anger,
The bitter gastric puke inducing realization,
Biting acid mucus burning understanding,
That They were still in Sheridan,
With pubic-stroking weekend passes
To Chicago,

When we were on the beaches
Of Normandy?
How clear can you make the division,
Between those who do the work,
And those who enforce it?

The pain of Fort Sheridan
Was not confinement,
Or wasting life's precious time
In useless activity,
Or inactivity.
We were accustomed to that
Standard Operating Procedure.
The pain was this:
We were placed
    Separated
From what we thought inherent
In all human relationships,
A standard of morality for us,
And for authority,
A standard of restraint,
A limit,
Beyond which no one goes,
Even in a prison.
The pain was in the twisting knowledge that
Our own would do this to us.
A massive, locked, steel-barred door opened to the cell blocks,
Three, one for blacks, two for whites,
Painted tan, as was the floor.
Quarter-inch steel straps, two inches wide,
Running horizontally,
Running vertically,
Woven with the width of an open palm
Between,
Formed boxes, longer than wide,
Maybe ten to twelve feet tall,
Inside each, three rows of double metal bunks.

Back to the lobby.
Three of us, brought in from the Milwaukee County jail,
Were told to undress,
Our clothes taken away.
A guard, shotgun slung,
Ordered us to stand, hands on knees
With the tips of our noses touching the wall.
Try it.
When our noses lost contact,
Or when our foreheads made it,
The guard kicked ass,
Hard enough to knock us down.
Civilian workers, male and female,
Walking through from office to office
Passed by,
The circuit from eyes to jaded brains
Broken.
We were not there
To them,
Our noses grew from the neutral wall,
Only a part of many daily games.
We shivered in January Lake Michigan air,
Earning kicks.
This went on for thirty minutes,
Or more.
Under guard to the laundry
In the basement.
We were given clean clothes,
Wet,
And told to put them on.
Old style blue fatigues,
White "P" stenciled on the back.
Upstairs,
Wet, cold, and miserable,

An interview with a second lieutenant
Of Military Police.
Name, rank, and serial number, etc.
Plus a gratuitous lecture on Patriotism,
Information on how we were impeding the War Effort
By putting Them to the expense
Of locking us up
With the Gorilla.

Into the cell block,
Assigned a bunk,
I sat down, and was immediately gigged.
Gig, noun, an official report
Of a minor infraction of regulations,
As in school or the army,
A demerit, meriting punishment,
Which was
No evening meal.
There were many gigs per day,
Every day.
Rations were drawn for three hundred men.
Three hundred, less gigs, were fed.
Rations were drawn for three meals a day.
Two were fed.
Rations were drawn for regulation army breakfasts.
We were fed
Oatmeal, no milk, no sugar.
Our unserved food
Went to the Black Market
In Chicago.
The gig I earned was for sitting down,
Forbidden until after evening chow.
Sitzen Verboten!
No sitting on the floor.
Compliance guaranteed by keeping
One inch of water on the concrete,
At all times.

Blankets must be kept stretched tight.
A coin must bounce when flipped upon the bed.
No bouncee no eatee.
Wall space at a premium,
Less space than aspiring leaners.
Evening chow meant more than food,
It meant sitting!
On the outside you can sit at will.
You can get up and sit down again.
At Fort Sheridan even the toilets had no seats.

No books allowed.
Made sense from Their point of view.
I got my hands on the one exception
At chapel,
In the mess hall, every Sunday morning,
Ministered by a Fundamentalist.
They did not deprive us
Of our religious obligation.
Everyone attended.
At chapel we sat down.
Each Sunday the sermon was the same,
Remonstrations, admonishments, supplications for us to
Repent, for sins against our Government.
By a Man of the Holy God of Punishment.
Jesus was not mentioned,
Except in the rote prayers read from a book.
As we left the chapel
A prisoner asked
To see the Chaplain, privately.
His bunk was next to mine.
He came back soon.
The Turnkey called his name.
He left.

We never saw him again.
Rumors said they threw him in the Hole,
Where he died.
We hoped that wasn't true.

Lights out meant little.
Lights within the blocks were dimmed.
Floodlights above the cages shined on.
Talking was verboten after lights out
But it wasn't quiet,
Coughing,
A chorus of coughing,
Throughout the night
By men who stood in wet shoes
All day.
Nine o'clock.
A black prisoner talked in his sleep.
The Turnkey heard him,
Came in with a guard, stood beside his bunk.
He thrashed and moaned, calling out.
The Turnkey threw him from his bunk and hit him
With his fist.
The guard beat him with his club.
They dragged him off,
Brought him back,
Bleeding.
No one helped him.

Next day:
Authority astir, general hustle-bustle,
"Surprise Inspection" coming up!
Real breakfast, lunch, no gigs,
No water on the floor.
Sitting!
The beaten prisoner safely out of sight,
In the hole.

The General, inspecting,
Passed through our ranks,
Asked how the food was,
Moved on before the answer.
Left smiling as a good General should.
The beaten prisoner
Removed from the hole,
Dead.
I saw that.
This is a litany of evil.
Reading it now you could find it
Unbelievable.
If you've never been a prisoner of something,
You can't know.
And I'm not finished yet.
The guards' knock-out game
Went like this:
The leader was the night Turnkey,
Worse than his daytime twin.
A prisoner was selected by some unknown criterion,
Which we endlessly tried to fathom.
To me, the only way
Was to become invisible,
To occupy no space,
Shrink into the walls,
Become blue fatigues only,
No face.
It worked until one night at chow
I became visible and was selected,
As an example,
To stand while I ate,
No problem except sitting was postponed.
So thereafter I ate upright,
And sat down later.
The night Turnkey came into the blocks periodically,
Trouble always.

We shrunk,
Straining to suppress
Any human emanance.
But he always picked one and his pillow,
Which was placed in the space
Between the steel straps of the cage.
Back of his head jammed into the pillow
The prisoner received
A blow to the forehead
From the heel of the hand
Of the guard contestant
For the prize, unknown to us.
The winner knocked the prisoner unconscious
With the fewest blows.
No marks,
No evidence
Of this patriotic fun.

Roused at 5 A. M.,
We let go of sleep and dreams
Reluctantly,
The dryness of our beds surrendered
To another day in that goddamned inch of water.
Make the bed to the bouncing coin.
Stand up till oatmeal at seven.
Then roll call out front.
Double time past the Turnkey,
His heavy kicks hard but slow,
Hit only one for three.
Timing was the thing
To get through the door
Successfully.
Outside, standing in ranks,
Breath steaming,
Feet steaming,
Waiting for the Lieutenant
Of Military Police

To call the roll.
Everyone was always there.
I longed to hear
That at least one of us was not here,
But we always were
All there.
Cruelest of all,
Time and place coincided
Roll call with the bus,
And the route by which
Young girls walked to headquarters,
Where they typed
The orders of our confinement.
Chattering, walking,
Heels clicking,
Hair and skirts swinging.
God, how good they smelled,
How good they looked,
Passing in review before
Rows of shivering men,
Made derelict
By the very ones
Who made them chic.
At rollcall we counted off,
A method by which some were selected
For outdoor work.
My number came up,
A lucky number,
Except that it led to an embrace
By the Gorilla.
We were taken by truck
To a mountain of pea coal.
From half-way up the mountain
We filled truck after truck
With coal from our shovels.
Guards for work details were called
"Prison chasers,"

Recruits, newly inducted,
Waiting to be shipped out for basic training.
Some were 0. K., some were mean.
They were all scared
Of us.
They carried loaded shotguns.
Most of them had never seen one before,
Waved them around carelessly,
Frequently in our direction,
Unintentionally, I think,
But they fired accidentally,
Occasionally.
It was a worry to be around them,
But not as bad as the inch of water.
At noon we rested for an hour
On the coal pile.
The chaser was relieved for lunch.
The truck driver, a civilian,
Passed out cigarettes and matches,
Both forbidden to us.
The chaser didn't mind or notice.
The driver went to eat.
We sat and smoked on the side of our mountain.
Five o'clock,
Back to prison.
Searched.
Oh stupid!
Stupid me!
A book of matches in my breast pocket.
An interview with the First Lieutenant
Of Military Police.

The Hole
Had a heavy hinged iron door,
Over which we walked on our way to chow.
Not deep enough to stand,
Nor wide or long enough to sit,

Or kneel.
One position possible,
Back and rump against the wall,
Knees and head against its opposite.
The iron door-roof slammed shut
An inch above my head
With a roar like a gun blast.
It stunk.
The breath of the Gorilla.
Out once a day, I think, to the latrine,
At night,
A cup of water, a piece of bread,
Handed down.
The time before They first brought me up
Was the worst.
I didn't think I'd make it.
The rage would explode my mind.
The things I loved saved me.
I talked with Laurence, Eli, Betty, Pete, and Nicola
About Joyce, Proust, Dostoyevsky, Van Gogh.
I listened to Schelomo and Petrushka
Over and over again.
I swear I heard every note,
And really learned the music in that rancid darkness.
Lost track
Of how many times I'd been out,
How often the feet above me
Shuffled to chow.
When my time was done,
They had to lift me out
From the bowels of the Gorilla.
I felt hate and triumph.
I'd been too tough
For Him to digest.
He had to spit me up!

One day Corporal Berardi,
Of the 519th, came to escort me back to Fort Niagra
For Trial.
Leaving the Courtroom,
Verdict and sentence in hand,
Mimeographed the day before:
Guilty,
Six months hard labor,
Fine:
Two-thirds of my pay,
The part left over after deductions.
Two months later,
Called to the office of another Second Lieutenant
Of Military Police,
Confinement at hard labor
Suspended,
Fine continued.
Overseas to England.
Made the invasion of Normandy
Free of charge,
Still no pay, or G. I. Insurance.

Fort Sheridan
Closed,
Prime Lake Front Property
Waiting for an appropriate sale
To a well connected, disinterested
Defense department consultant,
Moving through the revolving door
To the Guardhouse site,
On which stands a splendid
Gleaming Condo,
With a hole.

Tanure Ojaida
(1960-)

fatalities

Those who make their looks their armour deceive themselves.
Our proud king could not intimidate his assassins, only
confirmed to them knowledge of his vulnerable part, nor
the beauty queen hold off time with her face from disfiguring her.
The lion has no horns, yet pads the land with honed steel.
Do not sing your praise-name before the contest,
lest you bare your tactics and in the end cry of folly —
many losers have been driven by impatience out of their minds
into the fatal snares of their far weaker rivals.
Never beard the sun because you are tall;
the mahogany lives at the mercy of the earth and sky,
and its fall will not end the world, unlike the sun's.
Never speak disparagingly of the condemned in your judgment;
you are yourself sentenced to the human concession from birth,
It baffles, how we erect pyramids for the dead who need only a pit.

Maureen Owen
(1943-)

england and scotland are the paradise of walkers.
Thomas Grey himself walked the Lake Country in 1769
and after a long day's tramp found the inn's best
bedroom damp and dark and so went flamboyantly on
for another 14 miles to Kendal and an inn with a dry bed
O Thomas Grey I would have come too
through 14 miles of blushing crepuscular forest   and Europe
under my feet at last   I even skip the
pastoral beauty unbound   the sound of all those waterfalls
the sparkling lakes that turn completely black when the
long shadows of the mountains throw themselves down
I don't even mention at all the fresh trout   and partridge
the oaten cakes   young mutton   and the good country-brewed ale
I don't rave on about the Druid circles of stone
the serene villages!
is it so much to ask   Europe and a dry bed!

tightly woven fibers of virtually anything that
could be woven into fabric   flax, linen, or
cotton
                    The Sail
for as long as man has braved the sea   he
has relied upon the force of the wind   to move his vessels.
Sails of Rotterdam   sails hung from the masts   asleep
& dreaming of the Indies   anchored
at the doors of houses   Sails that have captured the wind
& the Nordic trade   I have waited for sails
Presenting myself to the sea like a stupendous fjord
I have reduced myself to a brush for the deck
lowered myself to the most ignominious extreme
assumed the look of one so abject   the foggy canals
offered themselves   as a promise of something better.
I pulled rejected animals from the drowning murk and
slime and they followed me home   immediately resuming
the heinous personalities that had caused someone
to chuck them into the canal in the first place.
I surrounded myself with these lives that hated the world.
We gathered in the lichen and fungi, liverwort and fern,
on the broken vegetation   that adjoined the cement boundary
of the canal   and wept drearily into the fog
bonded by a lover's rejection and common misery
we knew what hard luck was   & I think we made the most of it
we dragged back and forth along the grey wall
waiting for sails   in an artistic pose. . . . .

Now   here is a shirt   sown from Old Sails
patched and mildewed, weathered and stained
Sturdy sails   prized possession of the sailors
authentic old sails   changing tack on the open sea!

My mother has given me this shirt made from Old Sails
&   I have put it on.

"He flies to Bangkok every now and then   just to jack off"
and a flattened thatched cottage arrives in the mail
with a message from M.
I was leaning an the glass display case at the party   and
someone said   "The islands"   but I was looking for him
thinking as usual   "HA! He hasn't seen anything yet."
Trying to appear less desperate than before   throwing myself
forward into the noise   the thumb-sized rose at my navel
blushing soft petals of unnamable tortures and fevers
But not unhappy
a person in such a state can be perfectly happy!
someone who realizes their own hysterical clumsiness
is a person in control of herself.
O my arm that traps your hair against the pillow
my elbow in your shoulder   my knee in your groin
the night you called from the bed — "See if you can
raise the window-shade without putting your foot through
my guitar and knocking over all the plants."
What a destiny   to be the inexperienced actor in Agamemnon
who, whenever he moved his head, caused clouds of powder
to rise from his hair   because
in the 1st act some foot powder had accidentally been spilled
on his head
So past personal history puffs over us and identifies
outrageous failings   we work so hard to put them all behind
When I had finished all the tasks he simply
found more for me to do   the pressure remained
at a constant level   While pucks of rain hit the windows
saying, "Cairo"   "Cairo"   "Cairo"

Thank You, America

And   Oh Wheaton!
                for your shirtless hot youths!
  intoxicating chests buffeted by the breeze
in the rolled-up sleeves of their faded levis
     terrific muscles under their open shirts
I could smother in caresses   a posture
just between the cab of Dodge pick-up   and
the gravel drive
standing on the springboard of a red grain truck
tan-armed hand on the rolled-down window rim
I weep on the dashboard   kissing those locks of hair
Hugging the necks of that wild shyness
Where is the applause of a crowd of enthusiasts
for a jaunty torso   barely inclining forward
sliding from the seat   I press to my eyes the image
OH Moocher of my peace   A body slightly in the air
halfway to the ground
all bravura and boldness   before the grain elevators
Armfuls of sky!   Heavy dark boots and light tousled hair

       Such beauty rips me limb from limb!

     I'm not a crazed sex maniac   it's anatomy
these supple joints   the sporting step   that takes them
dazzling blond hair brushing their shoulders
blue eyes dashing forward
     bounding up the feverish drowsy streets of
      Wheaton, Minn. pop. 2,209   Right past me
sitting here   the hottest blow job in town!

Will Peterson
(1950-)

She saw the Sawtooths first at night
when they were just a silhouette
over the lights of Stanley.

The next morning she was alone
when she went for supplies
and I was basking in Basin Creek Hotsprings;
the river high that year.

So when we saw them together
coming around the last bend I confess
they took my breath away; more beautiful
than the Tetons.

It was a long drive: over Galena Summit,
through Ketchum and Hailey, over Timmerman Hill
and the long view of the lava country
and the butte by Shoshone like a woman's
dark nipple; by the time we got home
I was hurting, so I just crawled into bed.

She came in, knelt over me
her hands warming my neck;
I respond to kindness and afterwards
when she said, That was as good as the Sawtooths,
I had to ask myself
how could I not love her forever?

This house on the East Bench
used to be beachfront property;
now we're just between seasons.

Those farmlands and six volcanos
used to be the sea; but
that was before Bucyrus Erie skipped town
with the overhead machinery
in the Naval Ordnance Plant
and Union Pacific axed all those workers;
and it will take somebody at Idaho State
to confirm whether those are whales
above Pine Ridge Mall
or just sharky prototypes.

It would be nice to think, my love
that we could get along
if we had whales to watch:
drinking champagne on your bed by the window
with twilight on the sea.

But I'll keep that afternoon
with neither coffee nor wine
my hand at the small of your back
my mouth in your hair
seeing the plain and the volcanos
and the reservoir like a sword
and the Lost River Mountains still snowbound
having in one moment everything I wanted.

Charles Plymell
(1932-)

Ten Years Before the Blast
(An After Dinner Monologue Interior)

I am always happy to see you, Allen Ginsberg,
I think you are a charming soul indeed,
I felt that too when you came to dinner the other night,
However, this time, there seemed to culminate
An arrears of communication, or lack of it,
Which shook me from our usual encounters,
Which haven't been that much, but down to earth,
Or if they were aloof I would concede, that
It was my fault entirely, because I really
Haven't been that eager to run around like a dream,
Picking up the surplus scenes, in this dissolving culture.
As gold in the gutter: So rapidly! All that Art marketed.
I think sometimes that all those thoughts we held so dear
Could not have turned from freshly created into
Chocolate covered dust . . . just as quickly as
Our brains began to scan about for every rotting morsel.
It is like the economy itself that was fattened on
The spoils of war, but now the words are lean, and dear,
and measured to these times. Those other times, my dear,
You jotted down, were built on excess and have Popped.

It is not that we've not had our spats before.
And I usually ponder over who called who "creep" first,
Instead of more important considerations of the problem.
But we do not have time in this vain contemporary culture
To go about knowing each other any better than before.
It is within this glut I was so smashed and irritated to
Enjoy the gossip, I do so, as well as you, and was
Surprised entirely to hear you reveal that you were
Mortally afraid of my every stance. I do hope that is
Not the reason you seemed so puppy dog obliging in
Our recent public meetings. Please do not inflate MY ego!

It is while you have been enjoying yr. Kalifornia retreat
I have been too much aware that humanity just can't
Help producing such sleazy sons-a-bitches that keep
Perpetuating a rip-off culture, in which we all partake.
So if we have our feud, I'll feud in words so
You can use your prosody so pushy, chanty
And so masculine. I don't think you've ever understood
The pentameter which lends itself so delicately feminine
To those cherished generosities of a family life,
But yet so dangerously cunning to any outside threat,
Like simple responsibilities of food, and shelter, and jobs,
It is in that case I will stand inflamed against the
Elite and bureaucratic souls whose very jobs indict the artist.
To titillate and bandy about with gala obsession, to
Those names in news, is not quite enough for me to trust.
The proletariat you can never be, not the fanged toothed
Protector of the family, no redneck farmer you, but the
Saintly intellectual who can go to India and be holy
Where they feed the rats and let the booming babies starve.
will you soothe their bellies, Allen, will you straighten
Their bones? Will the drunken master you benefit with your poetry?

And if you have given up the poesy as has been reported
In sleazy pulp, then why bother to say those things, have
Published and bound, which most people wouldn't bother at all,
(as whispered to me by our contemporaries) but is it not in vain?
Though I'm sure your tender scribblings will be affectionately
Remembered by those same contemporaries . . . enough is enough.
And since you prattled up to Mr. Pound, before he died, with
All yr. rock records for his ear, was indicative to me that
There was no more important poetry you thought was being done.
To break that tradition may well have broken yrself
As you & Mr. Williams are not quite the most important poets
In the world, tho you hang right in there, kissing all
The most important ass, your Russian Rod McKuen, Yevtechenko,
Your superstar junk mail, Yoko, Lennon, Leary (I told you he

Was a phony 10 yrs ago when no one dared) . . . Lead all those
Fucking Lemming poets into the sea at sleaze Nixon's beach,
While all your faded superstars and big publishers clamor
For your junk mail and holiness and vision. It is not the
Baptist minister alone, who is the hypocrite with metaphysic slop pail.
You carry in those buckets and those journals slung to shoulder,
All those dead and desperate individuals who truck along
Like one more sucker, like the same dumb media you seem
So frightened to displease. Who would have known the mileage got
From one obscenity case. Who cd. have charted yr. path of assholes.
Your book award was a sleazy Nixon gesture to a sleazy American book
And if there is anything you must know, it is that your sufferings
In this universe are actually mild. So you got mugged. Welcome
To the world my worldly friend. I remember bleeding to the steps
of Fillmore ballroom. But it wasn't enough to be treated & washed up.

So when of late we discussed who shot up Ray Bremser's house
I wouldn't know, nor care, though old fleabit Ray is more the
Beatnik Buddhist than you'll ever be. Even with his dreadful habits.
I felt you had been waiting with a bug up your ass to
Call me creep, though I know you didn't believe him when he told
You I ran him out of town, and because of that
Lie, I'd probably knock his teeth out if he
So much as mentioned my name again, except he wd dutifully remind
Me he has no teeth, as poetically just as he is, but a thief
They said, and it wasn't me who went after him, because we all
Are thieves in some way; and I am certainly, because at this
Very minute I am plotting to sell yr. hand writ journals you
Left here . . . either by personally contrived karma, or ethereal
Design, for tomorrow the winds grow cold and I still feed Ray's
Mangy mut, and I helped him cut the wood for other winters.
And you have helped with money too, for that we are all
Grateful, be religious if you must, meditate and purify
Your soul, but if you call yourself the poet, then your verse
Must stand as solid as the unwobbling pivot, and you with it
As long as you pump the life into the words. If not, stay clear, poet.

November, 1974

246

In Memory of My Father

To you who sung the riddles of that desolate Atlantis
while wind worn wagons swept a sunken trail into eternal dust.
To your sod, your grass, your easy hills of flint from glacial
slope to wanderlust. "Perfect cattle country . . . the best I've
seen since Uruguay." I'd oft heard you say, your dreams and maps
unfolded beneath those eyes that inventoried skies, could you
have known the winter owl's alarm where black beasts of Angus grazed?
I could not see as far, but went my way, you understood, and
watched the windmills tell their listless joy to silt and seam.
Life must be beautiful or all is lost . . . those bison of the clouds
were pushed from life . . . slaughtered for sport . . . now they are the
storm clouds watching us from eternity and far beyond.

And I did not know (when you showed me the lilies on the
limestone.) No . . . I did not notice you had grown old, your
hair had turned to silver . . . for I never thought you'd die.
I thought when this would end we'd all join hands together
like you told the babes at playtime long ago (that you hoped
we'd all meet in Heaven) in that dust bowl depression of Kansas.
It is hard to notice age in those who dream. As you knew,
dreams are like the youth, without them the world could not continue.
They are like the trees you always planted on sun parched steppe,
enjoyed by those who pause and dream beneath the steel of time.
0 fading America! Where is Thy promise! 0 catastrophic land!
This land you loved when newborn calf kicked up its legs . . .
you said everything wants to live . . . and expresses it.

The slap, slap, slap of tires on the hard concrete.
The tears on the way to the funeral. The biggest sky in Kansas.
"Wish I could find that old house where Grandmother lived,"
someone said, trying not to think, or feel, or sob.
You had told me you "might kick off" one of these days
but I could never see you anywhere but waiting for us
on the porch, arms folded always with finger prop't

against sunburned cheek, Stetson tipped back, calm grey
eyes anxious and kind through smoke of neglected cigarette.
We were coming for Christmas in a few short days with new born babe.

Giant cranes along the ditch . . . steel helmet'd construction
workers laying concrete pipe beyond all progress of the
Family Store T. G. & Y. or the old folks home you cussed.
Under that vast space you saw end product of wasted soul & hand.
You saw the time begin to change, you saw the day of the Atom Bomb.
You know the true nature of man, foresaw the greed and plastic goods.
Saw those old jaws of monster oil wells pumping the never ending
depletion allowance of blood of man and earth. "The little man pays
the taxes."
And you sensed the vacant stare in faces. You saw man change. You saw
him buy on time. But he had no time to talk now. No time. No time.
New car tires squeal on the road to nowhere to make a time payment.

Skull of memory, how will your lamp burn now?
How will the dust, like pages scorch that canopy of bone?
How will those eyes rest against the dark storm of tears now,
when ozone rests on sage, calming that stampede of time?
It was the day of mustangs, the day train whistle screamed that
Rockies' grade, when double header highballed and howled past
diesel trucks, water towers of unknown towns; soliloquy of
settlements and cemeteries beyond truck stops and salvage yard.

Your folks from Indiana came overland in covered wagon;
crossed the Muddy at Hannibal Mo. Mark Twain was 36.
To Belle Plaine and then on to "No Man's Land." You staked your
claim. I remember the joke about no birth certificate, and
how the neighbors were healthy because they had government jobs;
Charley Dumbell shot himself with a Colt 45. You told the kids
wild stories. Listened to Joan Baez, your favorite, with teenage kids.
You were always young and had to be active, you built the fence
you didn't have to build at all . . . for your daughter's horse.
Lifting beams bigger than railroad ties . . . against the doctor's orders.
Post hole diggers left in the hole; never used again.
But you had built the fences on the prairie sod. You made it straight.

I was coming to see you from school, bringing my family,
Your father died with the fence unmended, the calves got out,
he didn't feel like riding; waited for you to come from school.
Everything changes but the meaning, and the tenderness passed on.
I stand here beside the peaceful grave, I stand here on earth
for the first time without you by me; I take this land upon my shoulders.
The grain elevator over there is filled with harvest, the seed of
newborn day. The green Spring wheat. I am a father now. I know.

It was said you paid the ambulance driver before you let him go.
You dug some bills out of your old leather purse to hand him.
Through your hard span of life, you settled up so quietly no one
ever thought of you carefully. Nor do they care for unknown sages
in unknown town. The end of a man, an age. I neglected to hug or kiss.

Charles Potts
(1943-)

A Marijuana Poem

Especially for Mike and Kathy

In the last great toking inhale of my now so faulty
memory I reconstruct a few highs I can no longer get to
for good reasons I implore you to listen.

It was only twenty years ago when I first went to
sleep in a daydream of Rip Van Winkle on my merry
way to hear Duke Ellington conduct the homecoming
band behind a couple of joints from Bob and Frankie.

I thought I loved it, may bags later, some highs too
high, too dizzy to recall, an entire psychedelic
encyclopedia of images cascading across the 40 states of
Old Mexico and "My country tis . . ." not quite of thee.

Teetering on and off the railroad tracks in Marfils as
Chuck and I waffled our way toward town where Max
and others similarly enlightened would load us up. I
was never dizzier but never completely fell, even the
next day on LSD in the ruins behind the walls, behind
the ruin I've made of my life from the time warp in the
silver riddled hills of Guanajuato.

2
For over our adolescent objections to the ruling class,
far beyond the Celtic Sea wafts the classic odor of the
Lotus. There in the agony of youth at war in a time that
was plenty for a privileged few, the rest of us eked out a
happiness.

We wanted desperately to help with our years of grade school idealism and the only project offered was the ruinification of some especially God forsaken place named Vietnam.

We turned to drugs to see what else they might be lying about. We turned our backs on their project and they remain turned on that project for it was and is a shambles. The revisionist history is no closer to the truth now than it was twenty years ago when they were making it up as they went along.

It was and is their asinine intention to delete the environment from ethical consideration just as though it were a nuisance we could all do without, "Listen dear, they are playing our song, pacify, interdict, defoliate. . ."

Take it or leave it is intoned to the animals whose dignity enabled them to pack their genes and hop, skip, and jump out of evolution. We are left here with the steak and eggs and the small plans of the unrequited remnants who belabor us to accept them with their feeble pleas for associated domestification.

There are whales so completely surrounded by water that they think they are alone. They could be right.

A few days ago in a fit of uneducated pique I ordered Farley Mowat's new book, *Sea of Slaughter*. I shelled out the $25 and heard an expert speak to me on the subject of where the Spearbills and the so called Polar Bears went.

I can hear the shells of their eggs breaking across the centuries. I have to sleep with the animals prowling around in my dreams daring me to save them.

There is going to be a time for people to learn how to pray again. I am not referring to the so called services provided on this planet by the omniscient Christian, Moslem, or Buddhist religions.

The derelict Dutch demand that we "Kill the Pope." This is as rational as the European Tradition will ever get. Even if the most serious attempts are made by the KGB.

3

This is supposed to be about marijuana. I would remember more if I had never have smoked the shit. I have some idea what my life would have been like during those years if I had of been doing without it. I resent to this day the amplification of my paranoia the laws against its use engendered.

Marijuana softened our lives around the edges. I can think of some uptight sphincters still at large in the almost exclusively in their view, human universe, to whom it would do some good still at this rather late date in their probably terminal evolution.

Now I get high and cool on the most ordinary of levels, aerobic workout, up a 100 foot ladder, answering the door to dispatch the next remainder of the vision of the universe has promised to deliver.

There was a time when I didn't think I could live without it. I could have lived without coming home and finding my books all strewn around the room, my kilos gone, my hash, the whole psychedelic mess taken by a thief in tennis shoes who left his footprint on my kitchen table while I was out playing tennis. I should have stayed playing tennis.

I should have called the police. The police, like the rest of the state, have disappeared, just as though we had passed through the perfect communist experience. They are simply vines and detritus to be cleared away on a daily basis. The whole hippie ethic in the same kind of smelly tatters the rest of the all too Hobbesian universe unravels on.

4

We get high to get ideas. We got high to get out of our minds. We got high because you wouldn't listen. We aren't coming down for the old song and dance. We aren't coming back to the fold. We won't change in any way you'll be able to discern, although you believe we already have. From Hippy to Yuppy with the same straightforward questions as yet unanswered.

Our simple dramatic tension is created by the conflict between the American Ethic: make as much money as possible in the shortest amount of time with the least possible effort; versus the interior vision of a world fit even for wild animals, everybody and everything living at peace.

It won't happen unless we work on it. Has the widespread use of marijuana brought us closer to or taken us farther from the goal? Our cowardice is becoming more obviously regrettable in our lifetime. We have a chance to see it all disappear. Our tender neglect of the worthy effort to overthrow the anthropocentric ethic has God killing us one at a time. How incredibly bored God is with our witless human successes. How many people will be too many? How much longer do you think we have? How high do we dare get?

dan raphael
(1952-)

Pound of Head

When what was my head pounds unceasingly,
   skull my fat has grown to burst
   like pants in the sky heaving against the seams of
    habit, expectations,   caffeine,   deep fried salt.
I pull another paycheck shirt over the mucus bubble
  enshrines my head beneath the red white and blue strobes of
  christian police carving crosses into bullet tips,
   put silver mascara and Type O lip polish across their war masks
    overpsyched shoppers storm the mall's flypaper windows:
    discounts with credit cards, discounts to blood donors,
  no condom users allowed, keep touching everything that moves,
    keep moving against the tide of reptilian hands
   anesthetizing light with elevator music spreads like floodwaters
to wax our ears sullen, soporific, tingling with multiple piercings

and the chronic release of ions slowly transform the iron in our blood
   works the cracks in elemental pavements
    so the weeds grow downward
into caverns rich with landfill and forgotten cities we wear as hats
  tightening our crabgrass hair–
     no showers of diazanon or roundup,
    no deodorants applied with paint rollers
   to hold in the sweat to exude no animal scent
to bulge the eyes like prime time velvet paintings animated for sex
    no body could afford to find herself like a butterfly
chloroformed, bound, rasterized and tingling free in the internet
    of supermarket's ventilation,
the rise of video tuberculosis– they're afraid to call it consumption
  like you never hear of an american flu, an upper class virus:
    all diseases come from deficiencies,
   from disruption or inadequacies in the ease we slather on
like latex sandwich spread tween bread nutritious as wallboard,
    bread that will outlive us.

I have my lover search every inch of me
for the freshness date, a trademark, a bar-code
to drag across my tombstone's eye.

my kids worry about the price,
interest rates for those with momentum deficiency:
we now need vitamins M and Q,
our alphabets have gone multimedia,
a remote control imbedded in the thigh, a tv that knows your name
and reminds you of what's coming up
attune your heart to the electronic pulpit,
the silicon pituitary, a million pieces of data
how many can you link to what clothes in what club
through today's freshest door high below the city
we try to fly on top of elevator shafts
clogged with multimedia cholesterol
to buy   to lose your hand in
to come home not shivering with amputated dreams,
dreams where i'm falling   spreading
as thin vats of unbaked wonderbread   pour into the sea
untouched by fish, corroding the drift nets
making the sea safe for subdivision.
the water will be our new ozone layer–
taste it with your eyes,
smell is taboo, smell prevents overcrowding,
nothing gets through the plaster walls.

Who is feeding from the stairmasters, lifecycles,
commuting across illusory asphalt cities with nothing between
but dwindling farmland punctuated by 3 story neon fungi
swapping clothes   bodyparts   genetic codices
where the shoulds become shat under what circumstance
if who was when did what against memory
semaphore of war whoop silently corroding through
backstab decimal points sliding along the spine's escape route

an anti-tide of dehydrated rodent scuzz recalls like a slow
razor-sharp pendulum no matter how deep the death
how dark the tea how free the honey of neurotoxins.
i end up better ventilated and less mobile,
smiling more than i realize, scared more than i want,
struggling a little less thinking the ropes will age before i do
but my sinews keep chewing at themselves
my teeth clatter into electricity shrink-wrapping the earth
learning to pucker but no one to kiss,
whistling in ways the dogs no longer care to hear

hungry and frustrated? make a baby   lonely? have a baby
yearn for the stability of the past? be a baby,
the baby your replacement   your knight   your surrogate;
don't bogart that baby, what else is there to smoke,
how else can we cut through the fog we can't extinguish–
can't ask whose oxygen is fanning the flames,
who's hoarding wood, who's pissing gasoline
siphoned from our savings accounts
whose service charge is greater than the interest rate
coz the banks are doing us favors.
we should be grateful for these jobs, these burgers
made from test tube cows continually rebirthing
in jungles no one noticed except the satellites
constantly edited and directed.
satellites shed no tears, satellites remember only from the outside
pulling the earth up to them–
that's why we need bigger heavier shoes,
to counteract the pull of space, the urge for flight
heightened by the systemic strictures on fighting:
fight the mirror   fight the power
fight the enemies of jesus,   the enemies of the american way,
one of whom is me.

the american way is a manhole cover called depression,
in our food   in things we cannot be,
yearn to burn,   want more better,   want more better,
want you so badly so haphazardly,

ooooh,
anyone can be a record, necessary rages to riches,
necessary lotteries crashing symbols of hope,
answering the 64,000 question, i wanna be put in jeopardy,
i want to solve the missing letters in "bend over and spread 'em"
don't tax the rich coz someday you might get there,
uhhuh uhhuh,
no no one's laughing, the rich don't laugh at what they don't see,
when the rich take off their wallets they're invisible:

value is what someone else will pay
to take what you have, to climb your spine
skin on the wall, face in a jar
recorded for all eternity   etched into stone
frozen until technology gets further ahead of flesh,
the firmware within us
only cons of spiritual practice can re-etch, the ohm of DNA,
rosary of historical mistakes–

we are killed by overburdened hearts, hearts unable to forget;
we are killed by cells gone awry,
growth without definition or purpose;
we are not killed by natural time;
we are not killed by justice.

Waiting on the Progress Train

what's in it for me?
      since i am the earth, since all of my hope
is a thin stream of genetic happenstance, all the places i remember
able to die back and blow away in some holocaustic wind
of accumulated ignorance

          we work so hard to extend science
for profit and convenience, we need thicker and thicker
lenses   helmets   knee pads,   surrounding our sex organs
with impenetrable etiquette of fear

          we don't sing, we shoot.
the trees are here for us, like a shoulder to vomit on,
a guardian angel combining radar   computer   cell-phone
and cash machine, constricting utility belt
to emphasize buttocks and minimize gut.

          that's why i feel damn fine tonight.
fog so thick i'm in a tiny bubble floating through space at 18 million
miles an hour yet feel no breeze   apprehension   or need to navigate.

          are we here yet?
will effervescent trumpets muddle us through
the days of vampire capitalism: the slope gets so steep
our legs adjust to nose-bleeding attitude imbalance.

with so much toothless information, why bother having hands—
work harder and smarter to obsolesce the body's efficiency,
          to curl like bacon in a vacuum,
          to steep in tubs of one dimensional fantasy
embroidering our veins   earth-roots   channels of energy
          With alien monofilament, spiking my brains
          with a hemisphere of snowy needles.

I keep exercising in a sphere of comprehensive anatomy
evaporating effort to an imploding point of white narcosis.
stomach flowing like a river of unusual delight,
lymph glands work overtime anticipating inspection by
white gloved corpuscles unscrew the top of my skull
          and poise like naked parachutists
          on the brink of transformative chaos

Breakfast at the Globe (for Robin)

i watch my self go three different places, in different bodies,
   just one city and time springing from,
      blossoming in this tattered tornado of snow

today's affirmation is a collage of
   newsprint gravy pencil shavings & legless fleas
imitating the milky way like the landfill's swarming yantra—
   thousands of gulls, crows, sparrows, winged socks,
      miniature spaceships hidden in brownbags,
    weaving collisionless through each other
and signaling what i have no vantage to decipher by joining,
   dancing to unlock the spell that captures an anadromous mountain
    melting in all directions including backwards,
  spelling om in radioactive fish skeletons
    burn through the brains of birds
wanting to escape the egg of my skull, to remove the honey from
   my trunk,
  mindless of flannel bark and the stingerless bees of my resolve

i throw myself across the sound like a bear from the center of the earth
  arcing his undisciplined heat across the rivers, streets and veins
    of a world our bodies are acronyms for, cryptogram acronyms,
      written in strokes so much bigger than us
  yet seeking wormholes in our lungs, enough space
    to turn inside out to a land of other scales,
       of different physical laws and molecular properties
free me from now's dance, unique snowflakes melting immediately
      or congealing to melt later,
  some drown in rivers, some kidnapped into small windowless boxes
   they can't open
      yearning for vortex, for extremes & common sense
  to justify an arm's length horizon seen through the bottoms of
   several coffee cups
      re-injecting night into morning
    despite the clueless sky motivating chance
      like a white balloon that may be bigger than me
      shredding the city with indecision—
   do i really want to get out of bed and onto the streets
    when the balancing fire is centered so close to home
   rising without yeast,   accelerating without an engine

Kissing the Newly Dead

when the furnace dies,
when canada begins a weeklong inhale
and swirls of litter   dust   animal hair   & random donations
        flap aloft in cursive alphabets,
streets now so bare and bland
unpunctuated by evidence we live here, while the sky,
  so thick with trash, trash that won't dissolve, disrupts
the chaotic balance of weather only a tilt of the earth can cure,
a tip of the atmosphere rising above the surface
of biological necessity
                so thin and fragile, so picky and decadent,
returns to a month of potatoes and wheat, society failing apart
without pigeons and starlings i begin to hallucinate gaps in the air
where absences of energy wing across the scalp of my vision,
the radio dial full of bristling talk, words overlapping
        like anatomical transparencies or the encyclopedia's maps
            of tribal build and spread prove we're all half-breeds
            incapable of fulfilling genetic destiny;

i wander earless, unable to tell which way i'm falling
as the ground forgets its role and tries to communicate by varying
density–what else could my skin do but get lumpy and multicolored,
my organs balkanize and demand various orifices for feeding
separating vegetarian legs from non-lactic intestines
as my lungs play bingo across the periodic table
            inviting lichen and million-year-old spores
                to test-land curious cell-plots

truncate   capitulate   make the transition gracefully
  enjoy the lingering freon;
not all metal tastes cold,   no decomposition is unorchestrated–
        it's the art of destruction time practices so casually
brought to a more meaningful cadence, one we can dissect
embellish   shortcut   culturate   sleep-with   and prosper,

the sun emulsified into millions of orange stars
while night-sky time-elapses into halos and abstract zippers
fraying the void into occasional information and mystery,
parts of faces and almost legible signatures impelling us skyward
until the frustration puddles my flesh into reflection

      i rise to the parasites of 21st century health care
     and social order suffused with subtly leaden light,
         light that makes sudden movement difficult–
    can't think that fast, nothing to react against,
           pushups in zero gravity;
storms like drunken giants throwing hand grenades,
every night the 4th of july celebrating some symbolic
   independence:
freedom from hunger, from paying child support, from gun laws,
freedom from voting, from choosing a career.
every day is hunting season,   is that time of month;

after an hour without breathing, everyone wakes at six
when government sirens shrill like nasal muezzins
turning us to our mirrors: we squat in porcelain   baptize anew
  and don veils of musk, roleplay and promise

in dreams i'm never late for the train and don't care where its
   going,
i have no body, am always looking in wide angles and pans
as i run from those only the monitor can show me

     the cinematographer rises from my throat,
    removes his jumpsuit and looks through me.
the cellist adjusts a turn-peg behind my ear and bows my 2nd rib.
mapmaker.   knows me by my handwriting.
the label on the body part says its mine but i'm not missing any
   thing:

"no, this is something new.
     something you'll really like.
you won't know how you lived without it."

Mitochondriac

*"the mitochondria are scattered haphazardly, some grotesquely
misshapen, others with gaping holes in their membranes, still others
white and vacant, bled dry of everything inside"* (ron silliman)

*"we would develop (or grow into) a culture that would accept the
fact that truth can only be conveyed (not stated),and that
unconscious process must be allowed to remain unconscious"*
(morris berman)

    mystic experience as part of a puzzle, as a jigsawed map,
  a body constructed from four notes, five drums, six hearts storming
    each door you go through taking a lifetime.
a mobile home represents the liver,
a bio-frenetic pond represents the pancreas
    like a lawyer and advertising agent combined

    the body coming out of the body– the flesh,
the shredded aluminum where fat would be for the freezing–
    refines earth's body parts, works too fast
  with too much tension on the cords, stands erect
in an unknown vortex where trees grow in various directions
    seeking what never has been light as we see it.

the mitochondria within us living fossils of the first animals:
    powerpacks, blueprints, seed-pearls we've warped and woofed
around/upon began a self-dissembly, as so much fits on one chip,
    as living mass needs something to do
when survival comes through the data highway:
        heat goes down, velocity rises.
some leave their homes and merge with the infrastructure,
others close their doors and turn wireless

we get where we always have been, removing most of the possessions
    so the walls can talk, stripping enough layers from the floor

so we are held up by our abilities–know enough to not fall
through the suddenly created chasm of basement utilities
become so voracious as we break our addictions to them–

before we develop mass freedom from television
we must euthanize the sets, vcrs and satellite dishes
or face packs of them feeding on the semi-liberated.
and what of all the radio and tv signals set free
and no longer received,
as every partial cycle unleashes the forces of its incompletion,
though disruption can cook as well as the sun,
call beyond a phone execs wildest dreams:

i believe the visitors will come from within
or some undefinable sideways
cause 'Out There' is the cold vast vacuum consequence
of so much mechanistic striving.
the limit stays symmetrical–
how big / how small we see–
until we realize each direction
is seeing through the others and back around us
like strands of cosmic toilet paper whipping through
insubstantial as dna with no known source or structure
to cure the struts
divert the need as you would a river
though more subtly
the force of a structure with little or no mass
the more we dam
keeping the circle apart
polkaing with ghosts who hurl me back to childhood
skinny blind simple
return to weekly rounds of diarrhea;
specific appetites i can't control.
if i get big enough will a new me burst from within
or will my size break down barriers, momentum me to freedom,
approaching some critical mass, not critical but demanding,
remaking the rules without intention,
the ten commandments of zen:

we invented metals so we had something hard enough
        to shatter the rocks we dropped on them
      trying to release the art within,
the secrets the earth's been cooking so long

    the recipe means nothing
        without the gestures, without the smell unlocked by
            where and how the cook dances

        so many voices, like doors, these lives i'll never have,
      to peel away, a skin like 20 year old flannel worn each night,
        the conflict of removing the sweat and dead skin from cloth
          to sacrifice it to water and air, to put one's mind
        through the spin cycle, though we seldom remember
      to turn down the thermostat or firmly attach the helmet
          of held hands   of parental faces
      like the many combination-lock snaps on this body suit,
    scaled at the most vulnerable, once you've gotten that far
                                                that deep.

    let me release into something more comfortable/ organic/ ready.
      so undeveloped the muscles with nothing to hold,
        air my body merges with,
    air that holds still opens up distracts enough of my body mind
      for these quest-ions to continue their path beyond the crust
      charred and dissolving when touched, not what i was
      but needing more heat less mass
        to fly   to transit

      the way my love-heart travels on this nearly invisible wire
      you think it can fly & are so amused by the movement
      don't notice it's restriction as novelty
                what we put into
                what we think we're seeing
            when the only true confirmation is touch, which,
                at car speeds and weight is always damaging—
        my body is not a temple, it's a car w/cable tv and modemed mac,
          coffee teleporting from java central, a panel on my skull

264

to turn sun directly to glucose,
to turn wind into biosynthesis,
whatever the nerves need to be trained to let go of their defenses
and truly express their multi-functional potential–
we're so much more than wires, communicators,
electrochemical echolocation.

would you trade eyes for sonar in order to fly?

this body is a gravity junkie,
can' go long without a
floor   crawl space   intersticells derivative anatomy–

still something to hunt,
somebody out there who wants to breed with me or mine–
i shoulda stayed in the trees, kept my
head below the sea and warped with its 4 dimensional salinity;
handicapped by my nose and hairlessness
my species is the victim of millennial stress,
our nature to seek revenge against biology, thrashing
with all our gifts against the duality our cells can't shake:
good vs. evil,   energy vs. matter,   here vs. now,
what we are vs. a world where mankind's
the front wave of an evolving sea

Jon Reilly
(1941-)

Insect Lines

On a Wildflower hike
at Peninsula State Park,
the guide said the whole
purpose of flowers was to
produce seeds.

Plants could produce seeds
without getting so wild and sexy,
so part of the purpose of flowers
must be wild beauty and sex.

I liked her talk about "insect lines,"
the lines in flowers that guide
the insects in for sex and pleasure.

Is it polite in the field of botany
to tell flowers and women
that you love their insect lines?

A Beautiful Day

i set forth early with
plenty of energy
and hope
and my nose to the air
for the slightest sniff
of possibility
as I smell it out

in the streets
in the parks
in the restaurants
spotting finally
a tail that sniffs
of unimaginable pleasure
and irresistible beauty,
as my fingers dig
into the wood of the table
tearing loose a few boards
unnoticed by me
as i rise with one motion
approach the rare creature
trembling with the importance
of my mission
tell her by thin disguise
somehow that I like the sniff
of her general bearing
or being
she like a miracle
replies somehow
she does not mind my sniffing
somehow she doesn't mind
my eyes as red as an aroused bull
somehow rolls over with me
through any number
of fields of beauty
rolls with me
on every bed
off every couch
onto anybody's floor
tumbles onto
table tops everywhere
and laughing sweaty
we curl into each other
and fall asleep
rolling through fields of dreams.

Mari-Lou Rowley
(1948-)

The Blob
for Patti

My sister is very funny
    not very subtle
When she sees a guy she likes
    she says
      he makes her wet to the knees.

That's what I thought
    when I saw him
wanted his mouth on me
to taste how we would taste
    it was true   as good
      as she said.

He liked love in the blue glow
    of '50s horror movies –
It.
The Blob.
Invasion of the Body Snatchers.

It must have been
    the size of
      the wet spot
scared him off.

Ricardo Sánchez
(1941-1995)

dirge chicaneaux
a canto for César. . .

I.
keening sentiments
wail, I glide into
somber waves of grain
in this Palouse
where our faces
barely exist,

I see you, carnal,
caught within
the camera angle,
an agile, smiling
powerhouse, a brother
daring the universe

to shelter
the humanity
of farm fields
where hungry bellies
and gnarled hands
dare harvest

America's bounteous
dreams for some
and horrorfilled fears
for others, our people
bless the day
you came into existence,

César, you dared dream
a humanization
to be realized
by a raza at the margins
of this, our land in hope
and our prison in reality,

despair was never yours,
you always found a God
to undergird you
and the legions of farm
workers sowing goods
un-rereapable by us. . .

II.
we knew you, carnal César,
within Texas turnrows
and Arizona cottonfields,
along valleys in California
and outposts in the MidWest,

knew you in the plenitude
of Chicano Movement outcries,
in the felicity of culture
dancing/poeticizing the moment,
felt the potent songs

wafting from you
as you spoke of courage
being a loving statement
shared to stave off
the murderous hands

of hunger, ignorance and fear,
César Estrada Chávez,
you combatted severity and pain,
left the embossment
of your indomitable spirit

across the scapes of humanity,
we feel the loss, yet also celebrate
the magic woven by your humble voice
which said with passion that
we shall find our meaning

in the measure of our will
to struggle to create
a humanizing world
all about us, that a child
need not hunger,

that justice might become
the song of human realization,
you taught a pueblo
to demand their rights, to thrive
within simplicity,

dust lingers in the air,
falls dutifully to ground,
we seal the box, inter you
in the earthen sod you plowed
and sowed so lovingly,

our eyes do water,
our voices quaver,
our spirits sing you flowers,
carnal, tú fuiste
poema en todo campo. . .

April 28, 1993, Pullman, Washington

David Sandberg
(1938?-1969?)

moving
    in a windowed
      world

    or trapped
        into a response

    (steam rising from sun-soaked
    house roofs after rain

        picking images

from floors of stone
        wavering

stalks of dread

or
birds

coming at us

      an attack of the senses
      filling the mind
          an
attack of

    FREEDOM:

        coming sure-

    footed
      across fields at
      night
        I am carried

    on a blade of breath   far
    beyond
      my normal zones

what crimes must i commit (did & do commit) to make
an action, what motion is good motion. real motion? i sit
bewildered, & make the keys go faster. my shoulder so sore
still & pained that typing is harder & harder. i should be
a player piano.

i search to see, to give up, be done with seeking,
to find, or i think to hold something up, to myself mostly,
& say, something like, look here shithead, this is the way
to do it, but can make no models of sturdiness, & it all
crumbles in my four fingers (forefathers, flushers) demons
crowd my night, making vision an arduous & trying thing.
                                                            not
super vision, but an more ordinary kind.
                                          i don't even know
what i'm saying half the time, dont know what it's all about,
& run screaming thru labyrinthine corridors of my cell-body-
holy-ordering of things, grasping at flashes of light, which
are bloody fish which disappear as i reach for their lantern
cave-like eyes.

i bend, god i bend, & sway on some solid
foundation that i can no longer trace culturally religiously
morally hereditarily or even by drinking tracer fluid &
pounding on a dark voyage thru my veins.

maybe you should get away from 1360 before it caves
in, move into a tomb, or a fish box & pray from that kind of
home. i worry for your safety & at the shark toothed tiger
people, biting at your only flesh, & i sing to lose myself
in total reality dream.

i'll see you inside of 5 days. if not the floating
pieces of my body will drift over everything, a fine black
rain of dust. –

Bill Shively
(1952-)

There was a weekend for children. I went to a temple for
a special candle lighting they have every year. The temple's
nearby, so it wasn't much trouble, except we weren't invited,
but once we got inside it was all right. There are 8,000
buddhas here. Little stone buddhas many of which don't
resemble buddhas so much as stones and not a few of them are
dressed for the party in these little aprons tied up around
their necks (if you know what I mean) so's I guess you'd
call them bibs cuz after
all these little stone buddhas,
all these little stone buddhas, and these guys are all over
Japan, it just so happens that 8,000 are right here in Kyoto,
right down the street, and all these little stone buddhas
are for the kids, for the unborn kids particularly, and I
think that's unborn as in didn't make it rather than unborn
as in on their way. And everybody

who was invited, which was everybody less two, everybody had
candles and knew what they were doing and what they were doing
was walking along these narrow paths among the bibbed buddhas
and looking for a candlestick to stick their candle in and I
don't know if they're looking for particular stone buddhas,
ones they light candles at every year, or if they're just
looking for one that strikes their fancy, but some of them are
looking for a very long time, remember there are 8,000 to look at,
but maybe some of them just don't see too well because it was
coming up on this edge of dark about then, but they find what
they need and light their candle and watch
that it's caught and then they'd move on cuz there was quite
a crush and if you got over under the ginko trees or got over
by the little priest saying sutra in his little priest saying
sutra shrine you got a nice look at all these candles
glowing and all these stones smiling and figured maybe
the unborn babies would be doing okay.

Night Side

All that is left is the night side of time.

Shadowy raptors,
two-door semi-automatics cruising the edges of safe zones,
enforcers
with keys to the property
for which it stands,
crumbling on the nether reaches, the central core imploding.

Neon dealers
frisking knowledge brokers,
selling what has to be sold, stealing what has to be stoled,
tending the *tetons* of files,
trading access not for gold but for souls.

Bucket deep
with waferboard convictions, powerless politicos,
studying Shinola, the uncommon Communards, sheep
in sheep's clothing, asking
their flocks to forgive
forget and forego.

All that is left
is the night side of time.

Having basked in the rain
and socked away straw,
walk now that blade with me, scything
psychotic promises, gambling every breath,
beating the beaters,
shilling the shillers, saving the saviors and leaving
the killers live —
bark into the yawping darkness and howl

now,
they've taken
the moon.

John Oliver Simon
(1942-)

One Reason

One reason I was born, apparently
was to learn about relationships
though if I've actually learned
anything that would help you out
from looking over and over into
the same eyes of different women
I can't think of it now. First
there is the stranger, stranger
than fiction she calls me out
of her own eyes, none other
and if in some obvious way she
is known to be wrong I'll take
that for a hedge against commitment.
To sleep with her is not to fall
in love but the glory is to invest
our fall with all that aura,
fill the space between our eyes
with light, and so what if most
of it's reflected? I help and
she helps to construct a sun
between us that's painted with
both our faces. At first we
are both in love with this demon,
later we both hate this child,
anyway it comes to occupy us
to exclusion of the known world.
All that projection I put out
seeking my own glory in another
finding my own dark shit thrown back,

all that glory she puts out
seeking her passionate rider
from the early earth and finding
only a false-faced void to fail in
clutching her dark shit to her
breasts like a warm blanket,
all the words I have said for her
that were said for me in the hut
of the self that looks inward,
all the words she told me
that I could not recognize.
Commitment fails against the known
wrong and nothing will save
the us except commitment
but no one will be the first
to let go of the smeared god.
If I had put half the attention
into ridding the earth of nuclear
weapons that I have into all
these changes of relationship
the world would be at peace.

How There Come to Be So Many
Joshua Trees at Lee Flat

one time a man was looking at the little stars like a tiny
coyote running away from Orion and the Bull. six of them,
two ears pricked and long sharp nose, looking back over
his shoulder, and the other three are his legs and tail.

but his friend said – if you look hard they say you can see
seven. so he crooked his neck and stared straight up. and
after awhile he began to think he could see it, maybe by
the coyote's nose, or maybe right under his tail, yes –
seven –

and as he thought he saw it, his hair began to turn stiff
and green, he was staring so straight up, and just as he
saw it for certain he turned into a Joshua Tree.

they used to come from all over, aunts and uncles and
cousins, they all used to come to Lee Flat to look at the
Pleiades.

Adventures of the Floating Rabbi
(a novel in eight chapters)

Chapter One
the kindly mescaline chateau

an evening in the mescaline chateau, no
lamps, no bulbs, just clean twilight from
outside fingering thru windows, amphibian
shapes of the servants. you were told they
were colored people. they don't approve of
taking mescaline. and you say on no. weariness
of a fallen empire. you have forgotten
the ambiguous splendors of new york and
san francisco. dying you have forgotten this
is a dream.

Chapter Two
loosing the venomous arthropods

quite near the chateau, everyone was ready in the
quiet hillside town. the peasants turned out
with banners & the rich tourists with cameras.
weren't they surprised when someone let the
giant spiders loose. wow watch them go.

Chapter Three
many deaths and reappearances

thru the agonies of the spiders he taught
us death was a dream. he gave me antidotes

when I lapsed unconscious. otherwise battering
the brutes with sticks – tarantula
forepaws crushed, crab carapaces leaking
green and violet juice. always wake up &
run some more. on a quiet dirt hillside
he preached to us the resurrection of the
meat. then they took him away and his secret
antidote too.

Chapter Four
underwater near hiroshima

now you're in the jungle on your own. faces
of asian and australian soldiers lifting carefully
their rifles always get you. underwater
in the coral reefs off hiroshima you keep
coming. many white animals gliding like bones
in the mist. shark and barracuda. where else
can you go now.

Chapter Five
fred the schizophrenic

back in the chateau we had to cope with
a secret schizophrenic. posed an ambiguous
threat, definitely murderous but
gentle as a lamb and no one believed us
when we explained that he had to be
executed. outside the night was flecked
with scrambled eggs. he left a yellow
trail wherever he went in his insane
pursuit of the virgin. when we returned
from the store he had been eliminated.

Chapter Six
breakfast under the mountain

northward we sailed thru the ice river. I
couldn't remember which side was greenland.
old stone barn under a mountain. ate
breakfast in a viking cathedral and had
to change money explaining to the unseen
lady at my side all the places I had been.
later the tourists took a moral dislike
to the nationality of our guides and
split for the southland. more room for us
– shimmering empty water.

Chapter Seven
a ski race to your draft board

it ended on a snowy mountain. futile to
recount the immense journeys which brought
us here. we skied downward in the
fluid darkness thru thick trees. the last
pitch was an empty hospital waitingroom.
tilting downward and unlit. a cameraman
posed all the racers as they came. afraid
of his line of talk I said fuck it and
descended while he was unprepared.
sailing on thru the far door it turned out to
be the draft board. appointments for the
shrink, to save my ass once again, I took
a seat between my dad and the hashish
scarab.

Chapter Eight

Gino Sky
(1940-)

**Waiting for the Revolution
in My Garden Where It Is Spring
and There Is So Much Rain**

try and settle down in what
you are is
an emotion extended bi-laterally
past the crack-up point

the emotions distilled through
the intellect
located in what is known
as where you are pissing
and the visions coming into

focus

with each emotion containing
THE HISTORY OF MAN at any given
point in the geometry from A to Z
coming out as a world confession
with narrow hips
and that is getting into
the groove and ain't no rut i'm
talking about

just how much

you are willing to let loose

and demand

as the priest told
the bad gunmen when faced with
six shotguns

are you trying to threaten
me with death

and how do you measure
anyone's death
when he keeps on talking to you
about his plans for the future

just how far out are you
when you can look at the Big Geometry
with all the lies packed into those
10 volumes and keep on memorizing

as i began with
Chief Pork & Tallow who became
for me CHIEF POCATELLO in the marriage
of the legend
to the conquests of land breaking
the distances going outward
as protection
when the history was breaking down
as the sea without the moon relaxes

carrying the migration inward

outpast

the sound of IDAHO into the myth
telling of place

occupancy

back to where i sit with my flowers
waiting for the revolution
where there is so much spring
and the windows of my cathedral
are
by the traditions of my emotions
stained many shades of red

Edward Smith
(1941-)

Letter to My People

I wish I could be with you as when I
dream of years of lack of sleep and unnatural
lites in the sky. Noise. Radios. My intuition
of a past acceptance, other grammars,
loves, rain, victory. After years of reason
& struggle I saw again the hole we see you
live in in our racist dreams of warmth, perch,
welcome blood in the hole we find you in blood,
the smell. A proper eye for the natural
felicity of creatures sees the migratory birds
Lien discovered in the Arboretum – the deep
struct is "thick with trees", the appended
judgment "no permanent home." War may not be
part of it & the history tapes will garble the
names.
   Our version dreams of hibernation.
Blood does. The blood of the poet, of the
Tudors, heroes. Is it a part of life I find
myself in?
   The dying American soldiers lie down
with someone older than man wet Shale gives
off the smell of. The migratory birds of Asia
will not perch in a tree of; is it a love of
petroleum?
   In the final analysis I've failed my
mission. The way here has come to me damn few
times. Once in a dream breathing water. Four
breaths per minute. Is the life so slow? What
is mine here, & what is from before? Charles
Olson's work gets to an upheaval of Ocean. The
plains, the ocean, place, take place desperate
men & women.

Lien incessantly grieves. Her state
of happiness hi & sort of artificial. Yet she
too pulls our little apartment, the
blood-shelter, in around us.

Comrades, I fail. I do not speak any
language true. I force English. I am coming
home in dreams. This land whispers revolution.
Was it to destroy its power I was sent here?
What of the birds in the trees? The soldiers
are allowed to see what their hearts cry for
before they die. No way to touch.

Yesterday I formulated the law of the
power of the empire metaphorically conditioned:
what is true of all beings may be applied as a
test to man, what is true of man is dream if
applied to all beings.

There is something in this myth
referring to an alien origin. They are right,
not one with all. Some are beautiful & wise
in their cruel fashion. They do not know how
to die. I am weary of them but hope our
planet may accept them

Hexagram 46 — Rising

A high sound you could see Carolyn Sawyer
said it touched one on the eyes & I thot this is
not hell because we are able to keep our eyes open
& the Katie killed the cat as I cast its oracle &
wrote it on the shed & Elaine arose from the bed &
the black kitty's body rose & floated in the pine
needles & the mosquitos lit on my arms & there was
no reassurance with our eyes open to the Vietnam
napalm atrocity photo on the wall now that this
place was no longer could never be never again be
hell there was nothing beautiful it was Shanda to
wail me to have a care for Katie meeting her eyes
outliving Carolyn on the stair to sit eyes open
to me as a mother parceling blame such a high
sound have an eye out for the children to have
gone where they are sent, discovering in the
middle of the stairs where music sends where life
where it falls off too much to have bothered with
all that where the trees have no sound & then all
follow Paul off to bury the dead where hell where we
touch the earth allows sacrament communion &
honor together

Mother Earth a sweet vale by Sammamish slough
of hell in flowers gathers her men her dead have
called her mother & closes over us all into night
and what can be heard of the stars
      & always Carolyn her eyes fixed on what horror
has been nailed to the wall by the likes of
the Katie the Edward it throws her where mother
where no blame where the holiness of the eye cast
into the fire where the stair ends where children

& men who would wish to throw fircones & lurk in
the grass glad forever are cast up into the air &
cast off keening triumph & death & go with Paul to
give the honor to the only Mother to the place where
nobody need open an eye where those who are
of ending know so easily where in the earth-mother
to place this increase & close their eyes & make
a symbol it is a horror to every mother without
rites to her presence to her unsureness on the
stair to her left as blame is to her eye where
war would go endless despite how we eat what she
had made for us long ago & what we tell her in
the false sound she sees

    to her unending unsureness that rises to the
occasion as we do not with our dumb prayers to
something we stand on & as grim as we are sense-
lessly invoke as Mother in our fear of the Carolyn
herself not enough touching blame to see where
her end it

    life from life to her
    eye the signal honor
    I care for rises
        as the air
    that has no sound for
    the Edward to have its number
    eyes the horror
    who could call her on

The Queen of the Blue Fox

blue fox
sweet girls
to work

    out of &
    cant end
w/ brave bag of dresses
hair spray, movie mags
the poor
bus all the way from Guadalajara
to these cabs
of night after night after sex
& often like filmdom
sweet stare of his
& his eyes
    cant end it –
to dance naked
& receive the kiss of red spots
& receive between her legs kisses
    of all who rise to the rail
she bestrides, rise
as if a woman could stand w/ spread
    legs against life
against mouths moved
to adore her   stardom
    cant end it
blue fox blue fox
the lights along the Avenida de la Revolucion
name only the names & sports of the rich
O commerce
real no underwear flushed squat sweating
  barrel-chested gnome of short arms out
   of pig-eyes that seize, of real-life
   crude blotto northamerican cowboy &
   tough guy in elevator shoes
movie star, you've no business

at all touching her,
kissing this business
of where there is a dirt floor
somewhere in Guadalajara
from which this girl, rapt
in her sweet self against
all obscene glory
that you have / that has been
    made / HAD
all round the whole goddamn world
    MOVED
        here
where her body has become a legend
of money
Stuff her crevices w/ our
        imperial power-
        green currency
Her mouth twists, to you
    she complains–chee–ken!
& passes on, looks again
moves on to others
    who reach, who rise

O her borrowed eyes!

One night there was a sweet skinny blonde
girl who had come with husband from L.A.
who got softly very drunk & who
after she had insisted was lent the top
of a see-thru shorty nighty & otherwise
nude then mounted the stage. No sooner
done than she was set upon viciously by a
group of college boys who had to be restrained –
as they say bodily & so to avert violence
the management requested she put back on
her clothes. Back up the stairs she

slowly went, so hurt, softly crying

She is my very / Queen of the May

II

I look for love
in the way a girl stands.
in poor things, a collection
of a purse. in work
that went into ratted hair of years
ago. into walking carefully
not to split up the crotch of
tight boys' & girls'
capris, of now.
now they look for love
the young heads, whose hair
& words come in ringlets
out of visions in which great number's abstractions
of teen years. nights
in Pizza haven, Coffee Corral.
I look for love
& there's a war on
   that cant end
though thousands will pass
as 201 files thru
countless personnels
though our country is fighter-bombers, low
coming in with white phosphorus fire
our president looks into his flaming death of,
for love, do not mistake me 0 my
red & brave & desperate
Dong Hoi, Ha Tinh, Binh Duong
dirt poor people

& your nation a parking lot, some
say, I saying this
from a nation
that already is
a parking lot, un-
bombed.

cant end
cant end
cannot end
it cannot end, looking for love

I cant help
but again &
again see a
railed stage
with naked bodies
of each

sweet smell of 100 Mexican women
a queen & her whores' court of the may

Anything,
it can end.
You were poor
You worked the formulas
You put up the capital
You lied peace
You didn't make sense
You believed in God
You hankered after exotic cultures
You sat next to a Negro
You were rich
You plotted the targets
You voted Republican
You were a Democrat
You were a white liberal
You idolized Adlai Stevenson
You worked for Boeing
You were a virgin

Because anything
because I give you a stage of many queens
that you go about under a permission:

you may
get high

you may
die
you may
love me

My Queens, you are all my queens
    I am a queen
    once a soldier

let me put on my robes
let me take off my robes

I cried in my green spec 5 uniform
I cried in my bride's negligee

I am different from you
though I say I wish you to touch me
I bring you news of what
            you are for-
            bidden to touch

not search but song
against infliction of my heavy
sentences. of love

        "You you & you."
just be high
in my voice in my
borrowed eyes.

The Flutes of Gama

Elaine and I
took a big chance
& got married
like any two, not knowing
our roles
or fates
from her Grandma
Rose' cards,
Best man Richard Miller from
FSM & jail
but it was us cast as
lambs, or even
anarchists
somewhere in Burbank
Rosewood Wedding Chapel
under our four parents'
four looks.

Married in that place
by a judge, as their civic
writ couldn't divide
Jew from Gentile –
on her white a thin blue belt
she took pride in, not all pure,
blue belt of power
& potency the boy in the tale's troll-loving mother
stole from him & he at last stole back
& he beat the living shit out of his mother
          & she died
such a symbol a shocking breach in a bride
& I denied
the judge his last-minute plea
to bring in, to at least mention
God
if not the almighty, the everlasting
father

if only for the sake of our parents
            & few dear guests there
who did sit
       as we stood
               in fear
us both first children
         the ungodly
& that bastard
did bring God in
informally, in his go-ye-forth
after the rings
& before my big real-kiss
Elaine & all, shocked
I always wanted to do that,
& leaving

Going into marriage
heads so high
truth to truth
Prince to Prince
eye to eye
over 19 but like Rimbaud
wanting
me to be queen
her to be king
champagne flowed
crowds came
that afternoon
to the Kaufman's house
on Kenneth Road
Glendale
Elaine was relieved
it was over
I with the guests rode high
"a beautiful couple of people"
later leaving w/ Chetty & Delphine
divided from rest
& hollywood sunset fadeout ending

w/ Rimbaud
toward the garden of palms
divided from stroll
up the hill & very familiar streets
to Brand Park
and its palms
flowers, lawns & swings
of what fast were to become
our old times
                merge
                ego gone
                submerge

                ● ● ●

                re-emerge
                midnight
huge wands
of spotlights
of grand openings
reach into the air
                we are new
                we are two well-formed things
                we have wings
                we fly away
                into the huge shapes
                of the Verdugo Hills

                ————

this is the myth
the actual busride
was long, was hell.
we groped.
no place for 2 to be alone
no place for one to be alone
groping at
each other,
groping away

The myth is
that love rules
the night, comes
& POOF!
disintegrates
the jails
called male
& female
that love's power
then can flow
free as Viet Cong soldiers
over us
as if we were sections
of dark countryside.

It is only at the rises
        it comes true
Shakespeare got married
can you imagine
him & Anne
Titania & Oberon?
or any of your married friends?
        What's true in it? –
        All of it except
        the night, for
        it happens constantly –
        like, here dear
        here's an assface
        you'll adore
        & all.

Titania & the big O
fight & you're scared
worse you're scared
of their objectives.

If women
don't love you

you're pitiful
you prove Mother
you beg crumbs
see, I'm as vicious
as Shakespeare
who they say hated women I
What do you say?
Nevermind.
I don't believe you.
Don't tell me
about your cells

Timothy Leary is pathetic
He got married
was it one / month?
He wants it
but he can't have it
& maybe her either,
anyhow she
found out & she split.
Don't tell me
about yr cells
how about play organs
big enough to see
Jesus, you want to talk to a tree?
Talk to some broad.
Talk to me.

Plot is a plot.
We are free
One to one.
Shakespeare knew it,
wrote Midsummer Night's Dream
later served
one politician
one king
whose plots are cruel
shown in English tragedy.

I read
they would not allow girls
to play on the stage.
It is they
who do not have
the love of women
or men
with any brains.
Kenneth Patchen says
watch out, they are out
to kill us all.
I believe it.
its a cruel world.
it's fight or die.

I will not
bow down before them
Fuck their word of God
they snuck into my wedding.
I will bow down
& adore
& I shall kneel before
& give suck to
the powerful cunts of
certain particular women
who in love have
turned their faces
straight at me
and one girl who
now most loves me
I scream & cry & hear her out
she who came
she to whom I came
& come
to owe
the world,
Elaine,
the promise

is ludicrous –
play house,
play games,
put on
this hat –
it's gone
or stashed
with the rings.
I'm glad
I stayed.
You stayed
unafraid
to draw blood
in a fair fight
some one
can win
not a war.

New Living Room

if love was love
& not disguise
we touched under
what our eyes saw
in the quiet
& beautiful colors
of the paintings
you made of
          our struggle
I miss them now
& fear them less
than you
the new
will have the room
we make for everything
& therefore we must care
to fill it up
I think there must be a new
look on you too
& I must have you do
another one
          of me
for Edward Smith
          has died
& haunts our living room
along with Charlie Potts
& all the
hungry dead
a dumb mistake
I thot
you had survived
you tried to tell me
with another name
I thot was meant for other
ears than mine

& forced you back
beyond nine springs
the year your mother Roy
posed in all her drag
& coughed & shed
a dishonest tear
now you take
a few pictures down
I see! you dont
underplay it
Hanako
your name is
what is mine

II

with the courage to write again
I've discovered how it ended
the year the hippies died
& Sawyer & Costigan
called the tune
I missed the life
I lost too long
& cried
again & again
love was love
it had no defense
it's gone

who was I
when you woke up?
we are strange
creatures I see
to touch only
each other
& force no sympathy
beyond the past
or to some other
way of death

tho its a thing
all of them
sing now
or kiss the dead
girl's pussy
cause the living
one wont want to
pay that price
or show that gracefulness
without a deal
I love
you, Hanako
the rest, the artistry
is trash
to give away or sell
to cause the other
to split from the other
pain he'd wish to
dress her up in
it always
shared a life of that
disorder
"it makes me feel
so real"
is what is said
who'd go back
to that
        from here
that face of you
my only Malcolm X
        is gone
the uncomfort of keeping it
I'll lay on
a collector, OK?
& keep the change
like Paragons
I'm catching up
because of you

dawn stram
(1944-)

shall we

take

the   (stares)

and walk

out sooner

from a building

of stigma

called public

service

the

Japanese cherry

blossoms

into April

so Tokyo

must be

lovely

now

bond age

25 years of star-
spangled security
for ameri/i/cans
buying US
savings bonds to feed
another
anti viet
cong
attack!

You solve the equation
for the unknown
soldier
boy rocking sea
sick over the bar at Astoria
thinking
           that was
rough but he'll get his
sea legs
& it just mite be
that the sea will

get rougher
before the southern
cross is
not seen thru
eyes   that also

don't blink

at the purple
heart
his daddy proud
ly carries

home from Washing
ton in hands
clammy
from the touch of

Pow
er

6 years from pocatello

my mind keeps reaching back to my first memory

of you and i come up with a sunlit smoky room

on Wednesday afternoons where we all defied orders

written on the blackboard and made our own

paper ashtrays that filled up

w/ ed's Parliaments and my Pall Malls

you were always at the other end of the table

close to john hoopes and rocky sorensen

and across the table was Lord Byron

i try to remember your comments about my poems

and instead i remember Pal chanting his way to the street

breaking the silence after ezra pound

& i felt intimidated by your recent lapse

into the poetry i'd been trying for years to write

then it was summer & i was pocahantas washing

peed-on bedding in the bathtub & typing papers for you

about henry james giggling each time i had to type

"fanny assingham" and visiting professor herbert

n.m.i. ruhm worried that i was tricking you

into thinking you had made me pregnant

i was happy to run into you weeks later

on the streets of Ketchum

you wrote to me faithfully after i left

and sent me poems you were struggling with

sean was born and you were a budding young poet

i thought about the summer when we were

youthful poets laureate of idaho state

and then it was february and you and ed and i

dancing circles in the greyhound depot, portland

i presented my first born son for your approval

and he was beautiful

ed bought a carton of Gauloise for helene because she

liked them and i smoked in front of my mother

and she loved you both because i did

at the depot ed pressed a wilted flower into my hand

and I watched you with your noses pressed to the window

as the train took you a way and i ran crying after you

the bell-shaped blossoms dried on the shelf

and weeks later the seeds rattled softly inside

and there were sometimes unpostmarked cards w/

places scrawled illegibly so i couldn't find you

and the phone would ring from Kellogg & finally

Olympia and it was April a year later

judy & i came after you

because you didn't have anything to do and we broke

a fan belt and we heard leroi jones & drank at the union

station with walt and larry until i had to leave and you

decided not to go to california

i called you later from san francisco begging

to come live with you

June arrived and Creeley was in La Grande and i went

to meet you and ben and "bobby watson" thinking it would

have been so nice to have found you the weekend before

when i'd driven through with julie on my way back

from idaho and a five-year class reunion

i brought you home again & carlos

& barbara was enormously pregnant and you left again

for Olympia and finally Seattle

i came home late one nite

and found a message & took off at midnite for you

and Seattle and quietly knocked at a door

larry was up & he opened the door and hugged me

and was glad to see Stramie again

i shook your shoulder and woke you and was happy

to be in your arms hearing you cry that you loved me

& i knew you were drunk and scared of the draft

but i needed you and spent many hours and many months

driving to you and away from you reading and writing

my poetry turning on to john handy and off to oscar peterson

caught up w/ ed, elaine, larry, peggy, jack, litmus,

zig zag, farmer's market, poetry readings, acid heads,

at home typing pages of poetry for your mag and in

seattle shivering as we tried to activate a

multilith that had died long before

& you took the boys to the zoo and philip was

your flower and sean up-tighted you and I quit going

to Seattle

later it was briefly paul and cocaine, sgt. pepper

and dogs and cats and pot throwing, picking berries,

apples, electric guitar cases and stones & i got you

started for mexico

you came back sooner than anyone

expected and left again

for Seattle & Berkeley and got your mind blown and in June

I was afraid of the power and hate in your poems

and knew the worlds of laffing water and dawn

were far apart but I loved seeing allen ginsberg

take a second row seat to us

you called me from Oakland when I was cracking

without the boys

and I wanted you here but I was afraid

to commit myself

to marriage so I sent you away

because I couldn't take care of either of us

then the nightmare started again

and I started to

get straightened out and I called you and you

sounded good again and I got worse

& woke up one day wondering why all the men

and boys I was attracted to

looked like you

Ford Swetnam
(1941-)

Putting By

My parents must have wondered
What they had left to give
After the great depression
And the 4th Marine Division
Took them at sixteen and returned them
Strangers at thirty-one,
So they raised us tough and turned tough on us
If we didn't straighten to the sun
And get our lessons, which explained money
As men had once explained the Hun.

The little Eisenhower depressions
Must have felt to them like the first
Cough or wander in a used car,
So we had sudden livestock
And suddenly mortal chores,
Laying low the ditchbank weeds
And holding the boar by the haunch
As the vet lifted vas and tendon;
Mutton had been combat rations,
So we'd have no sheep,
But there were screams in the hams too.
Raised to the state of war. Stock up.
Trust your kin, but don't
Go into business with them.
Boil everything.

I know it was a kind of love.
The Punic veterans when the harvests failed
Callused thus their Anatolian children,
And hardened children live in Anatolia still.
But knowing from how far
Come the hurts we give,
I'd wish now to have given pity then,
And asked it for myself and asked for more to give.
The dirty times in lives before our own
Chained us to rocks with those we never saw,
And I have whipped my own son
With rope I didn't braid.
Dry summers still breed bruises.

If there's no pity,
We stand in the blowing dust
Between the pickup truck that works
And the one that doesn't
And bind ourselves with screams
And threatened violence and tears.

With pity,
We could shiver less when the markets tremble.
We could live on the ditchbanks we now waste.

Stephen Thomas
(1950-)

Stiletto Heels

A rattler isn't poisoned by its meat.
It swallows its kill whole. That's how it lives.

Maybe the first specimen of vertebrate with venom
had no stomach for it, died
digesting its first bite.

A little failure in the scheme.
We'll call it narcosaurus
for the sleep it now enjoys.

I made it up. Of course! So what?
The planet must have sired some such sometime.
Guesswork too can shed an honest light.

See then in the narcosaur's small failure
how the law succeeds. The planet
isn't hipdeep yet in oxymorons:
gophers freaking out in tunnels,
acrophobic eagles, fish
that panic out of sight of land.

Go ahead. Relax, since logic rules
and rationalists thrive,
like women dressed to kill, but not survive.

A Texan Jesuit Who Used to Play Left Field

The choices narrow down to these, he said.
You can perfect your art or self.

There are great fools,
failed men and women,
at the back of masterpieces,
cowards, bullies, drunks for whom love
is bent.

And saints are good for nothing.
They go up without a wisp of smoke.
They leave no ash, are rapt
in Godhead as the weather is in air.
Those whose names survive
were that much less.

Yet fate will not be fooled.
Serve one or serve the other.
Both you cannot serve.
Though neither is enough.
It's misery or disappearance.
Choose, he said, and fail.

At the Metropolitan

I wandered there into a sparse grove of marble,
where both ravished and appalled I gazed on the display:
dickless antiquities, nose- and earless, altogether headless,
limbless lopped trunks out of Goya's widowed fancy.

In another room were columns topped with heads,
busts broken from their bodies by history's hammers
in our hands,
or executed by the portraitist,
guillotined in the conception,
also nose- and earless, lacking in the chin.

Is there yet another room where curators retreat to howl?
Where elbows, noses, earlobes, dicks, nipples,
all the protuberant detritus,
hangs arrayed in ghost postures,
like bits of fruit in aspic?

Time is a disdainful portraitist
and doesn't love us much.
It sculpts away the finished marble,
finding the shape within.

True to its grieved and solitary genius,
what it shows us is ourselves alright,
senseless and dismembered.

The Wheel

1.

My daddy made me reinvent the wheel,
and this was every day. Yesterday's
invention never did. "That
just won't do," he'd say.

I did what I could
with parts and parts of parts,
with lefts and rights and
interchangeables,

until the theories and
abstractions fledged and
flew. I watched them,
half admiring and more than half

annoyed, resentful, staying
put, while all the little
yesterwheels, done and
abandoned, lay

beside their ruts beside the road.

2.

My daddy made me reinvent the wheel.
And I mean everyday.
Yesterday's invention never *did*.
"That just won't do," he'd say.

His own wheels, cartoon crude,
served well enough his ends,
but every day in darkness,
when we rose, he bumped me out

into the walking world. "O man,"
he'd say, the problems pressing in.
"Good God." It made him sad
to have to think.

I'd find the tools once more
on the wet lawn.
Their pale impressions stayed
where I had left them in the grass.

I'd set to work, and he would say,
"You give a man a fish,
three days and he'll curse you.
Teach him how to fish,

he'll curse himself."

3.

My daddy made me reinvent the wheel
out of darkness in the waking hour,
out of silence, articles of
light and sound, unpromising

materials, I thought, but
with the habit on me
strong almost as breathing
I made do.

And did I mention
it was unforgiving?
No. I see I didn't. Well,
perhaps it wasn't. Only

everyday to make it up,
whole cloth, seems harsh
from time to time, like
putting frozen fingers right to the fire.

4.

My daddy made me reinvent the wheel.
I don't mean lengths of logs;
the pyramids were up and running;
nothing crude fit in.

Not a tool mark marred the polished hubs.
The bearings in their raceways
whirred like smoke without
a click or tap or wobble.

Only tools with pedigrees were used,
their provenance traced in unbroken lines
to Lisbon and Spinoza, forged of carbon steel
as pure as Henry James' unsullied mind.

You see it wasn't just the drawing
board, not just conception
that the old man harped on,
not the *machina* that the *deus* used.

And not the baby pickled in the jar
of formalin. He wanted some
repeatability. "You show me how," he'd say.
"There is no *what* without it."

5.

My daddy made me reinvent the wheel.
I don't mean so to speak.
For him the fiction was the only thing.
The agony of parts inspired no pity in him.

How the tool steel screamed,
as it sank its tooth
into the hub block on the lathe,
the lathe which I'd invented more than once

and would again. The spoke wire
trembled like a martyr,
as I drew it out from the
extruder in the hissing workshop air.

But never, though the elements cried
out and the tools cried, never
did he say, "There. Make more of *that*.
That's what I call a wheel."

6.

My daddy made me reinvent the wheel.
and this was every day. Yesterday's
invention never did. I tried, of course,

and tried to steal the neighbors' wheels
or borrow even from my cross-town
enemies a little round, a caster

or jeweled movement. He
would catch me out. For
penance it was molecule by molecule from scratch, until

I'd had enough and swore
to be my own and own and Ouch!
it hurt each time I spoke

but spoke I did. I
had to. You
would too, if yours were mine.

7.

My daddy made me reinvent the wheel.
Year after year from darkness mixed
with light and unknown
substances, glimmers, notions,

feels. It was far more than he
could even start to understand-
or maybe just admit. I'd
got beyond his ken, the way

a son should do, I guess.
My wheels were not the kind of wheels
he grew to use and used to. But-
O, ever more important particle!

O, pivot of the universe!
which elsewise runs dead flat,
straight as a habit- But!
he let me go at last and him I let.

8.

My daddy had ideas and a disaffection.
"Wheels!" he hollered," Wheels!"
until the world grew dark
and distant and the turning,

unimaginably fast,
appeared almost as stillness.
All the wheels and all the wheels
within exploded, slowly, so it seemed.

I saw their milky ruts from under,
or above, and couldn't find
the sense of where I stood, until
the dark revolved. The sparks

flew from the [one remaining] dish and
hung. Then habit helped me out.
Dizziness went down, as I
bent, tasked, above my bench.

9.

At dawn each day and often
in the chill night at,
if I need add, my daddy's urging, I
would reinvent a wheel or so.

The moon spun on my finger,
gyroscopic, tilting,
holding against common sense
something of its own.

The spilled milk of the stars
gathered on my workbench
an assemblage of its own
pale peripheral parts.

10.

Daddy, I make wheels. It's what I do.
Wheels have become my be- and end-
almost. Were anyone like you to try stopping me now,
telling me, "That's enough! No more wheels now.

It's over." I'd say, "Who d'you think you are?"
And I would be afraid. Belligerence and fear
go rim and hub, arbor in spindle,
go in gone, round in around. But look!

There're *whee*ls and wh*eels*.
Whatever I put down comes up
and back. Around what goes around
comes. So: "Whatever," as Patty Borman's

father said and died. There's
nothing new, which means there's
nothing old beneath the sun,
of course, except the moon.

11.

When I awake, it's wheels, as
when I fell asleep, all
concerning wheels, their
reference, circumference and context,

wheels. And when an ambiguity
inheres, as when I say,
of him and me, "We'll tire
of this contraptioning

and folderol. We will
refrain from *tra-la-la*
one day. We will, I swear,
we will get off this wheel awhile,"

why then what
might and can and do
and ought and have and shall
I mean, but wheels, wheels.

The Sirens' Song

Call me Ulysses. Call me Prince of Guile,
master of more tricks and turns than Ptolemy.
There isn't much I stick at. Little disgusts me.
Most things I'll try twice.
                              Tales I have to tell
of Troy and of the sea of the Middle World,
tales you know already of the things I've been and done:
a war resister, faking madness at the plough,
a diplomat and breeder of wooden horses.
I've fucked witches, made old Proteus cry Uncle!
mocked the monster Polyphemus,
after I put out his only eye.
Derision long outlasts the pain of wounds.

And I have been among the gray dead,
asking questions, prying into things.
I've learned what I don't mind telling,
even if few believe, and it makes me mad.
The gods have set us up where we are proud,
like pins, and they compete to knock us down.

Things I could tell you make a strong man sick:
Circe's tricks, her cowardice, her harlotry,
and she a goddess in eternal bliss;
the snapping sound of human thigh bone breaking
                between teeth
among shrieks wherein pain and horror compete;
how war weary soldiers in the face of victory
kill everything that's enemy, even furniture,
cradle and wheelchair, in the grip of pure blood glee.
Ordinary soldiers, I tell you. Ordinary men.

I've also heard it said my wife of twenty years,
though only a year's bride the day I left,
kept company with no man in my absence.
Her name's become the watchword of fidelity.

Listen:
Anybody tells you that a woman in her prime,
who has offers and likes sex,
spends twenty years, the only life she has
without so much as a hand gets in her pants...
Don't marry the teller's daughter.
Don't let him sell you a boat.
His head is full of something, and it isn't facts.
There's something on his mind experience can't dislodge.
It has nothing to do with women or with boats.

Penelope is clear eyed, and she knows her station.
Queens cannot just fuck and walk.
Anyone lays a queen, anyone, that is, who is her equal,
doesn't want to be her equal but her lord.
That's how it is with property:
the more a woman has the more she's seen as such.
It wasn't her companionship her suitor's wanted.
It was oblivion.
They thought a king need never be himself.
They thought their gnawing emptiness could be
              evaded by command.
They thought and proved the value of their thinking.
What they knew...They knew nothing.
Now they groan in hell.

Penelope should be the word for perspicacity.
She saw what her suitors wanted.
Not a strong willed, handsome woman with dark eyes,
equally eager to laugh and to lay.
Not an equal. Not a wife.
They wanted Ithaca, a stage for posturing.
They wanted to strike fear in other hearts
to eclipse the fear in their own.

I've been among the exhausted dead. I know.
I have authority which neither badge nor office can augment.
Doubt me if you will;
I've heard the Sirens sing.

The tale is plausible, I think, like all my tales.
Believe who will. It goes like this:

When we returned from Hades and Persephone's cortege,
Circe entertained us on the beach,
the men with wine, myself with anecdotes of the immortals.
The bonhomie among the crew gave place to brags,
the brags to brawls, the brawls to bonhomie,
until at last like children angry with fatigue,
their bickering subsided into sleep.
Then I, who shared the goddess's bed,
kept watch beneath the circling stars,
while Circe set to fill my heart with fear.
She planted images in mind, what lay ahead,
the Sirens, rocks and maelstroms,
monstrous presences and holy cattle,
the commonplace encounters of a hero's youth.

Point by point she laid out every danger, every choice,
enjoying, as I saw, in her imagination
    my prospective horror.
And she warned me not to venture into earshot
    of those fishy witches called the Sirens,
who would see me dead of false promises
    and pretty noise.
Knowing me as well she might, considering my long,
    bewitched sojourn there on her island,
she knew that I would have to hear what had destroyed
    my kind before.
She knew I would insist as children will on having
    what must harm me.

And she told me how to bring it off.
Everybody knows the story nowadays:
how I informed Perimedes and Eurylokhos what to do
once I had stopped their ears:
to bind me to the mast
and, when I struggled, double up the bonds.

I asked myself...I should, that is, have asked myself
why Circe would assist in this.
Why would a goddess in immortal bliss,
who owed me nothing in the scheme of things,
reveal this trick to me?

Strange humors move the gods.
To ask their motives is to interrogate the wind.
We sail among their wills.
And all our mastery of seacraft
is the knowing of the limits of ourselves and of our boats.
We choose at their direction.
Their will will be done.

                Soon after dawn we sailed.
I told my men enough, not everything of course,
lest desire and fear make mutineers of them.
I led them to believe I had no choice
except to listen to the Sirens' song.
And so, of course, I could not choose but choose.
I stopped their ears with kneaded beeswax,
and then I had them tie me to the mast.

I got to know that mast, its rough spots
and its smooth, its degree of taper,
how it widened downward,
tightening my bonds when I relaxed.

    And what occurred?
                I stood awhile
against the mast anticipating,
like a young man at his wedding, when his bride
in silks casts long and knowing looks upon him.
Everything illicit in her father's house
will, in some hours, be allowed.

The oarbeats measured time, like spoons of honey,
    slowly, slowly out.
Longing and uncertainty together stretched
awareness taut. And time stood for a time

completely still. Repeated oarbeats seemed
the one beat caught in an endless, undiminishing
echo. Noon it was and summer solstice.
Thirty-seven twenty North by twenty-seven East,
The zenith and the nadir of my years.

Sweet music came across the glass green sea.
An open candid air in harmony
One clear soprano and a husky alto,
redolent of sex, the kinds of voice
that draw me like an insect to a lamp.
The tune was such I heard it in my belly and my groin.
My scrotum tightened and my sex got hard.
Delirium took hold of me from inside,
like a hunger or strong wine, and I was overcome.

As often as I've told the tale,
I never would admit until this moment
that the words I heard were vivid as a dream and
dreamlike disappeared except for a nagging trace.
I think they offered endless willingness,
vigorous invention, pure transparency.

Everybody knows how married love has its opaque corners,
where unfathomable otherness is lodged.
The best intentions of a hero's will meet this and quail.
No force of arm or mind can make it yield.
It is the man in the woman, the woman in the man,
the other other in the spouse who breathes against all will.
The Sirens' song dismissed opacity, promising
compliance, telepathy, pussy as pretty
as the crease in a just ripe peach.
Everything a man knew how to ask for,
more than he could know to ask.
All that was needed was a leap of faith.

The ribs of shipwrecks stood around that coast,
like pickets of a French fence. The beach
was littered with the putrid carcasses of seamen,
as the banks of spawning streams are

littered with still salmon.
The stench was overpowering, the sight sickening.
Yet the Sirens seemed to sing to me that this
was an illusion, just a test of courage.
If I could dismiss the evidence of my senses,
I would possess their beauties always,
live always in their sexual embrace,
coming in great spasms, like the Nile at flood
fucking the very sea.
I wanted to believe them. And I did believe.
I looked upon that horrorshow.
I saw how empty were their images,
shadowy hags tricked out for midnight show,
beckoning from under awnings, under tawdry wigs,
distance and desire coloring what nearness would
    rinse blank.

Even while I knew their vacancy, I cried out,
    "Let me free!"
I wanted what they promised,
the shallows, the variety, and the lies.
My stomach rose into my chest.
My heart throbbed in my throat.
My head spun round as if with wine and smoke.
By god, my sex had swollen huge,
as huge as wild Achilles in his battle dress,
as huge as Troy in flames, as huge as Ithaca,
as huge as Greece herself.

Perimedes and Eurylokhos arose from their
    opposing benches, pinching at their noses,
    doubled up my bonds and went back to their rowing.
The oarsmen altogether gazed astern,
their eyes averted from that horrific shore.
Then the song grew visual.
It erased the picketed wrecks,
covered the corpse littered shore.
The stink itself transmuted from the rottenness of meat
to the sweetly salted ammonia scents
    of a woman's wetted sex.

The singers came to me as blondes and redheads,
statuesque black priestesses with full red lips,
brunettes in all attires and none,
beauties of all statures and complexions,
manners and desires,
full heaving breasts and parted thighs.

They were all beauty, all desire, all willing,
all in all in all and I could not get free.
The fetters cut my wrists.
Splinters worked their way into my back.
My tongue was dry and swollen and my lips were cracked.

Even so I might have spent myself before all eyes,
if we had not pulled slowly out beyond their voices' length.
Then, as the vision faded and I felt my age,
I heard among the dying notes a lonely cry,
as if my mother, Antikleia, bowed with age,
were keening for her father, Autolykos,
were keening for her lost youth, beauty, life,
wantonly recalling bouts of sex, and
angry with me, as with all my gender,
for our crimes and for the crimes of fate.
I shuddered then, as if I were King Oedipus
recognizing in his aging wife his aged mother.

And the singing died.
I was exhausted, sore and thirsty.
I had seen and heard too much
and even so felt my desire untutored,
for I hearkened back again to the Sirens' visual song.
Yes, I had more to learn.

I caught Eurylokhos' eye
and mouthed the words "Release me."
He gestured to Perimedes, who rose.
Then looking over me, he shook his head.
The mother of a willful child who hurts
himself and in a rage denies his hurt,
transforms his pain to anger and, once-burned,

determines he will teach the fire a lesson,
the mother of such a child casts such a look
as did Perimedes on me, before
he drew another loop across my chest,
cinched it up tight and went back to his bench.

Then I began to learn about desire.
I heard my heart above the oarbeats.
I felt the life in me those heartbeats
    made and measured.
How it ran away.
How rapidly I fled through time,
like wine out of a torn skin,
like blood out of a deep wound.
My hands were numb.
A fiery, small pain developed
underneath my shoulder blades.
Time moved in two contrary rhythms,
rapidly toward death, slowly on toward evening,
when at last the sundown broke the spell that
    held my oarsmen to their clockwork task,
and they rose to untie me, but not to set me free.

Karen Waring
(1944-)

The Letter

You flinched
from the water flying into our faces
one year.
You cannot drown.
You drowned the kitten
to spare it death.
It sneezed under your chair
before you could silence
what suffered.
Think of all the rooms
we have known
we could not live in.
There were so many windows
and what came through
was a crack of sunlight
to hide under my heart.
I couldn't keep it for you
in spite of your frightened mouth
at my breast
my pain in bed when color would not rise.
What filled my mind was flat
what filled my life was faces
want could not bring
to anything.

Poem for My Husband

You were one Hell of a man,
a hot summer of a man,
a long, long night of a man,
a long distance runner of a man
running me down
until you hit the dead-ends in my eyes
and you could not turn with me.
You spun the bottle
until the kisses were gone
and when the kisses were gone
there was the full moon of whiskey
and streets where you could not find me,
poems you could not bring me out of.

write of moon in june
they say
sex isn't nice

so I write of moons in june
but not the drums, the golden puke
of sorry, kites dangling from high tension
wires, prophets on the corner of ninth asking
for spiritual alls, the slime of a snail
sparkling the walk with spasms of demented sun-
light, cut up negroes in the park eyes rolled
toward the sun, tattooed god on the back of a
sailor

hell has no ceiling

i
write of
toilet chairs rusting in the garbage dump, skins
of zarathrustras hung and dried, sagging men on
sagging porches on sagging tits of time, jack
who crawled into a spiritual sax and died with desmond
stinking on his kiddies breath, frank who got shot
by a mulatto while walking down a street in a
seattle dusk and his achille's soul throbbing with
wedge of cold lead imprisoned, louise who got
propositioned by a fifteen year old don duck & called
him back to beg a dime to call father lemure in the
sake of god, & jim and carol who got married in spite of
the ghastly awning beneath which they existed and
aborted called all in all all is well until, the
markets dappled with flesh of fish and man in spangled
draught, and mack didn't really have a knife but a
spiritual gun

but i luv the people people people roots & lips of
people, dark hairs on the men's open chests, answers
and cigarettes curled from women's lips, souls

hyphen split and god with an apostrophe & people dizzy
diamond-eyed in the street heady with success loved
in spite, love like the clang of tincans beat by a wind
off puget, the web of a spider with a face like a poet
darkening my window with unstrung words wound up
like ulcers in the belly

i shall write of moon in june and empty rooms
i warn you all against sex and pretty colors
sex isn't nice
either are family reunions

moonlight censures the world

Poem for Katherine Seven Years Ago

we went into the darkness
of your high school
& i made up a boogie woogie

on a broken piano
we both knew that
would end   we both

knew the janitor would
frighten us away
waving his fly

i once tried to tell
you the facts of
life but you thought

the boys at the edge of
the lake were merely
being friendly when

they asked you to lie
down   i was ashamed
of your heavy white breasts

trembling in the cloth hands
of your bathing suit. i was
skinny but hid in the water

as they made remarks about
us. you didn't know
the meaning of cock, cunt, & fuck

the boy who kissed you
the first time later bit a
young boy's throat in a

movie one night but you
had laughed happily & asked
"are kisses always wet?"

sending us into hysterics
thankgod you weren't
good looking. i wasn't

either but found enough love
to consider shabby rooms
& didn't write you then about

the tavern where i played
the piano & lived on
beer for weeks   you

thought everyone was nice
you mentioned god
you drank coca cola

i broke my high heels in
a cocktail lounge   you
read montaigne & wrote

poems about home
& mother & things.
you cracked up once

but still smiled beneath
the christmas tree like
little lord Jesus

would jump out of a box
& cuddle in your lap
like a kitten   i'm

married again, you're an
old maid writing pleasant
letters on flowery

stationery   i'm
afraid if i looked you up
i'd find you at that lake

jiggling in a bathing suit
some old man asking you
to lie down you're tired

& i'm afraid you would
wrinkles on your face
seeing god over his shoulder

Exposed to the Elements

1
Lives are mountains
with brushfires and ice caves
and deceptively beautiful high meadows
beneath which
glaciers sicken and cough blood
behind blue hands.
There was danger of avalanche
the first time you saw her,
there was snow on her shoulders
the first time you touched her
with trees
and there was no coming back
from her white slopes
and thawing eyes.

2
Mt. Baker ate them alive,
broke her husband's ankle
and left him to die on a ledge
with a heart condition
and a ten year old son.
The experts said
it took the boy a week to die
exposed to the elements.

3
Marriages are mountains
with people lost in them
and she is still alive
in the wilderness
of another marriage.
Mountains give up their dead
in the spring, hearts do not.
The mind
retains the high meadows
and the heart stretches
like an ice age
across the coupling continents.

Child's Poem

i loved you
when i was ten
& dared you to kiss my knee
& you did with dirty lips
blackened from a fall from a tree
we climbed together
& i loved you when you
collapsed
& the children built chains around you
holding you in
from the doctors & police came
& i loved you when you bought binoculars
& spied on me
chopping wood in the yard
& you were ill and far away in a window
when our dogs fought in the yard
& i loved you
when we built a camp in a snarl of brush
& found one dead cat for the purpose
of burying it there
& later dug it up and got sick
because the dirt was sticky and found
a lump that didn't break apart when poked
with a stick
& i loved you when you were a greasy rink
& hollered names at me on the schoolbus
& deliberately stood in shadows
to frighten me as i walked in search of eyes
& i loved you when i crawled out of my window
at midnight to find you waiting in the brush
with oyster shells and grey pearls found within,
& i loved you when we walked under the trees
& found nothing to be afraid of
so crawled in the window again & slept

& i loved you when i went on my first date
& you rubbed my stomach in the movie
& i cried and told father
& said i never wanted to grow up
because i was afraid of your hands
& the things your eyes did when they saw
me barefoot rooted in the summer
still determined with baseball bats & science fiction,
& i loved you when
a boy named Black dared you to kiss me
& you threw me on my back in the grass
& kissed me for three minutes & the grass sweat
& the backs of my legs were green when i went home
& i loved you when i was 15
& in a roller rink with my parents
& i loved you when i skated into a locker
and kissed you back with a black eye
& i loved you when you came from Germany
& i loved you when you put my heart on your dashboard
& it dangled there for weeks as we
screamed through cities and family expeditions to granite falls
where i fell over a chain & broke my mouth
& you held my breasts all the way home & made me dizzy
i loved you when my skin
spilled out of my blouse
& i loved you when you said you couldn't touch me
& went toward another girl that stared at you
from her bedroom window across the street
& i loved you when you came from Denmark
with burns all over your face
& i tried to teach you grieg's piano concerto
in the practice rooms at school
where we hid after class behind stage curtains
& invented things to say to people we would never
say to people because we were not popular
& couldn't honestly get turned on by a football game
& i loved you when we skipped class
& hid in the boiler room and talked about building

a boat & going off in it to get lost
but didn't
& i loved you when you came back
with nervous hands & a Christmas present
& a marriage
though it happened before & the trees screamed
as we found it in your brother's car
& i loved you on our wedding night
when the blood came
& the dawn brought a face for the shadows to fall upon
when the rocking of the bed had ceased,
& i loved you
when we came back from Vancouver in the rain
& ate two boxes of strawberries
& got a nosebleed
& went to bed early every night for three months
& i loved you when you punched me in the breast
& it turned green & you cried in my mother's house
& i loved you when i was pregnant
& jumped into a truck with you & rode all over
Washington picking up junk to sell so we could eat
& i loved you when the baby crawled out of me
& had your eyes & hair,
& i loved you when you discovered me on the bus
coming back from working
& we talked about my husband who was mentally retarded
& you said it must be beautiful being married to him,
it was like being married to a child,
& i loved you when i deceived you
& skipped work one day and walked across seattle with you
& stood in the shadows of hotels we couldn't go in
& i got sick in a restaurant & couldn't eat
simply because you were there talking to me
& i was so happy
& i loved you in the library
when i had an orgasm with my hands on the piano
& i loved you when the bus came & we rode back to edmonds
& you caught a cold on the beach & wanted to be left alone

& i loved you
when you took me home & i slept on your floor
with a book of psychology & i loved you
when you wept with your wife in the bedroom
because a child had walked into her bones
& i loved you when you followed me in to the basement
& held me
& you closed your eyes & the bathtub overflowed upstairs
& you said it was no good,
i should write novels,
i should get a job & did taking care of a sick woman
who couldn't wash herself & whose husband watered gardens
but loved you long after that tho' four children happened
since then,
& i loved you when you tried to die
& they found you in dick's driveway
& pumped your stomach out as i laughed somewhere else
not knowing,
& i loved you all the time i was alone
& thinking of cracking up,
& i loved you when you followed me into the depot
& tried to touch me in a telephone booth
& i cried again
& i loved you in my red dress
& said – don't go there –
pointing to a street,
& i loved you when i got in the car with you
& you stopped in a strange place
& told me to do it,
you didn't give a goddamn about the poems,
& i loved you when i walked back alone,
& i loved you at the party
where ronnie got drunk and thought of suicide
& you spun me around the room & told me a story
& later jerked off in the car
in the middle of a philosophical argument,
& i loved you in saunders
in your dirty clothes & desire to hitchhike to new york

& loved you when you read your poetry over the telephone
& food burning in the kitchen,
& loved you when you showed me what would happen to me
if i did not stop loving,
the way the edge of the face breaks when it is touched too much,
& i loved you when you built the forest for me
& i wouldn't come
& i loved you when you drowned in the coffee cup
& collapsed on the highway & went back to your wife
& i loved you when you said you had a disease
& were going to die,
& i loved you when you were cold and skinny in your jacket
& i wanted to take you home with me
because you were so old somehow
& didn't write poems anymore
since the doctors found that dirty word in your chest
& were giving you a few weeks to find your eyes
& my parents wouldn't let you in
because you were skinny & dirty & didn't have a clean jacket
& we sat in a garage & smoked for hours
hoping the neighbor's dog wouldn't attack us
& i wouldn't come with you,
i wouldn't give you that because my father was making
hot cakes in the morning
& my mother wanted to go to the bon marche the next day
& you got sick in the street
& fainted on the bus spending you back to seattle
& i could not eat the next morning
because my parents were happy & eating all the breakfast
up as if nothing had happened,
& i loved you when i lost my poetry on the bus
& you found me crying on a corner of the night
& i loved you when you walked me all the way up to the bus
station to get it, & we pounded on the door for a long
time until somebody came & not only returned the poems but
gave us coffee to finish the night on,
& i loved you when we found the music
& tried to go in

& act 21
& you failed and had to leave,
& loved you when i found you again
laughing over funny papers when i was with someone else
& no longer writing poems,
& i loved you when you asked me to write a poem about
rain because you found a poem in a puddle of water
& couldn't' pick it up,
& i loved you when you strangled in the saxophone,
strangling on violent, gypsy hair
& i loved you
when you sat across from me & couldn't speak a word of english
& touched me all over
tho' six people were between us glaring all over,
& i loved you when you were working in saunders
& talked to me about the second WW
& everybody else laughed because you had a scar,
& i loved you when you closed the restaurant up
& we washed dishes in greasy water
alone with a four o'clock in the morning color all around us,
& people banging on the windows with newspapers,
& i loved you
when you put me in your room
& made terrible shadows on the wall
& the clothing fell. off,
& my soul broke under your foot as you jumped from
bed to get an instant breakfast drink & cigarettes
& my shoulders shriveled
when you touched me in the car on the way home
& later tried to kill me when i wouldn't answer the phone,
& i loved you when i came from you
& sat at your feet struggling with lines
& the body the fire brought out of the shadows
& i loved you when you told me of a girl with your child
somewhere growing old in a rented room you paid monthly
visits to with empty pockets & long golden hair,
& i loved you
when we laid in your bed until the apple trees grinned

through the window,
singing songs & getting sleepy with each other
& i loved you
when you fell asleep upon the greasy pillow
& i wandered alone through your house looking for her,
& i loved you when Monty
came in the next morning with his fruit truck & wanted
to spend the day at the beach,
& the 3 of us slept together,
nothing happening except the poem,
nothing moving except the mind as we slept together like
children in a grandmother's bed on Christmas eve
& i loved you when you said you could destroy me & did
handing me a stale sandwich the next morning
as i ironed your shirt
& nothing was said about letting me love you again,
& i loved you when i caught the bus alone,
leaving your blue shirt in the house,
leaving my eyes in the room where rachmaninoff climbed
the hill alone,
& i loved you when my eyes got scared
when i said i was going away
& i loved you when you suggested prostitution
to me as a way of keeping my poems
& i loved you when i called you a bastard
& we fought in my room,
&i loved you when you fell asleep
as i cried staring out the window at the olympic hotel
& i loved you when i was starving
& couldn't get the bus fare to go home
& i told you to go away & you did
& i loved you when i found you once more
sandwiched in between old walls
& i loved you when you sighed & wanted your back rubbed
& i rubbed cities into your skin
& i loved you when you sold your first painting
& told me i was like your sister
as we sat in pizza haven

& i loved you when you stood at the window with me,
a window framed with terror abstract,
& you told me about love, as a machine grumbled & i aped
across the dirt into a hole where man crawled with tools
& misery,
& i loved you when suddenly the sun melted our eyes
into a single eye

& you said love

& the city disappeared taking all the hills with it.
& i loved you
when you came from india
& got drunk in the taxi & called the cab driver
a goddamn fool & then asked laughingly, "is this the
way you do it in america"
& i loved you when you laughed in the chinese restaurant
when I slapped a copy of why i am not a christian
down on the table
& some businessmen stared
& you read a passage to me from the book
in every conceivable kind of dialect
& i loved you when we argued philosophy
& your head finally fell on my shoulder
& you stared at the accidental part of me
& i loved you
when two taxis took us in wrong directions
& we never met again,
& yes, i loved you,
when you came into america illegally on a forged passport
& hid from the authorities in a dirty restaurant
on a dark street, washing dishes
& stumbling quite accidentally over the poem
as it was handed to you in a moment of drunkenness,
& i loved you
when we went up to your room to talk
& i drank up all your vodka
& laughed on the bed

because the window shades had legs
& they were all kicking the back of your head
as you sat there & read your diary to me,
& i loved you when
you laid beside me & kissed me
& helped me up,
& helped me find a friend because i didn't know where i
was going, & i was tired, & the poems were getting
heavy,
& i loved you when i wanted to die,
& went out taking the food with you to give to friends,
& i loved you when i was in county general
& nobody came with flowers
& the snakes on the wrists were real
& i loved you when you brought me a book to read
& i loved you when you said the hell with it all
& we got married
& got drunk together on two o'clock morning walks
down the avenue toward coffee corral
& the trees shook dead hands above us
& the rain was an umbrella itself
& i loved you a year
& nobody came,
nothing happened out of the fire,
no one came to mend the stair,
& we didn't mind that no one could come up
& find us screaming on the pillow
& i loved you
when i fell through your face
& found myself in a place where no people were
because my blood was so thin it covered everything,
& i loved you when you stood by yourself
because the poem was hammering into my face
& it had to be torn off
& fitted to other things,
& i loved you when we walked & counted all the spiders
on the university bridge at midnight,
& i loved you

when you put your hands on my throat
& your mouth told me you wanted me to die
because i could not stop giving birth,
& i loved you
when you cried on me
& got tears in my armpit because you were sorry,
& i loved you
when we opened the door & looked once more
& i would put a stop to this poem
if i could

Bob Watt
(1925-)

Introduction

This poetry is written to take you into excellence by the way of inferior poetry.

All other poets claim their poetry is superior to mine; I will allow them this.

Some of these poems can rock people off dead center.

I can bring you to excellence plus enlightenment using inferior poetry. I will not leave people unrocked, so don't try to stabilize before me.

I may be able to lighten your load even at this sitting. If I can, you will be working just right: on your self.

I will lighten your load even though you have been able to stay struggling under it to date. Nobody can talk me out of it by telling me how much better their poetry or their favorite big bull poet is.

The best poetry is still in the air and has not been written yet. If we can lighten you even a little, or even come close, write and tell us as this will be a major breakthrough for me, and even more for you.

New Family and Family Goals

The family must be extended.
Two people are not enough to start a
family. We need the love of three or
four women and vice-versa.

All families of six or seven must be
open to lose or gain new members at
any time.

Each house will have a light sign on the outside
so we can see the goals of
each family, if we can add anything
to this family we could stop
to see them.

This poem is not clever enough to convince
but a life of ordinary suffering may do it.

Holding Hands with a Flower

Turn yourself in if you want to. No
poem could deliver the promise of the title.

We invented heaven because its so handy.
Heaven invented earth for the same reason.
If you need reasons to begin with, holding
hands with a flower will hardly bring you
enough freedom, to want to hold hands with
more flowers.

All flowers, are the same, so don't just
melt before one kind of flower. Any flower
likes to melt in with you. Flowers share their
beauty with everyone equally, true saints.

"Seasonal Love"

Winter is a love white puritan poem.
Spring is a poem of free love.
Summer is when you sweat out payments.
Autumn is when you make big payments and
look for new loves to pay for.
the next spring you look more intensely,
becoming real masochistic. You're willing
to pay more & more and women are skeptical
as to whether you can physically pay for
two or more of them.
Only dogs will love you now.
I haven't given up hope for summer to bring
more love & power and hope by fall dogs will
lose interest, then your love becomes curtailed–
only curs will tail you, now.
You allow yourself to dress a little sloppy to
be less attractive to dogs. This will help to
cur-tail love.
Because I'm in love with so many dogs, women bite
me in jealous fits of distemper and in the confusion
of fur, flying hair, dogs, cats, women bite each
other in necks. I am off again, scot free,
loving dogs & women whichever I can attract or
afford at the time.
I am cool and collected in the center of this rolling
ball of dogs, cats and women. Fur and hair mixing.
I know I will not get emotionally involved
in a show of force. I remain aloof and
intellectual, U of Wis. training.
I may yet return to my old country and teach
mumbly jigg to my people. Asians have suffered
enough: you have suffered; they can move on;
you can move on; easy: now Watt; easy: –
don't turn on your full flow of power. You could
frighten some.
Let people press up against anything this season,
for extra love. Please don't get hung up on
anything, this season, which is all of your life.

Over Entertainment

While staying with two girl social workers
and having sex with one, the door
slipped open by accident. Girl's roommate
threatened to move out and did so.

This seems to be a case of accidental over-
entertainment causing everyone to move from
the neighborhood within a week and these
were liberals in Milwaukee. Can you imagine
what a conservative is around here?

Bull Dykes

What is wrong with them
they get women started in love don't they.
    The better lovers they are
the more loving their girlfriends become;
so isn't this going in the right direction
of loving.
    Why do fems want to run off
with bull dykes
to begin with or am I being naive asking?
    Do bull dykes ever buy fems for an
evening.
why does all this have to be so secretive,
why isn't there more in the papers about
it.
    Do bull dykes
ever go queer & start loving other bull
dykes?
    Is it against the law to be a bull dyke,
if it isn't why
don't they have parades
so they could attract more fems.
    What if you fell in love
with a bull dyke what would happen.
    Why don't they teach us some of these
things in high school or college.
    Why don't we invite bull dykes to our
poetry readings so they could explain
bull dyking, & a bull dyke love affair.
    I like that name
bull dyke. Bull dykes should have rights.

Mild Sprees

A girl I know wanted to go on a
penis sucking spree for a few days.

All kinds of people tried to talk
her out of it. They would sooner
smoke, drink or run around in fast
cars, fight with their wives,
boyfriends or husbands.

This girl was healthier than these
various self-destroyers.

I know a couple of girls entered
the field were thrown into local
insane asylum just when they were
having fun with various boys.

Poetry
and
What Should Be Done About It

Why should I go on as I am, when I can buck
      right into something new, yet unknown.
Practically everybody wants me to go on in
      the same old vein not realizing how close
      I am to breaking into several new
      discoveries.
If people could realize my potential or their
      own, for invention and growth, they
      would be very exited and ready to blow
      their cool at any minute.
I promise not to blow my cool until I have
      invented something that will give all of you
      a lift and a third way of living.
Now that I am in this poem, I hardly know
      what it is supposed to be about and
      what to do with the tangle, what are
      poems supposed to do for you anyway.
I know what they are supposed to do but do
      the people who read poetry know what
      it should do for them
I would like to ask our poetry readers or the
      general public what they expected from
      poetry, to begin with.
Poetry is supposed to have effects on you
      and one day I will blab on about this as I
      don't want to tighten you down too much
      right now.
I don't want to lay any more rules down as
      we may have too many inside us already.
New poetry will come as we lay less rule
      on each other.

Eric Wegner
(1959-)

The Miller

Last night the mill broke down and I was
baptized with flour dust, rolled and breaded
like a fritter ready for frying.
And the noise and the dust invaded me and
left all my cells ringing and white.
and I carried the smell of warm, friendly
ground flour home with me, leaving puffs of white
as I passed, like a trail of pheromones, an attractant
to bakers.

This morning, like bread or Lazarus, I rose again
feeling stiff as a crust from my labors of last night.
Heading to the mill with two cups of coffee and a
question grinding in my brain:
Did I fix it last night—will it work right when I
throw the switch?
And it does, and the roar of the mill sings to me
as I put flour in bags, and the truck comes to take
what I have milled, and the flour is still warm as we
load it into the truck.
I love this job. I come to work with a blue collar and
leave with a white collar. Every day is a promotion.

Loki

This morning I woke into foolishness.
The worries I had laid down upon were broken and strewn
across the room like an orgies' remnants,
and from the lightness between my ears where reason
once prevailed there came echoing laughter.

Divine fool.

I had forgotten you in my dark accounting.
Now in your wake I see my clumsiness and laugh.
Plans that unravel, deeds that misfire are but
the blast of your seltzer water.
The flowers I see all wait to squirt vinegar in my face
and I will laugh until I blow milk through both nostrils.

Has it been that long since you last possessed me?
I remember that dark time also, when all was vain
and only death by grisly means made sense.
And when things could not have gotten worse,
you came and made it all twice as bad
(but I cared less.)

And in the face of your manic grin and crossed eyes
I found my wobbly knees pulling free from the muck,
and beneath the cream pie on my face my eyes were
watering tears of ecstasy, and when you did leave
my life was wrecked but I slept for the first time
in weeks.

Welcome back.

Keith Wilson
(1927-)

The Poem Politic x: A Note for Future Historians

When writing of us, state
as your first premise
THEY VALUED WAR MORE THAN ANYTHING
You will never understand us
otherwise, say that we

cherished war

> over peace and comfort
> over feeding the poor
> over our own health
> over love, even the act of it
> over religion, all of them, except
> perhaps certain forms of Buddhism

that we never failed to pass bills of war
through our legislatures, using the pressures
of imminent invasion or disaster (potential)
abroad as absolution for not spending moneys
on projects which might makes us happy or even
save us from clear and evident crises at home

Write of us that we spent millions educating
the best of our youth and then slaughtered them
capturing some hill or swamp of no value and
bragged for several months about how well they died
following orders that were admittedly stupid, ill-conceived

Explain how the military virtues, best practiced
by robots, are most valued by us. You will never come
to understand us unless you realize, from the first,
that we love killing and kill our own youth, our own great
men FIRST. Enemies can be forgiven, their broken bodies
mourned over, but our own are rarely spoken of except in
political speeches when we "honor" the dead and encourage
the living young to follow their example and be gloriously
dead also

NOTE: Almost all religious training, in all our countries,
dedicates itself to preparing the people for war.
Catholic chaplains rage against "peaceniks," forgetting
Christ's title in the Church is Prince of Peace;
Baptists shout of the ungodly and the necessity of
ritual holy wars while preaching of the Ten Commandments
each Sunday; Mohammedeans, Shintoists look forward
to days of bloody retribution while Jews march
across the sands of Palestine deserts, Rabbis
urging them on....

THEY VALUE WAR MORE THAN ANYTHING

Will expose our children, our homes to murder and
devastation on the chance that we can murder or devastate
FIRST and thus gain honor. No scientist is respected whose
inventions help mankind, for its own sake, but only when
those discoveries help to destroy, or to heal soldiers,
that they may help destroy other men and living things

                                        Be aware that
Destiny has caught us up, our choices made
subtly over the ages have spun a web about us:
It is unlikely we will escape, having geared
everything in our societies toward war and combat.
It is probably too late for us to survive
in anything like our present form.

THEY VALUED WAR MORE THAN ANYTHING

If you build us monuments let them all
say that, as warning, as a poison label
on a bottle, that you may not ever
repeat our follies, feel our griefs.

Daniel Zimmerman

(1945-)

MTBF: Pass & Stow

the best thing is most of the time
entropy goes unnoticed.
I used to think so but now I don't.
every minute adjustment,
snazzy epicycle, dims Ptolemy's stars,
no, blots with fractalized coherence
& gives us for steady state *trompe l'oeil*.

today I shave with Ockham's razor
& cast the devil into hell.
I used to forget but now I resemble.
it isn't the compression it's the bounce
that counts, sometimes enhanced
with English, but usually fine as is.
a round for the Liberty Bell.

heavens to Betsy

starlit speculation
drew heaven from earth
the whole wasteland in elegant path
trodden by none but the chosen dead
inevitably in profile
having learned nothing
& therefore entitled to their gold watches
& we to bawdy lays of their ineptitude
attentive to a kindred destination
salting feathers
treading more the fire than the flood
laughing longer to laugh last
weathermen botching the forecast
sending our men to the moon
silver-suited with a flag
spring-strung to guarantee
eternal wind
where a brick would do
perpetually arcing through
the Pentagon window

the mice will play

stagehands in black, sometimes invisibly
sometimes soliciting indulgences,
inattentions, snake the scene away,
slither in new scenery,
never till now pausing long enough to mate

ships in the night ninjas
shadows stepping over their names
their properties their prints
as if in snow, black snow, converging
then reversing, stepping back out of the emptiness

& then these banishers
of scenery, these actors, thrashing
on the lances of desire burst
like President Kennedy's head & disappear
behind the billion versions of their history

The Decline of the West Rag

not the Portuguese foothold in Japan ended the West
   but Perry
1853 & steam
made a mess of the rising sun
so long Lilioukalani
Tahiti Bikini Gauguin

it wasn't battlewagons wasn't carriers was subs
not kamikazes not even kaitens
taking out the Indianapolis
the last last stand against
row after row after row of the teeth machine

eclipsed the frontier as it drifted horribly back
to redden the lips of the East with Frederick
Olmstead's parks now muggers' paradises
horribly with malls & ghetto projects urban
renewal bussing Gordian

mutilations of the compass needle
itself still true
though deviated convoluted macaronified
if properly attuned to declination
north by North by Nautalis' screw by '58

& only Arne Saknussem to overtake
& Neil Armstrong, Jacques Cousteau
churinga-dowsing through the Bardo
to break up Jupiter's rope-a-dope with Mars
& boomerang the sphere of fixed stars

Teri Zipf
(1954-)

What Awaits Me

Maybe it's the rusting barge
abandoned in the river on its way
to Lake Washington that makes me think
something is going to happen,

perhaps it's the turbulence that lifts us
into more thin air, but the plane
approaches the runway,
the landing gear drops

with a thud and suddenly we are airborne
again, rushing upward over the hangars,
back through the clouds,
dipping our wings over Mt. Rainier.

I do not pray. For perhaps the first time
in my sometimes superstitious life, I do not
knock wood or offer bargains
to God and I don't care that nothing

is probably what awaits me
on the other side. I don't think
about my lover, who I just left
in San Jose, or all the things

I haven't done.
All I regret is being late-
my children waiting
for an airplane that never

arrives. Lately I have become
painfully aware that my destiny
is often beyond my control. My neck
vertebrae have crumbled

like the mortar between old
bricks, and it occurs to me
what a mess my life would be
if we crashed and I survived. And yet

I walk constantly on a sea
of faith. For every self
important businessman who pushes past
me in the aisle, three strangers step

in to hand me my briefcase and carry
my bag, If I drop
a twenty dollar bill, unknown hands
reach out to return it.

When the voice of the Captain
explains that a Cessna broke down
on the runway and this is why
we have circled Seattle,

the desire to land in my home
state grips me, a fierce passion. Once again
we pass the rusting barge,
once again the crowded freeway

seems precariously close,
once again the prospect of coffee
in Seattle revives me, but this time
I know we will arrive safely.

Even so, with my good left hand,
I touch the window of the airplane,
offer it my frail human blessing and thank it
for its strong, man made wings.

The Way the Blackbird's Song

My days are orderly as tombstones
at Arlington, soldierly rows of identical white
slabs. But between the long parentheses

of my life I had hoped to avoid
this regimented order. The Dixie cemetery
has a more natural symmetry, angels have fallen

as often as they've flown off with the souls
of children who would be gone by now
anyway. It's surprising how many dead people

I had forgotten. Markers lay face down in the dirt,
marble ornaments like cannonballs rest beside
the graves, weeds grow tall until Memorial Day.

I know I shall lie here with the Lambs and Laidlaws,
my pioneering ended in the Blues. Perhaps someday
the pattern will soothe me, or I'll find new geometries

in the curve of earth. The way my children
break the smooth expanse of sky. The way
the blackbird's song defines the air.

Acknowledgments and Notes

Sherman Alexie's poems are reprinted from *The Business of Fancydancing* ©1992 by Sherman Alexie, with permission of Hanging Loose Press. Alexie is a Spokane/Coeur d'Alene Indian who lives in Seattle, Washington. His most recent book of poems is *The Summer of Black Widows* from Hanging Loose Press and his latest novel is *Indian Killer* from Atlantic Monthly Press.

Diane Averill has published three books of poetry: *Turtle Sky*, © 1996, the source of her poem here, by 26 BOOKS, 6735 SE 78th, Portland, OR 97206; *Branches Doubled Over with Fruit* from the University of Central Florida Press–a finalist for the Oregon Book Award; and in 1998, *Beautiful Obstacles* from Blue Light Press in Fairfield, Iowa.

mel buffington, born in Baker, Oregon, lives in La Grande, wrote and published his first poem at St. Patrick School in Walla Walla in 1953. His poems here are reprinted from *The Temple* 1, the book *One, Two, Three*, and *Blitz*, a magazine buffington co-edited with Jan Kepley. "Poets, Poets, Poets" is from the book of the same name by The Sacramento Poetry Exchange, Ben L. Hiatt, publisher. All work © 1998 by mel buffington.

Charles Bukowski's poem is reprinted from *Poems Written Before Jumping Out of an 8 Story Window*, published by Litmus in 1968. All the current books in print of more than 50 titles by Charles Bukowski are available from Black Sparrow Press, 24 10th St., Santa Rosa, CA 95401, John Martin, publisher.

Casey Bush's poem here first appeared in *The Temple* 4. He lives in Portland, Oregon, and has a book, *Blessings of Madness*, in the 26 BOOKS series.

Andy Clausen's poem is reprinted from the book of the same title, *Extreme Unction*, © 1971, 1974, published by Litmus. Born in Belgium, Clausen has traveled much of the known world and lived for a time in Florence, Oregon. The most recent of his eight books is *40th Century Man* selected poems from Autonomedia. *Without Doubt* (Zeitgeist) 1990 comes with an enthusiastic introduction by Allen Ginsberg.

Jack Collom's teaching brought him for a time to Salmon, Idaho. He lives in Boulder, Colorado, and has published many books of poetry including *Arguing with Something Plato Said* (1990) from Rocky Ledge Cottage Editions. His poems here are from *Ice* © 1974 and *Little Grand Island* © 1977.

Abelardo Delgado is often referred to as the father of Chicano poetry. Originally from Chihuahua, he has taught all over the West and lives in Arvada, Colorado. His many books include *Chicano*, *It's Cold*, and *Bajo El Sol De Aztlán*. "Totoncaxihuitl" is reprinted from *The Temple* 1, © 1997 by Abelardo Delgado.

Richard Denner founded, and ran for many years, Four Winds Bookstore in Ellensburg, Washington. From his many books of poetry, the selections here are from *The Scorpion* © 1975, the D Press, Berkeley, and *Flake on Flake* © 1981 also by D Press, then of Ellensburg. Denner is taking care of his father in Santa Rosa, California. New titles are *Too Many Horses, Not Enough Saddles* (1994) and *Sambhogakaya Cowboy* (1996).

Edward Dorn's appearance in Donald Allen's *New American Poetry* anthology in 1960 introduced his work to the general public. He remains an inspiration for contemporary poetry, especially in Idaho, with his teaching for many years at Idaho State University in Pocatello. Dorn lives in Denver, Colorado. His poem here is from *Recollections of Gran Apachería* © 1974 from Turtle Island Foundation and is reprinted with permission.

Sharon Doubiago's poems here are taken from her book *Psyche Drives the Coast, Poems 1975-1987* © 1990 by Empty Bowl Press of Port Townsend, Washington, which won the 1991 Oregon Book Award. Her many other books of both poetry and prose include the epic poem, *Hard Country*, *El Niño*, *The Book of Seeing with One's Own Eyes*, and *South America Mi Hija*. She lives in Ashland, Oregon.

Bruce Embree's poems are reprinted with permission from *Beneath the Chickenshit Mormon Sun* © 1995 and *No Wild Dog Howled* © 1987, both published in fine letterpress editions by Limberlost Press of Boise, Idaho. He published poems in *Rhododendron, Famous Potatoes, Cloudline, Mountain Standard Time* and *The Slackwater Review*. He worked on the railroad and lived in Inkom, Idaho.

Michael Finley's books include *The Movie at the End of the Blindfold*, Vanilla Press, 1978; *Lucky You*, Litmus Inc. © 1976, from which "This Poem is a Public Service" is taken; *Water Hills*, 1984 Salthouse Press; *The Beagles of Arkansas*, 1978 by Rockbook; *Home Trees,* 1978 by the Minnesota Writers Publishing House; and *The New Yorker*, 1995 by Kraken Press. His other poems here appeared in *The Temple* 1, © 1997 by Michael Finley.

Charles Foster's poems here are reprinted with permission from *Victoria Mundi,* © 1968, edited by Judith Foster, Art Rudd, printer, Marysville, California; and © 1973, published by Litmus in cooperation with The Smith Press of New York City. Foster's other books include

Outrider for the Lady, © 1974 from Rainbow Resin; *Dial Artemis*, © 1975 from Aldebaran Review Press; and *Peyote Toad*, © 1975 from Litmus Inc. A story, "The Troubled Makers," appeared in *Writers in Revolt* in 1963 published by Berkeley Medallion Books, edited by Terry Southern, Richard Seaver, and Alex Trocchi.

Hugh Fox's energetic presence in American literature has resulted in more than forty books in English and Spanish. He is a multiple Fulbright and OAS scholar and a professor at Michigan State University. "Jurassic Seas" originally appeared as a Mudborn Press broadside © 1979, and "Will the Real You Stand Up, Please!" is reprinted with permission from *The Temple* 5, © 1998.

Ed Foy's most recent publication is in the anthology *Water Works*, edited by Scott Forland. Foy has been an active participant in the literary scene in Walla Walla, Washington, as a member of the Poetry Party, as the host of his own spoken word radio program on KWCW, and the host of an extensive open mic series at Pangea coffee house on Boyer. His poem here is reprinted with permission from *The Temple* 1, © 1997.

James Grabill's most recent book is *Listening to the Leaves Form*, © 1997 from Lynx House Press, the source of his poem here. He won the Oregon Book Award for Poetry in 1995 with *Poems Rising Out of the Earth and Standing Up in Someone*, also from Lynx House. *Through the Green Fire* from Holy Cow! Press was a finalist for the Oregon Book Award for Literary Nonfiction in 1995. He lives in Portland, Oregon.

Darrell Gray (1945-1987) with the *Actualist Anthology* and the Actualist movement in American poetry took poetry places where it had never been before. His poems are reprinted with permission from *Something Swims Out*, Blue Wind Press, © 1972, and *Scattered Brains*, Toothpaste Press, © 1974. *Essays and Dissolutions*, 1977 from Abraxas Press, are fundamental texts of discovery and creation.

Adam Hammer (1949-1984) died in an automobile accident near Tallahassee, Florida. His books are available from Lynx House Press, published by Christopher Howell from Spokane, Washington.

Carl Hanni's *Night Shift*, © 1996, the source of his poem here, was published by Quiet Lion Press as Vol. 1 in the Off the Beaten Track series. Hanni produced *Talking Rain: Spoken Word and Music from the Pacific Northwest*, a CD on Tim/Kerr Records. Hanni lives in Portland, Oregon, but is moving to Arizona. He ran the literary arts program for Portland's Artquake Festival for many years and produced the "Poetjam" Parties.

Robert Head's poems here are from *After Word Comes Weird*, © 1969, written with Darlene Fife from Quixote Press in Madison, Wisconsin. Fife and Head edited and published *Nola Express* from New Orleans, the quintessential alternative newspaper. Other books are *I Once Was Alive* and *In Praise of Caveman* from Samisdat.

Mary Heckler published poetry in *Wild Dog, Reason, L.A. 201*, and other magazines during the sixties in Pocatello, Idaho. Her poem here is reprinted from *Wild Dog* 16 with the author's permission, © 1965, 1998. She lives in Eugene, Oregon.

Dennis Held teaches at Lewis-Clark State College in Lewiston, Idaho, where he is also the faculty advisor for the *Talking River Review*. His poems here are to be collected in *Betting Against the Dark* and originally appeared in *Poetry, The Temple* and *cold-drill* from Boise State University, reprinted with Dennis Held's permission, © 1998.

David Hiatt's poem is from *Vanish* © 1974 from Litmus Inc. in Salt Lake City, Utah. His other books include *Rewind* from Grand Ronde Press. He currently operates David Hiatt Literary Agency and was co-founder of the Walla Walla Poetry Party in 1990. He lives in Enterprise, Oregon.

Daniel Jacobs' poem "Baby Blue" was first published in *The Temple* 3. He was a member of the 1997 Ann Arbor National Poetry Slam team and is a graduate student at the University of Michigan, working on a project to integrate the appurtenant history of U.S. Highway 12 into school curriculums.

Zig Knoll (1940-1997) published two books, *Not My Mother's Child*, © 1971, and *Dancing Girls Are Different*, © 1996, from which "Rabbit Drive" is taken, both by Noel Young at Capra Press in Santa Barbara, California. Zig was a mainstay and inspiration for the poets originating in Pocatello, Idaho, during the 1960s.

Peter Rutledge Koch's poem first appeared in *Aldebaran Review*, Berkeley, California, in 1968. It was reprinted as a Litmus first edition in 1974 with variants. Koch, a world-class poet, is also a world-class printer, originally from Missoula, Montana, now of Berkeley, California. His print-work has recently been featured at the New York Public Library, the San Francisco Public Library, and the Houghton Library at Harvard.

Ron Koertge's poems are from *Men Under Fire*, © 1976, Duck Down Press, *Sex Object*, © 1979, Little Caesar Press, and *The Jockey Poems*, © 1980, Maelstrom Press. The recipient of an NEA grant for poetry, Koertge writes young-adult novels and his new and selected poems, *Making Love to Roget's Wife,* was published in 1997 by the University of Arkansas Press.

Richard Krech's poem is from *The Incompleat Works of Richard Krech*, © 1976, Litmus Inc., Salt Lake City, Utah. In his 50 plus years on the planet Richard Krech has been a civil rights activist, astronaut of inner-space, poet, printer, father, husband, and is currently a criminal defense lawyer in Oakland, California. He has traveled in Africa, Asia, and Europe. His poetry has appeared in anthologies and magazines.

Barbara La Morticella's *Rain on Waterless Mountain,* © 1996 from dan raphael's 26 BOOKS series, from which her poem "The Underground Economy" is taken, was a finalist for the Oregon Book Award. Her poem "A Liturgy for Trinity" is from *Even the Hills Move in Waves,* © 1986, published by Leaping Mountain Press in Fort Collins, Colorado. She is co-host with Walt Curtis of "Talking Earth," a poetry program on KBOO in Portland, and was a founding member of the San Francisco Mime Troupe.

Eugene Lesser's poems are reprinted with permission from *Poems of an Acrophobic Steeplejack,* © 1967 from Magdelena Syndrome Gazette Press. *Drug Abuse in Marin County, 1968-1973,* and other books are published by Michael Sykes at Floating Island Publications, PO BOX 296, Cedarville, CA 96104.

d.a. levy (1941-1968) committed suicide in Cleveland, Ohio, under circumstances of prolonged and intense harassment from the police. His poems here are reprinted with permission of the publisher from *Collected Poems,* © 1976, Druid Books, Ephraim, Wisconsin. The cover of *ukanhavyrfuckincitibak,* a 1968 collection of levy's poetry, displayed a photograph of the author beneath a billboard that read: It takes a lot of hard work to be a good American...but *it's worth it!*

Lyn Lifshin's new book, *Cold Comfort,* is published by Black Sparrow Press. Her poems here are taken from *Black Apples,* © 1973, and *Upstate Madonna,* © 1975, both published by The Crossing Press of John and Elaine Gill. Lyn Lifshin is the most widely published American poet of the thirty year epoch from 1968-1998.

Gerald Locklin's "kids" is from *Son of Poop,* Mag Press, © 1973. "we almost had twins" is from *Fear and Paternity in the Pauma Valley,* Planet Detroit, © 1984. "No Love, Please; We're Americans" is from *tHE iLLEGITIMATE sON oF mR. mADMAN,* Slipstream Publications, © 1991. "Friday: 3 p.m." is from *Sunset Beach,* Hors Commerce Press, 1967. Locklin teaches English at California State University, Long Beach. For thirty-five years, hundreds of his poems appeared in *The Wormwood Review,* edited by Marvin Malone.

Lucky Luckenbach's *Who Knows, Some of This Might Be Real,* was published © 1973 by the Hellcoal Prison writing series at Brown University, edited by Jaimy Gordon and Bruce McPherson. Luckenbach also published in *Concours* at Westminster College in Salt Lake City, Utah, and participated in the Trubador Poetry Festival on early leave from the

376

Montana State Prison at Deer Lodge.

Denis Mair translated and published several books by Chinese poets Yan Li, Bei Ling, Li Lu and Meng Lang through his Between Dreams and Poetry Around presses in Seattle. Mair divides his time between Seattle, LA, Taiwan, and China, working as a translator for the Lords of the Universe Seminary. He is editor for Chinese poetry at *The Temple, Gu Si, El Templo*, the poetry quarterly published by Tsunami Inc.

Robert McNealy studied at Cornish School of Applied Arts in Seattle, Washington, and at Idaho State University in Pocatello. Originally from Buhl, Idaho, he lives in Vancouver, BC. He spent many years working as a journeyman archaeologist in North and South America. His work has been shown throughout Canada, the USA, Europe, and the Middle East, and is represented in many private and public collections.

David Memmott's "The Storm That Put the Phones on Hold" is from *House on Fire*, 1992, from Jazz Police Books, Wordcraft of Oregon, which also contains the Rhysling Award winning poem, "The Aging Cryonicist." "Too Many Windows; Not Enough Doors" was first published in *The Temple 5*. His cycle of poems, *The Larger Earth: Descending Notes of a Grounded Astronaut*, was published in 1996 by the Permeable Press of San Francisco, California. A new book, *Within the Walls of Jericho*, is forthcoming from 26 BOOKS.

Jo Merrill's poems are from *Woodspurge*, an unpublished collection. They also appeared in *Waterweed*, © 1976, from Litmus Inc. Merrill, originally from Fairfield, Idaho, is well-known as a painter and poet. She lives on Beaver Pee Farm near Ladysmith, BC, on Vancouver Island.

Ray Obermayr, also well-known as a painter, is a retired professor of art who lives in Pocatello, Idaho. *Double You Double You Too*, poems of a WWII experience, from which "Fort Sheridan, Illinois" is taken, is published by Rick and Rosemary Ardinger's Limberlost Press, HC 33, Box 1113, Boise, ID 83706.

Tanure Ojaida of Nigeria taught at Whitman College in Walla Walla, Washington. The poem "fatalities" is from the book, *the endless song*, published by Malthouse Press of Lagos and Oxford, © 1989. Ojaida has published several other books of poetry and won the Africa region Commonwealth Prize for Poetry in 1987. His work also appears in *The Fate of Vultures*, BBC prize-winning new poetry from Africa.

Maureen Owen's poems appear in *Big Deal 5, The Poetry of Maureen Owen: a brass choir approaches the burial ground*, © 1977 and *The No-Travels Journal*, © 1975 from Cherry Valley Editions. She is the author of eight books of poetry and her title, *Amelia Earhart*, won a Before

Columbus American Book Award for poetry. *American Rush*, her selected poems, is forthcoming from Talisman House, Publishers. She makes her home in Guilford, Connecticut.

Will Peterson operates the Walrus & Carpenter Bookstore in Pocatello, Idaho, and produces the annual Rocky Mountain Writers Festival there. He published an anthology, *Mountain Standard Time*. His poems here are from *Luctare Pro Passione*, © 1995, published by the Walrus & Carpenter, 121 South Main Street, Pocatello, ID 83204.

Charles Plymell denies he was ever a Beatnik, although he used to live with Neal Cassady. Author of many books, his poems here are from *The Trashing of America*, © 1975, from the Kulchur Foundation. His classy classic novel, *The Last of the Moccasins*, has just been reprinted by Mother Road Publications, Albuquerque, New Mexico.

Charles Potts' "A Marijuana Poem" was first published by Mike and Kathy McKettner in *Catalyst* in Seattle and is reprinted from *The Dictatorship of the Environment* from Druid Books, © 1991. Other new books include *100 Years in Idaho* and *How the South Finally Won the Civil War*, both from Tsunami Inc. *Rocky Mountain Man*, selected poems, was published by The Smith Press in New York City, 1978.

dan raphael publishes 26 BOOKS from Portland, Oregon, featuring many of the Northwest's finest poets. His own books include *trees through the road*, *Rain Away*, *The Bones Begin to Sing*, and *Molecular Jam* from Jazz Police, © 1996, from which four poems are reprinted with permission. "Breakfast at the Globe" originally appeared in *The Temple* 2.

Jon Reilly founded the Madison Co-op Bookstore at the University of Wisconsin in Madison. His poems here are from *Insect Lines*, © 1976 by Druid Books, illustrated with nude and nearly nude photographs of young women in playful rather than pornographic poses. Druid Books also published *A Bukowski Sampler*, d.a. levy, and several significant books by Bob Watt.

Mari-Lou Rowley was born in Edmonton, Alberta. Her poem here is from her first book, *a Knife a Rope a Book*, © 1990, from Underwhich Editions in Toronto, Ontario, which also produced an Audiographic cassette of Rowley's work. *CatoptRomancer*, © 1997, was published in a limited edition by Revelation Publications of Vancouver, BC, where Rowley lives.

Ricardo Sánchez (1941-1995) was a professor at Washington State University in Pullman, Washington, when he was diagnosed with stomach cancer. He was a paragon of strength and publishing in the bilingual bicultural West. His poem is reprinted from *Amerikan Journeys::Jornadas*

Americanas, published by Rob Lewis in Iowa City, © 1994 by Maria Teresa Sánchez. *Canto Y Grito Mi Libracion* was published by Doubleday in 1971.

David Sandberg, deceased, dates unknown, was an editor of *Out of Sight* with Gino Sky in San Francisco during the mid-sixties. His poems here are reprinted from the San Francisco *Oracle* and also *Litmus Loads Tone*, © 1971, in Salt Lake City, Utah.

Bill Shively's *2nd Edition*, © 1989 from emPo Publications in Seattle, Washington, is the source of his poem for children and "Night Side" comes from his latest book, *Terminal Bar* from 26 BOOKS. Shively has performed all along the West Coast and in Japan where he was the poetry editor for *The Kyoto Journal*. He belongs to the band "Coincidences of the Realm" which continues the multi-voiced presentations of Ultra-Poetry he pioneered with the ensemble "Life As We Know It."

John Oliver Simon's "One Reason" is from *Lord of the House of Dawn*, © 1991, Bombshelter Press. *Adventures of the Floating Rabbi* is © 1968 from D.R. Wagner's Runcible Spoon Press. Simon has published many other books and translates Spanish poetry and travels extensively in Latin America. *Son Caminos*, his poems in Spanish, is published by Hotel Ambosmundos in Mexico City.

Gino Sky is a poet and a novelist whose poetry books include *The Year of the Fat Flower* and *The Ball Tournament Specialist*. His novels include *Appaloosa Rising* and *Coyote Silk*. His poem here is reprinted from *Out of Sight*, one of many magazines he edited and published, including *Wild Dog* during its second phase in Salt Lake City and San Francisco. Sky lives in Boise, Idaho.

Edward Smith's poems are reprinted from *The Flutes of Gama*, © 1976. Smith had another book from Litmus Inc., *Going*, © 1977. He has written a novel and was enthusiastically received as a poet while in Seattle, Washington, in the late sixties, securing a degree in Chinese at the University of Washington after his service in the United States Army in Vietnam.

Dawn Stram's book, *Roots and Wings*, was published © 1968 by Carlos Reyes' Presna de Lagar Press in Milwaukie, Oregon. She published in *Wild Dog*, *Litmus*, *Salted Feathers*, *Padma* and several more magazines. She is a cultural anthropologist and doctoral candidate studying the school experiences of "juvenile delinquents" in Boise, Idaho. She edited and published in *Windows and Mirrors* in 1997, a collection of stories and poems published by the Boise State University College of Education.

Ford Swetnam's poem "Putting By" is from *Another Tough Hop*, published by Walrus & Carpenter Books of Pocatello, Idaho, © 1991. His book, *301*, © 1995, was published by The Redneck Press and Penelope Reedy. Swetnam lives in Pocatello, Idaho, and is a professor of English at Idaho State University.

Stephen Thomas teaches at Cornish College of the Arts, University Preparatory Academy and the University of Washington Extension. Several of his earlier books were selected and collected into the major edition of *Journeyman*, published by Tsunami Inc., © 1997, from which his poems here are reprinted with permission. Thomas lives in Seattle, Washington, and is also the poetry editor for *Point No Point: A Blue Moon Reader*.

Karen Waring published regularly in *Litmus* and other magazines in Seattle, Washington, in the sixties. Her poems here are reprinted from *Litmus* and her © 1976 Litmus Inc. title *Exposed to the Elements*. Her poetry has generated high praise from Douglas Blazek, Edward Dorn and numerous other reviewers.

Bob Watt, a painter of Indian style art and an ex-exterminator, is from Milwaukee, Wisconsin, and a founder of the Wisconsin Poetry Alliance. His poetry here is reprinted from *The Ten Bulls of Zen Made Easy*, © 1970, from Morgan Press, Madison, Wisconsin; *Woman Poems*, Madison Book Coop, © 1971; and *The Selling of Wild Women by Cats in Love*, Druid Books, © 1971.

Eric Wegner is a miller and a practitioner of Neuro Linguistic Programming from Pullman, Washington. His poems here first appeared in *The Temple* 1 and were taken from a privately circulated manuscript, *An Implement That Cries Aloud*.

Keith Wilson's poem here is reprinted from *Graves Registry*, Clark City Press, Livingston, Montana, with the permission of the publisher, Russell Chatham. It was first published in *Midwatch* from Sumac Press, edited by Jim Harrison and Dan Gerber.

Daniel Zimmerman's poems are reprinted from *Indian Rope Trick* (*House Organ* #9), Christmas 1994, Lakewood, Ohio, Kenneth Warren, editor. This whole issue of *House Organ* featured Zimmerman poetry. His most recent work, a collaboration with the late John Clarke, *Blue Horitals*, © 1997, was published in Amman, Jordan by Stephen Ellis' Oasii Books.

Teri Zipf's first book, *Outside the School of Theology*, © 1997, a Tsunami Inc. first edition, won the William Stafford Memorial Award for Poetry in 1998 from the Pacific Northwest Booksellers Association. Zipf, of Walla Walla, Washington, has been a Fishtrap Fellow and received the 1993 Artist Trust Fellowship in Literature, funded by the Washington State Arts Commission and the National Endowment for the Arts.

Tsunami Inc.
Book distribution

Michael Finley, *Lucky You*, Litmus Inc., 1976, ... $5
Charles Foster, *Victoria Mundi*, Litmus/Smith, 1973, cloth, ... $10
d.a. levy, *Collected Poems*, Druid Books, 1976, ... $10
Charles Potts, *How the South Finally Won the Civil War,*
and Controls the Political Future of the United States, 1995,
Tsunami Inc., cloth, 11 maps, index, 200+ works cited, ... $29
100 Years in Idaho, Tsunami Inc., 1996, ... $10
Loading Las Vegas, Current, 1991, a satiric novel, ... $10
The Dictatorship of the Environment, Druid Books, 1991, ... $10
Lettered & signed cloth bound limited edition, ... $25
Rocky Mountain Man, The Smith, 1978, ... $10
The Opium Must Go Thru, Litmus Inc., 1976, ... $5
Cover and illustrations by Robert McNealy,
Quarter bound in leather sewn into boards by the author, ... $50
A Rite to the Body, Ghost Dance, 1989, ... $5
Edward Smith, *The Flutes of Gama*, Litmus Inc., 1976, ... $5
Stephen Thomas, *Journeyman*, Tsunami Inc., 1997, ... $15
Teri Zipf, *Outside the School of Theology*, Tsunami Inc.,1997, ... $10

Pacific Northwestern Spiritual Poetry, an anthology of 50 poets,
Tsunami Inc., edited with an introduction by Charles Potts, ... $20

The Temple, Gu Si, El Templo, an 80 page quarterly of poetry
in English with Chinese and Spanish poems along with English
translations: sample $5; Set of volume 1, 1997, issues 1-4, ... $20
one year subscription, ... $20

Tsunami Inc.
PO Box 100
WALLA WALLA, WA 99362-0033
1-509-529-0813
<http://www.wwics.com/~tsunami>
<tsunami@wwics.com>